I0812100

POSTCARD HISTORY SERIES

Angola and Steuben County in Vintage Postcards

POSTCARD HISTORY SERIES

Angola and Steuben County

IN VINTAGE POSTCARDS

John Martin Smith

ARCADIA PUBLISHING

ISBN 978-0-7385-1916-6

Published by Arcadia Publishing
Charleston SC, Chicago IL, Portsmouth NH, San Francisco CA

Printed in the United States of America

Library of Congress Catalog Card Number: 2001093323

For all general information contact Arcadia Publishing at:
Telephone 843-853-2070
Fax 843-853-0044
E-mail sales@arcadiapublishing.com
For customer service and orders:
Toll-Free 1-888-313-2665

Visit us on the Internet at www.arcadiapublishing.com

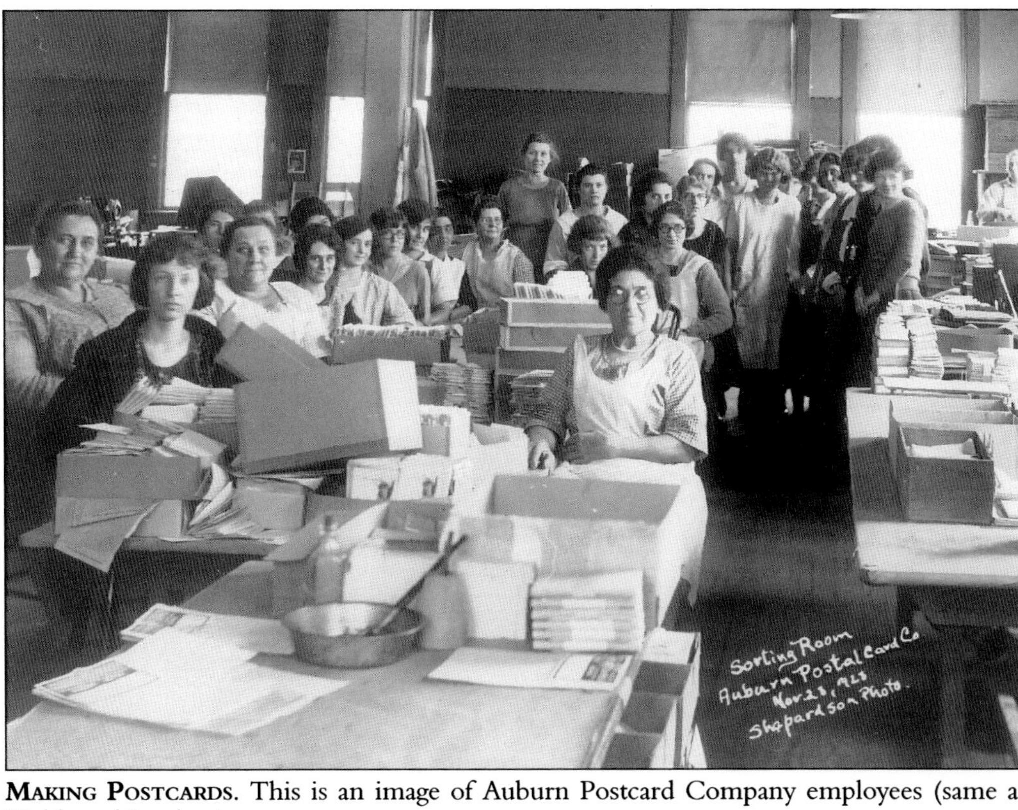

MAKING POSTCARDS. This is an image of Auburn Postcard Company employees (same as Noble and Steuben).

Contents

Acknowledgments 6

Introduction 7

1. Angola 9

2. Fremont 39

3. Hamilton 47

4. Hoosier Hills 53

5. Hudson 55

6. Lakes 59
    - A. Buck Lake 60
    - B. Clear Lake 71
    - C. Crooked Lake 78
    - D. Fox Lake 84
    - E. Hamilton Lake 85
    - F. Lake Gage 95
    - G. Lake George 96
    - H. Lake James 101
    - I. Pokagon State Park 109
    - J. Silver Lake 112
    - K. Snow Lake 113

7. Metz 115

8. Orland 117

9. Pleasant Lake 119

10. Ray 127

ACKNOWLEDGMENTS

The author is indebted to several people who have contributed to production of this book:

My wife, Barbara Clark Smith, has participated in the collection of these postcards for nearly 40 years. I thank her for her patient search through thousands of postcards at antique shows and antique malls to find those relevant to Northeastern Indiana.

My son and law partner, Thompson Smith, has made law office facilities available to assist in the production of this book. His paralegal, Tricia Hertsel, has done the computer input and organization. My secretary of 32 years, Sharon George, has also assisted.

Arcadia editor Ann Fugman has been of great assistance in getting the book into print in accordance with the high standards of Arcadia. The quiet behind-the-scenes efforts of a good editor always makes an author look good!

Lastly, I am indebted to those photographers and merchants who had the foresight and vision to create and distribute the original postcards. While postcards have a fleeting, ephemeral quality to them, those "packrats" who have collected and saved them have provided us a legacy of our towns that would have otherwise been lost after the click of the camera and the thunk of the postmark!

John Martin Smith

Introduction

After my grandfather died in 1961, we found a box of old postcards which were exchanged between my grandmother, Viola Smith, and her sister, Iona. They both lived in Butler, Indiana. I arranged the cards in chronological order and scanned the messages. Some were postmarked the same day.

With a little research and questions to my father, Walter M. Smith, who served as postmaster in Butler from 1950 to 1976, I found that beginning in 1907, there was mail delivery twice each day in the town. Therefore, the sisters could exchange messages the same day—i.e. "Can you and Carl come for supper at 6PM? Iona"—"Yes, I will bring an apple pie, Viola."

Some of the cards had floral and holiday scenes on the front and others had real photographs of buildings located in Butler. Postage was 1¢. I later sorted out the scenes of buildings and started looking for others. At antique shops, flea markets, antique malls, and auctions I found more postcards from Butler. This search then expanded to all of Northeastern Indiana. Over a period of about 30 years I have accumulated hundreds of postcards. One of the best sources now is Ebay on the Internet. Since most of the postcards were sent away from their place of origin, many are listed for sale from places far from Northeast Indiana. This source has enabled me to augment the collection presented here.

The history of the use of postcards centers around United States Postal Laws and Regulations. The printed format of postcards also enables one to generally date postcards. The sequence is as follows:

1893–1898 Pioneer Cards
These cards are quite rare and are sometimes labeled as "Souvenir Postcards."

1898–1901 Private Mailing Cards
These cards are labeled "Private Mailing Card" on the address side and usually also state "Authorized by Act of Congress of May 19, 1898."

1901–1907 Undivided Backs
Postal regulations did not permit a message on the back—just the address. This was also true of the Pioneer and Private Mailing Cards.

1907–1915 Divided Backs
On March 1, 1907, the United States Postal Service approved the divided back card, which permitted the address on the right side and a message on the left side of the back. This change made the use of postcards much more prevalent as a means of communication.

1915–1930s White Borders
A change in printing techniques resulted in a printed image with a narrow white border.

1935–1955 Linens
These cards were printed on cardboard stock with a "linen" like surface. The publisher started with a photograph but modified it to make an idyllic image that was also colorized.

1945–Present Chromes
These cards are printed in color on a slick stock.

The foregoing date categories overlap considerably. Sometimes the same basic photographs were used for several postcard versions. Pre-linen cards were frequently colorized in various ways. For example, a black and white image would be overprinted with a brick color on a brick building. The Auburn Postcard Company was known for its "Blue Sky" cards, which were a black and white image with the sky overprinted in light blue.

From about 1900–1915, many cards were "Real Photo" cards. That term is used to describe a photograph printed by the photographer directly onto postcard stock. Sometimes only a single postcard was made. Usually, the number of cards printed was limited. Real photo cards are sought by collectors due to their relative rarity and sharp, clear image. Real photo cards were also issued in the 1940s and 1950s. A real photo card and a printed card can be distinguished quite easily by magnifying the image—a printed card will have a pattern of small dots to create the contrast, whereas a real photo card will have a solid image.

The bulk of the images in this book date from 1910–1915, which was the golden era of postcard production. It is likely that the local use of postcards waned after the telephone came into general use. As automobile travel increased, postcards were used by tourists to send a photograph and message back home. Many persons also collected postcards, which led to friends and relatives sending them postcards for their collection.

There were several local postcard companies in Bryan, Ohio; Fort Wayne, Indiana; and Auburn, Indiana. The Auburn Postcard Company was a major international publisher of postcards. The Whitten-Dennison Post Card Company moved to Auburn from Maine in 1910. They built a small factory on East Seventh Street adjacent to Cedar Creek, which employed five women. The name of the company was changed to Auburn Post Card Manufacturing Company in 1913, and to Auburn Greeting Card Company in 1929. In 1933, D.E. Messenger acquired the company and changed the name to Messenger Corporation, which is still in operation at 318 East Seventh Street and is a major printer of religious calendars and printed materials for the funeral home industry.

How were the subjects of postcards chosen? Generally, they were chosen by local merchants on the basis of what would sell in their drugstore, restaurant, or bookstore. In some cases, the scenes selected were designed to show off the town. The most common are scenes of the courthouses and principle streets. They were ordered in quantities of 500–1,000, so the merchant wanted to make sure that they would sell.

The images selected for this book are designed to present a representative selection of images for Steuben County. The space and format of the book did not permit the use of all cards in our collection for this county. In some cases, the messages on the back are as interesting as the image on the front. I have incorporated some of these in my interpretations. The bold type in my captions repeats the caption of the card. If the date is not contained in the caption and the card is postmarked, the postmarked date is stated "*c.* 19—." If the card is not postmarked, or if the postmark is not readable, no date is stated. I then supplement the caption with other information when appropriate. Some images simply speak for themselves, so I refrain from any further comment.

While not originally intended to document a town or place historically, I find that they are a great source of local history and images that is otherwise unavailable. As persons restore buildings to their original design, a postcard may be the only source of a period image of that particular building.

I sincerely hope that my readers enjoy and use the images and captions contained herein to appreciate their heritage and sense of place.

John Martin Smith

One

ANGOLA

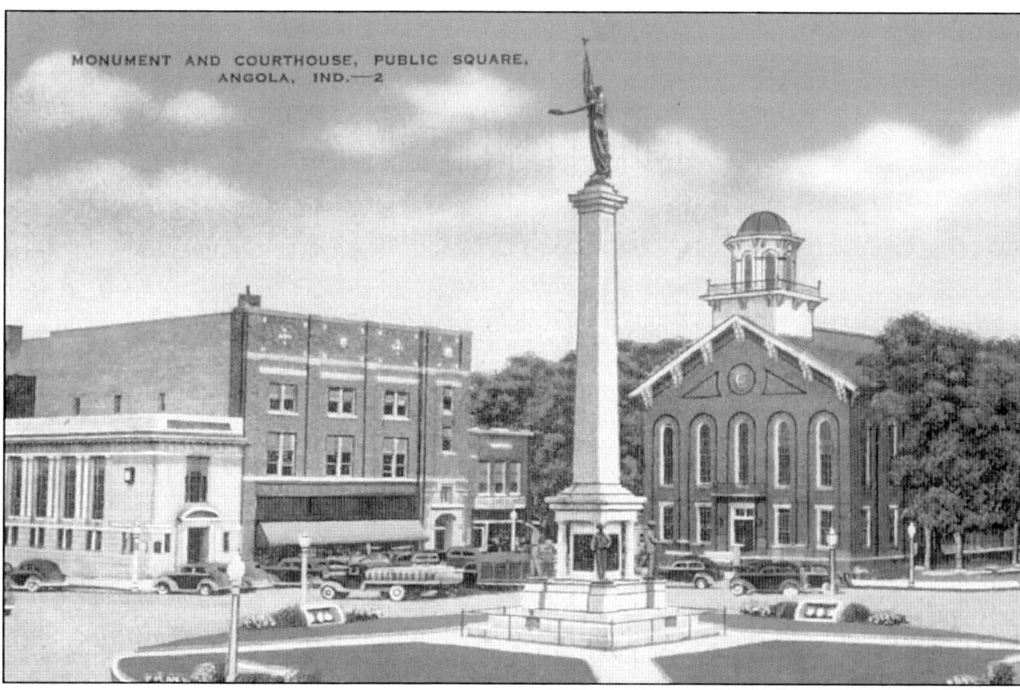

MONUMENT AND COURTHOUSE, PUBLIC SQUARE, ANGOLA, INDIANA, *c.* 1945. The Public Square is the most common subject for Steuben County postcards.

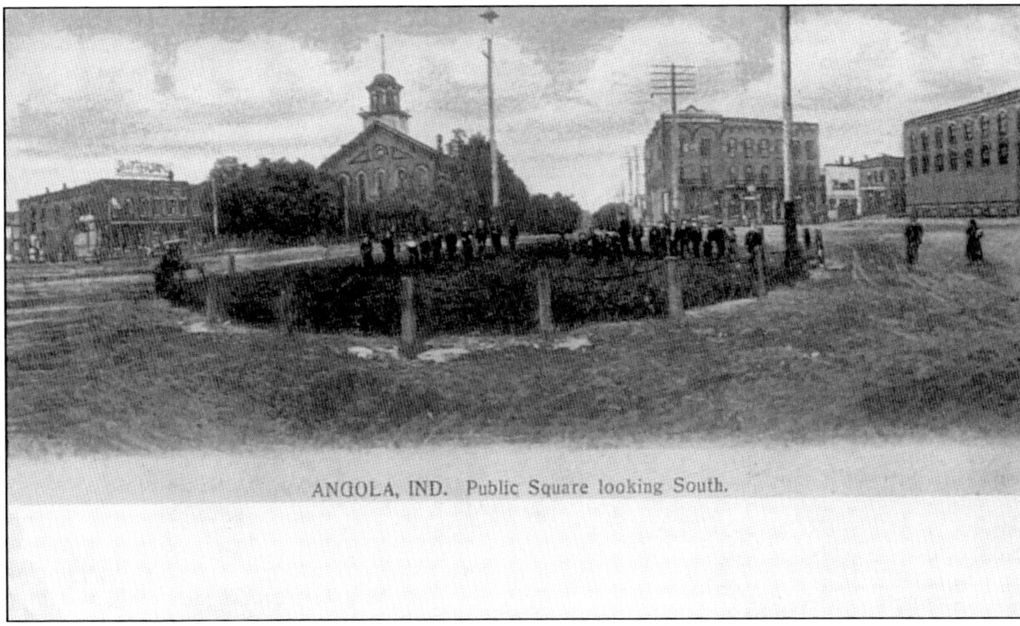

ANGOLA, INDIANA, PUBLIC SQUARE LOOKING SOUTH. This is a "Pre-monument" view. This photograph was made with a "Cirkut Camera." It was placed on a tripod. A spring wound mechanism slowly turned the camera while the film inside advanced at the same rate of speed. The result was a panoramic view. These cameras were even capable of making a 360-degree photograph.

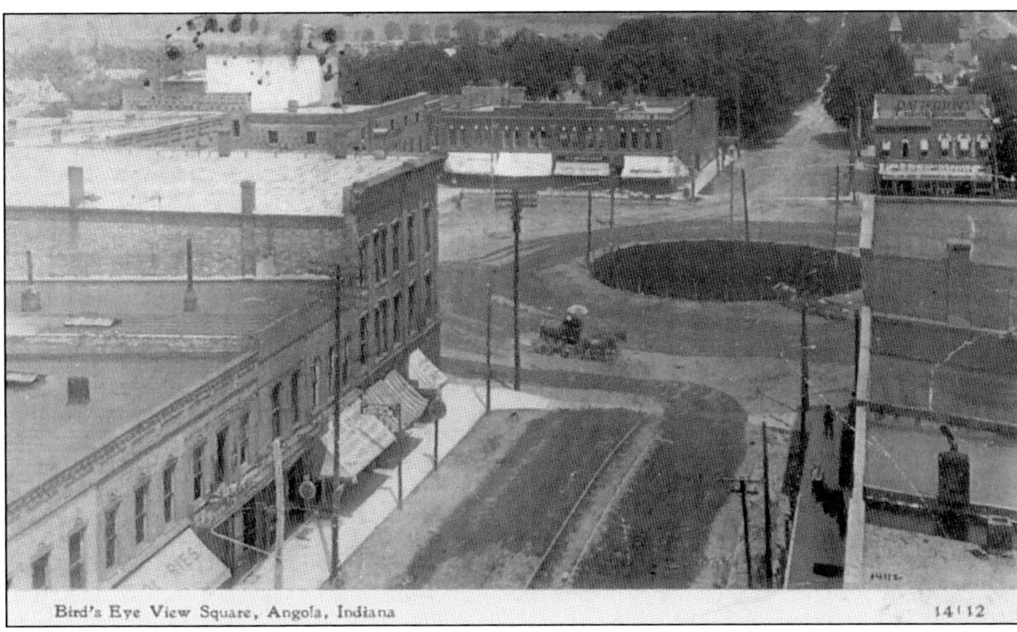

BIRD'S-EYE VIEW SQUARE, ANGOLA, INDIANA. Some call this area the "Square," and others the "Circle." Still others call the area the "Mound." All terms are correct. Angola's town plan is of New England origin. Most of the early settlers of Steuben County came from New England.

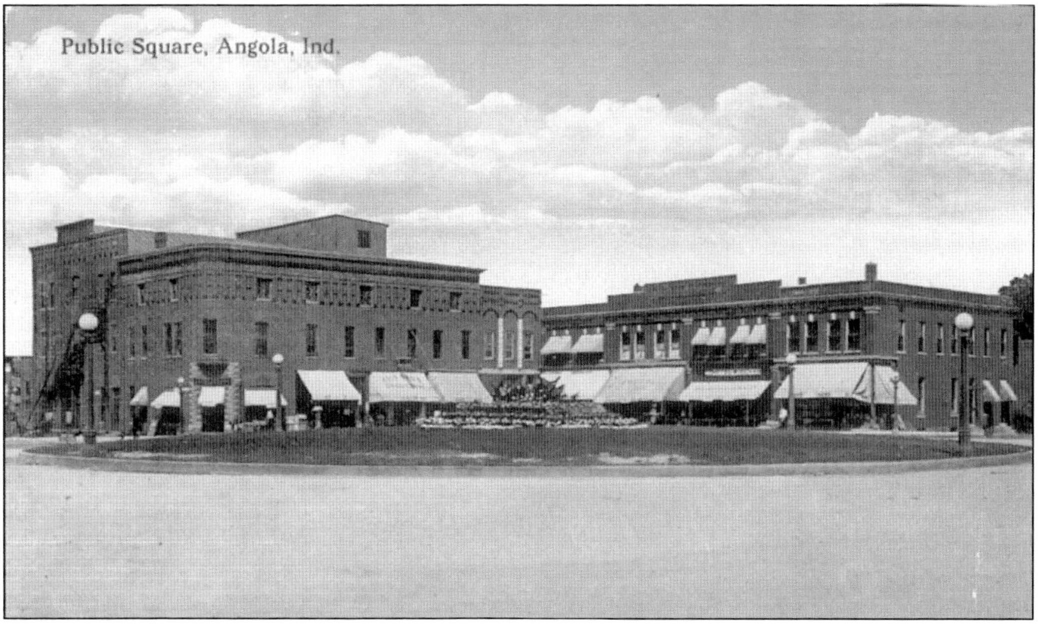

Public Square, Angola, Indiana. This view shows the flowers in the center of the Circle. Note the awnings on the buildings. This photograph was taken from the west with the sun behind the photographer.

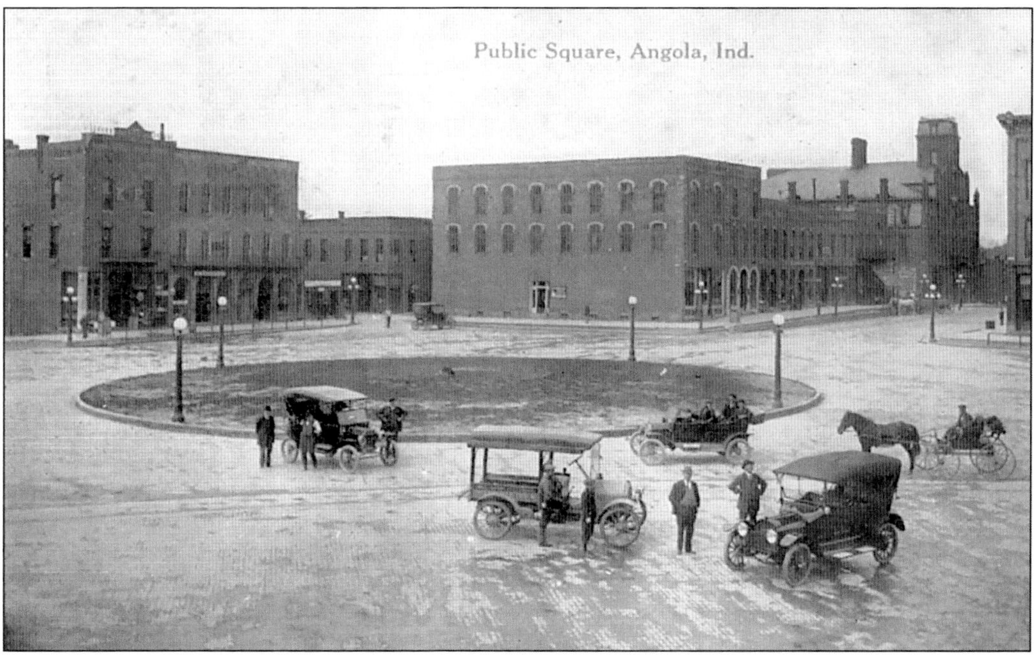

Public Square, Angola, Indiana, *c*. 1918. This view is looking southwest. Several proud owners have lined up their automobiles and horse and buggy.

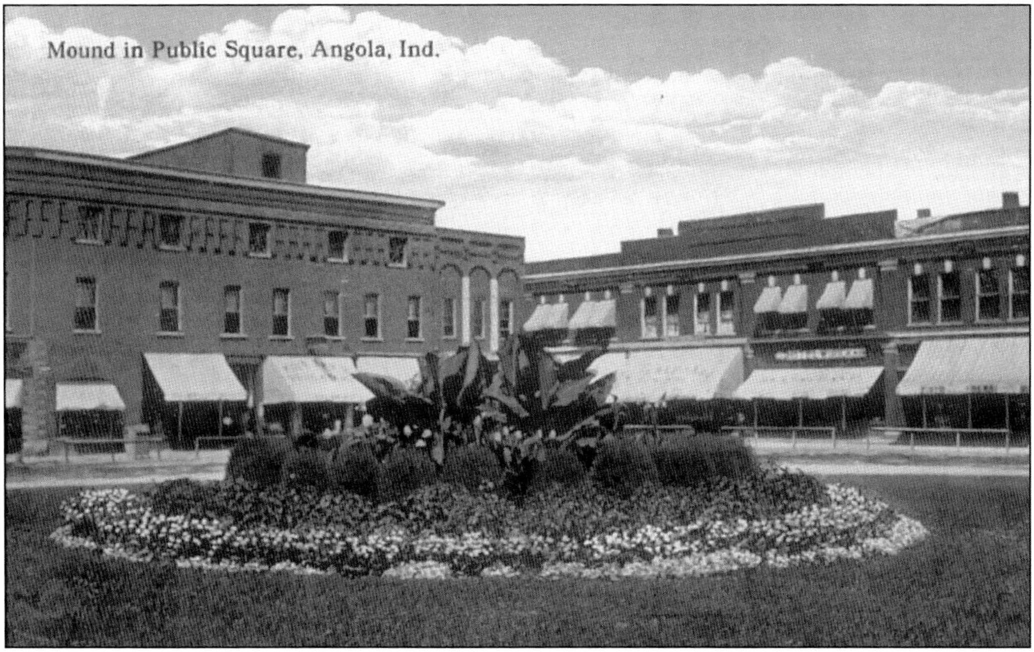

Mound in Public Square, Angola, Indiana. This is a close-up view of the "Mound."

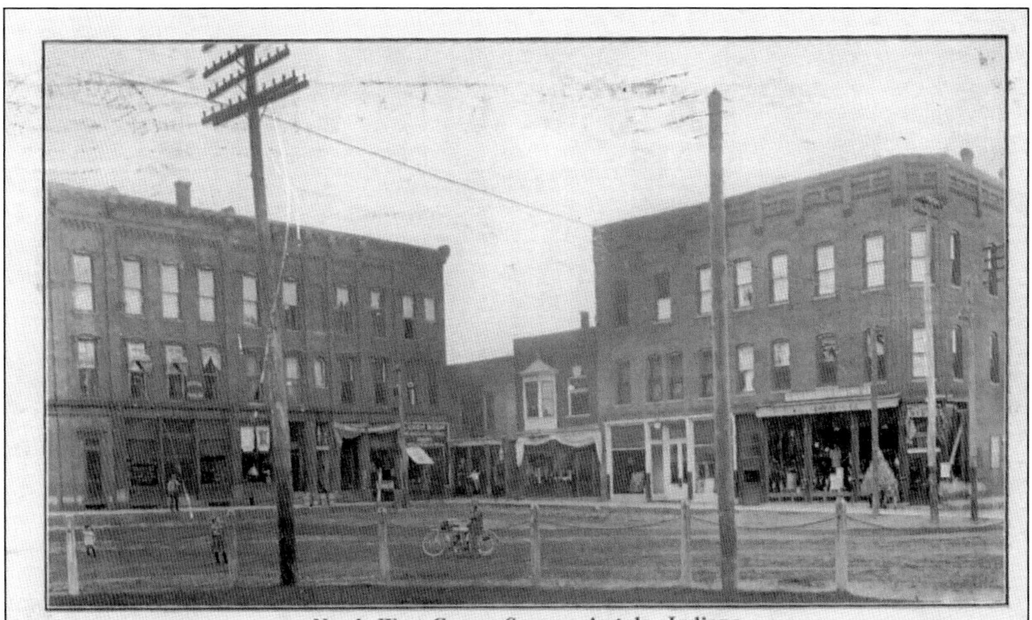

Northwest Corner Square, Angola, Indiana, c. 1913. Seen here is a fine view of the northwest corner.

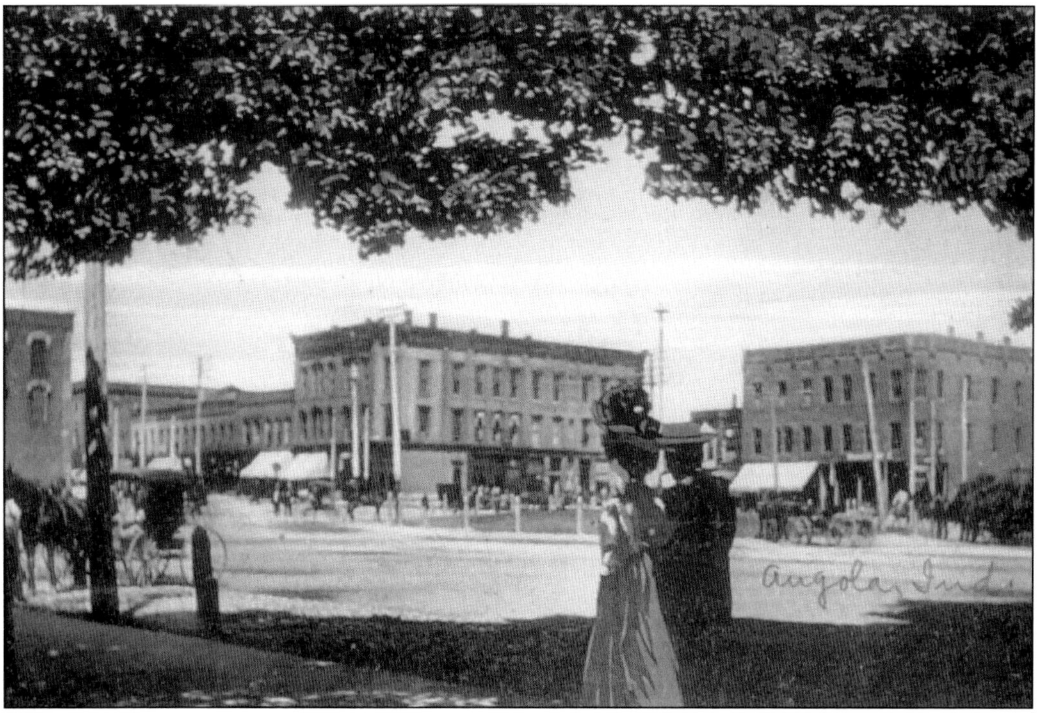

Public Square, Angola, Indiana, *c.* 1910. This view shows typical activity, including a well dressed couple.

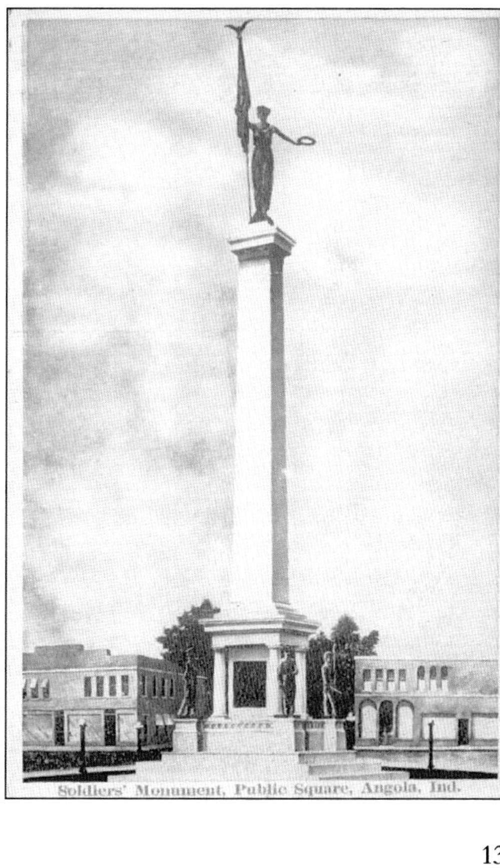

Soldiers' Monument, Public Square, Angola, Indiana. This is probably an artist's conception, as the buildings in the background are not correct.

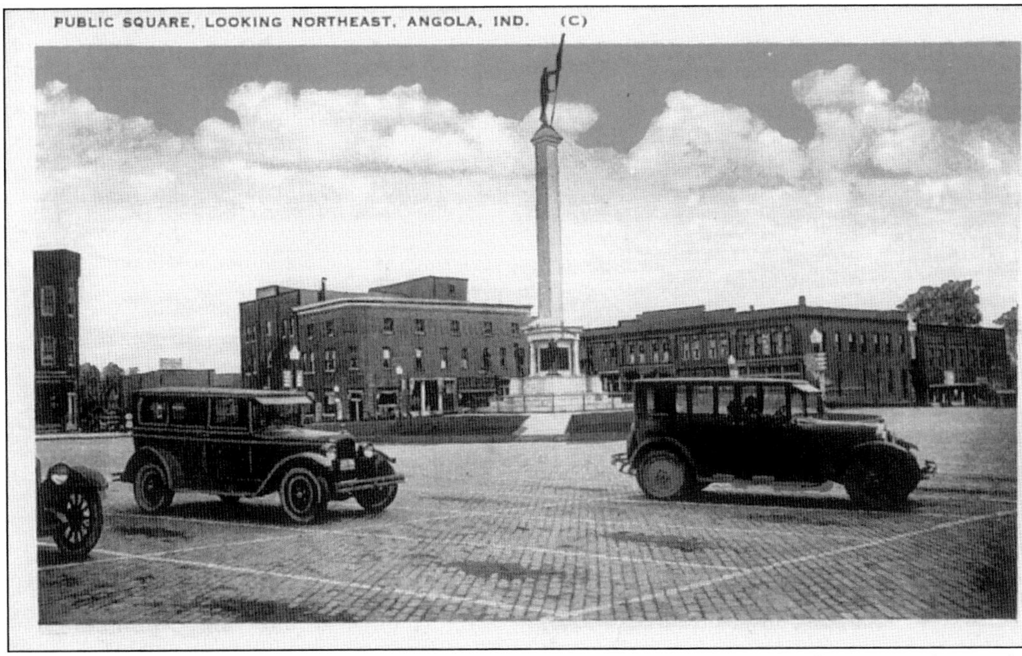

Public Square, Looking Northeast, Angola, Indiana, c. 1929. This view shows the brick streets and some cars parked between the lines.

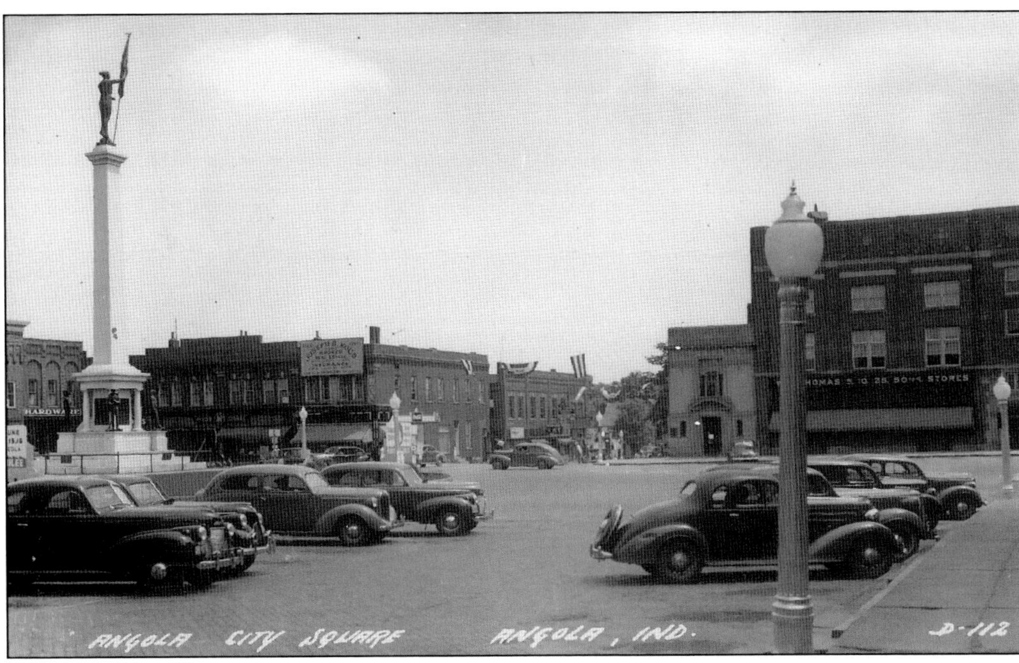

Angola City Square, Angola, Indiana, c. 1940. The flags and banners are out, and the street lights are new. The large sign in the corner building advertises "Joseph B. Kolb—Broker—Real Estate—Insurance."

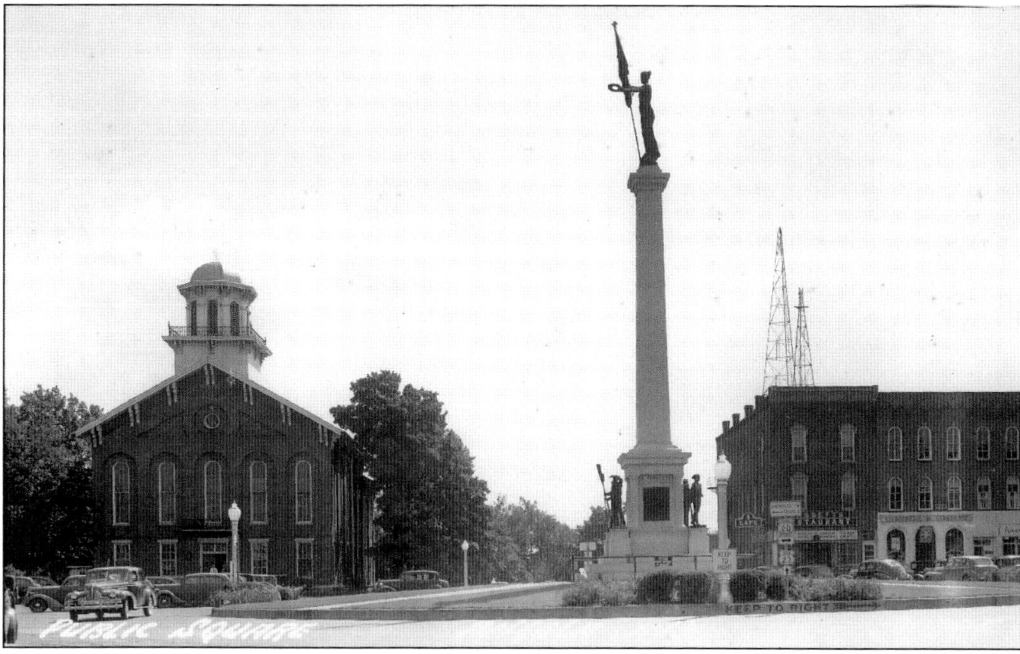

PUBLIC SQUARE, ANGOLA, INDIANA, *c.* 1940. This view is looking south. Bassett's Restaurant and Campbell & Company are to the right of the monument. Note the tower on the building to the right of the monument.

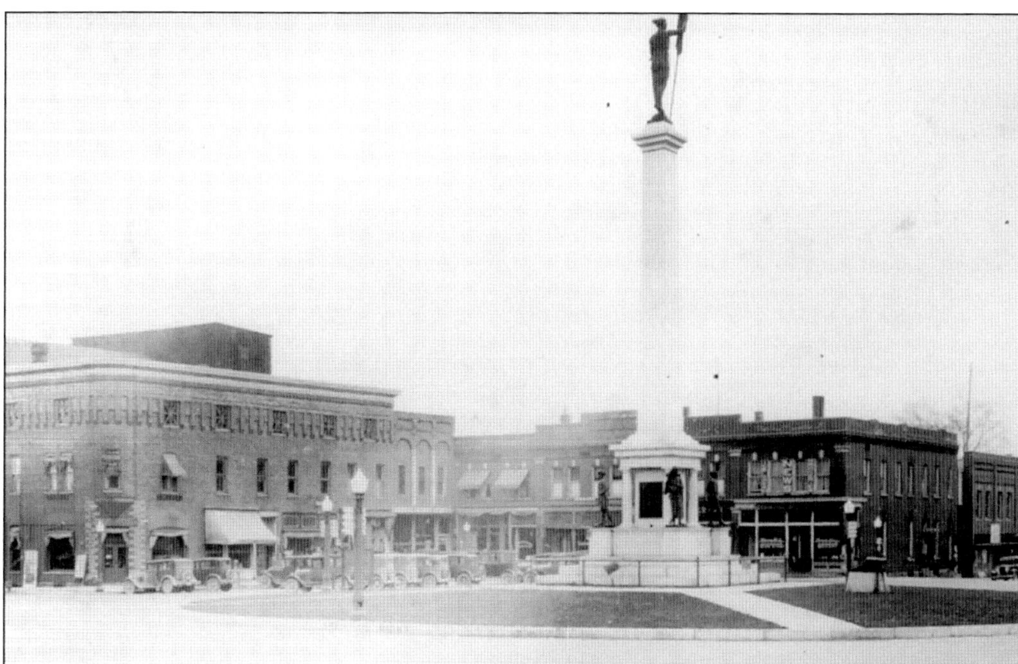

MONUMENT, ANGOLA, INDIANA, *c.* 1928. This view looks northeast.

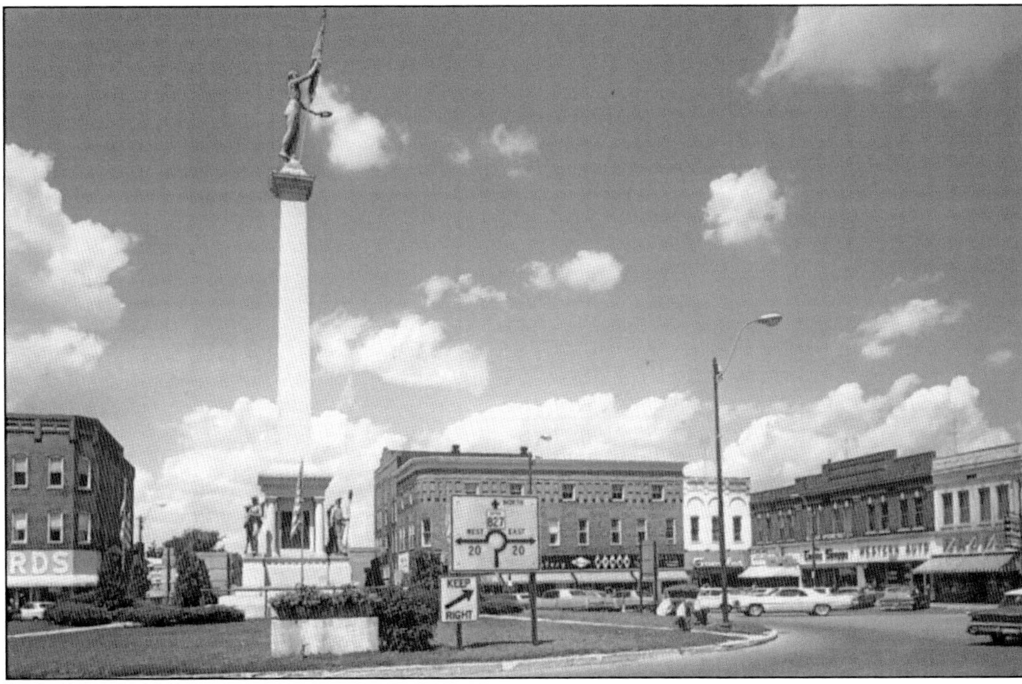

Civil War Monument and Square, Angola, Indiana, c. 1955. A chrome card is seen here looking north.

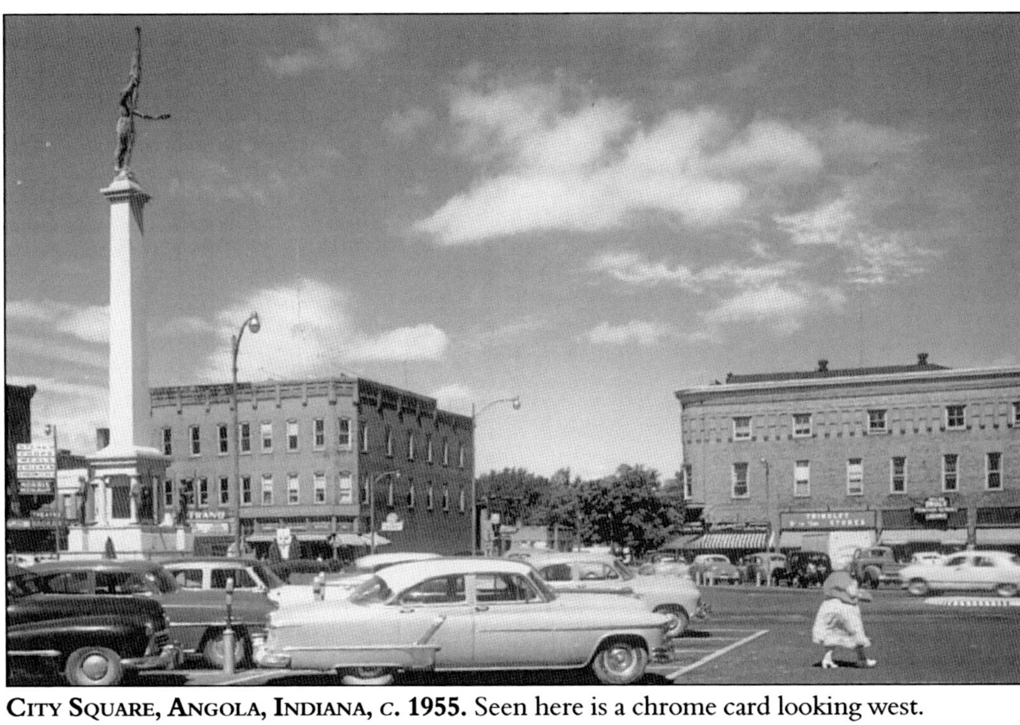

City Square, Angola, Indiana, c. 1955. Seen here is a chrome card looking west.

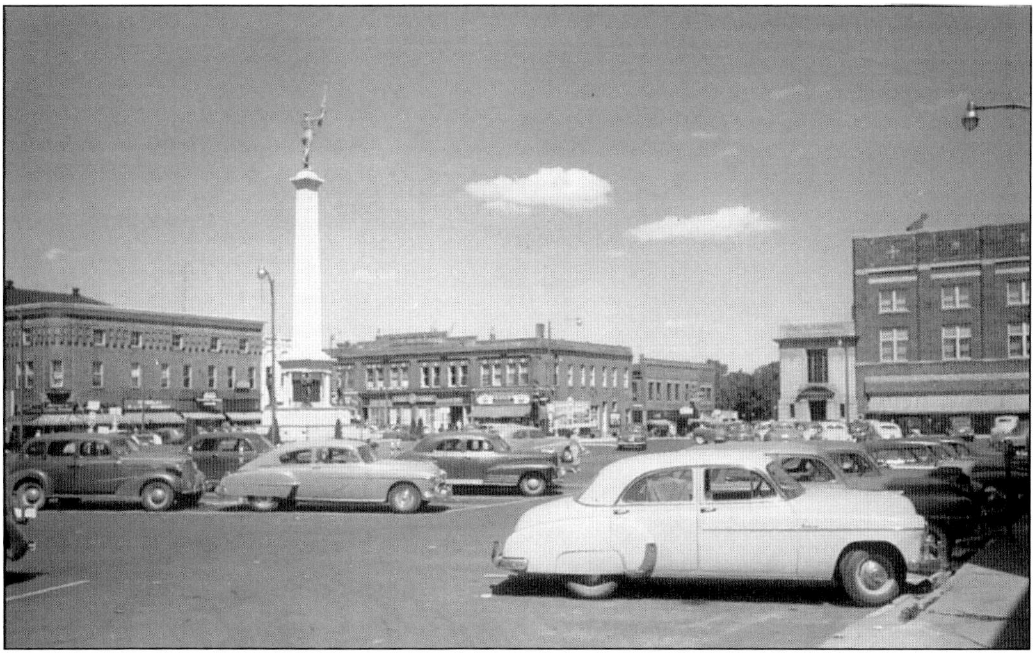

CITY SQUARE, ANGOLA, INDIANA, C. 1955. Seen here is a chrome card looking east.

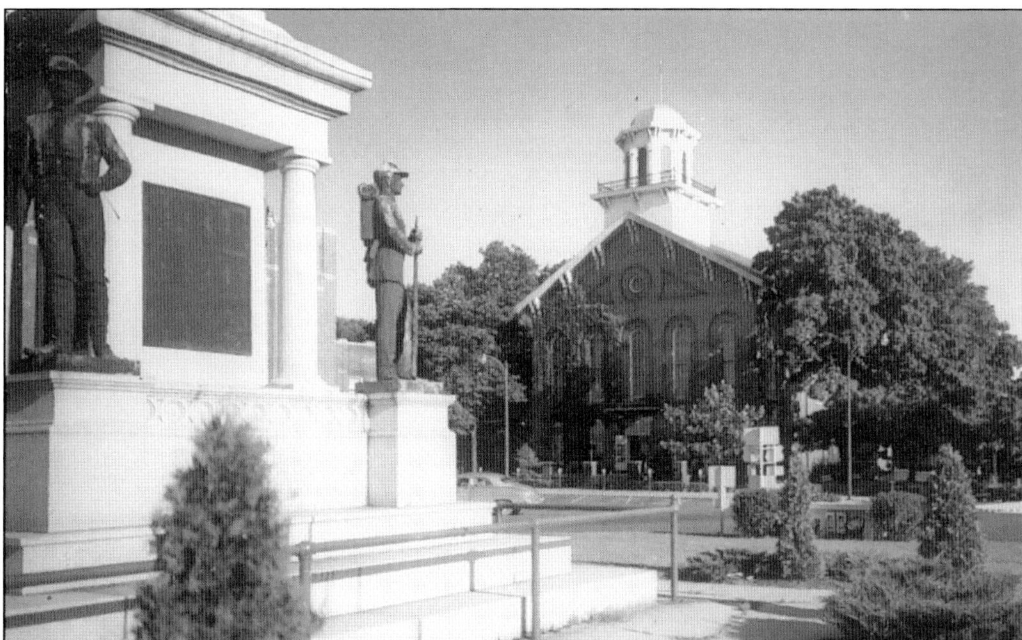

CIVIL WAR MONUMENT AND COURTHOUSE, ANGOLA, INDIANA, *C.* 1955. A chrome card displays the base of the monument and the courthouse.

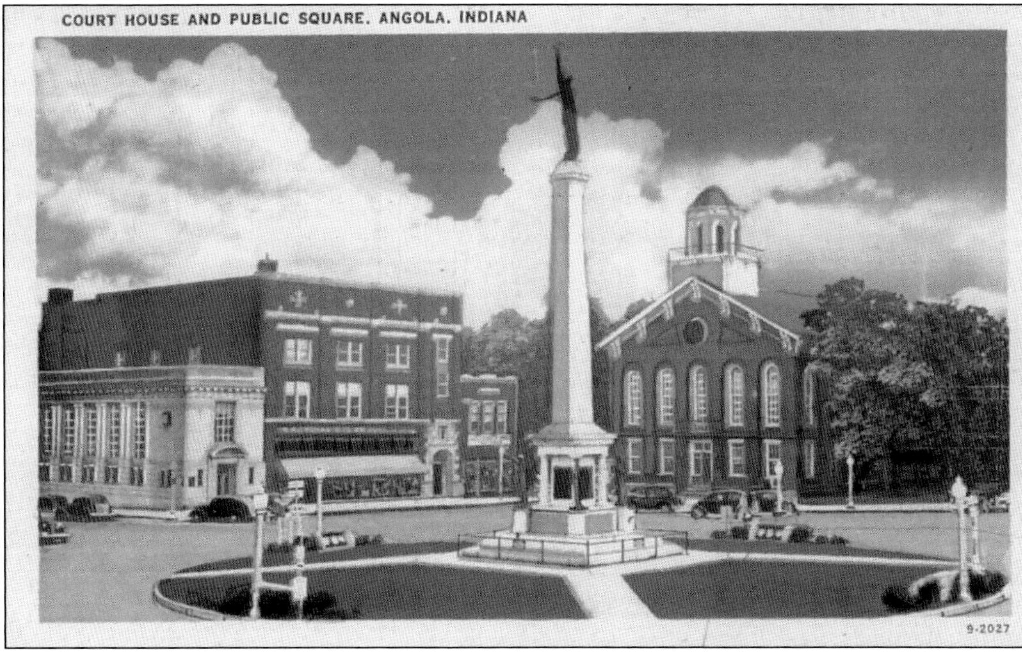

COURT HOUSE AND PUBLIC SQUARE, ANGOLA, INDIANA, *c.* 1935. This is a linen card looking southeast.

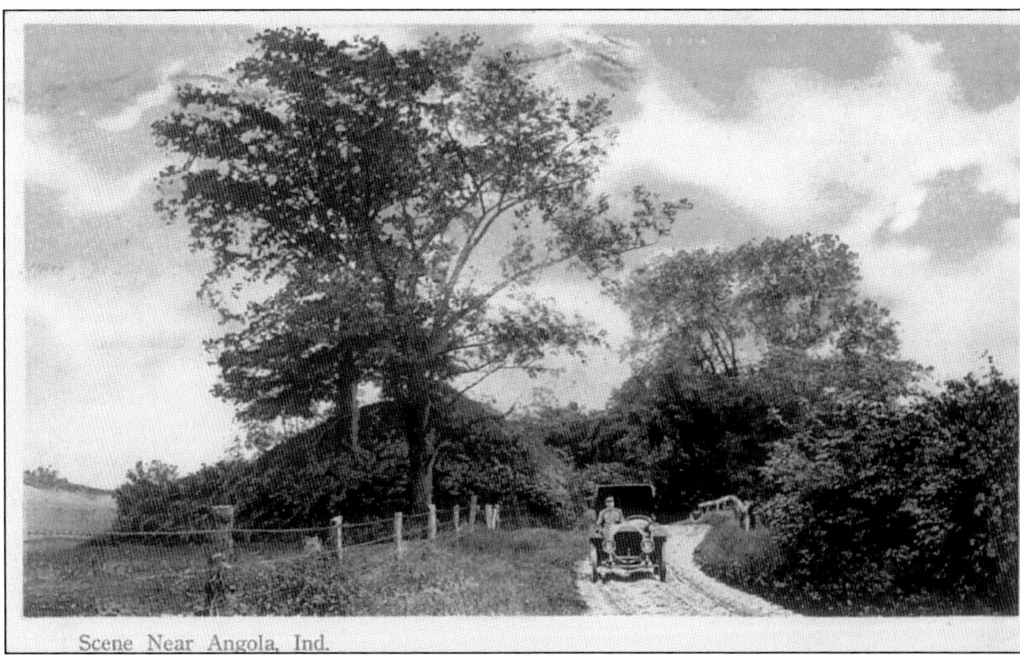

SCENE NEAR ANGOLA, INDIANA, *c.* 1916. Although this is probably a stock scene, it is similar to real scenes in the Angola area.

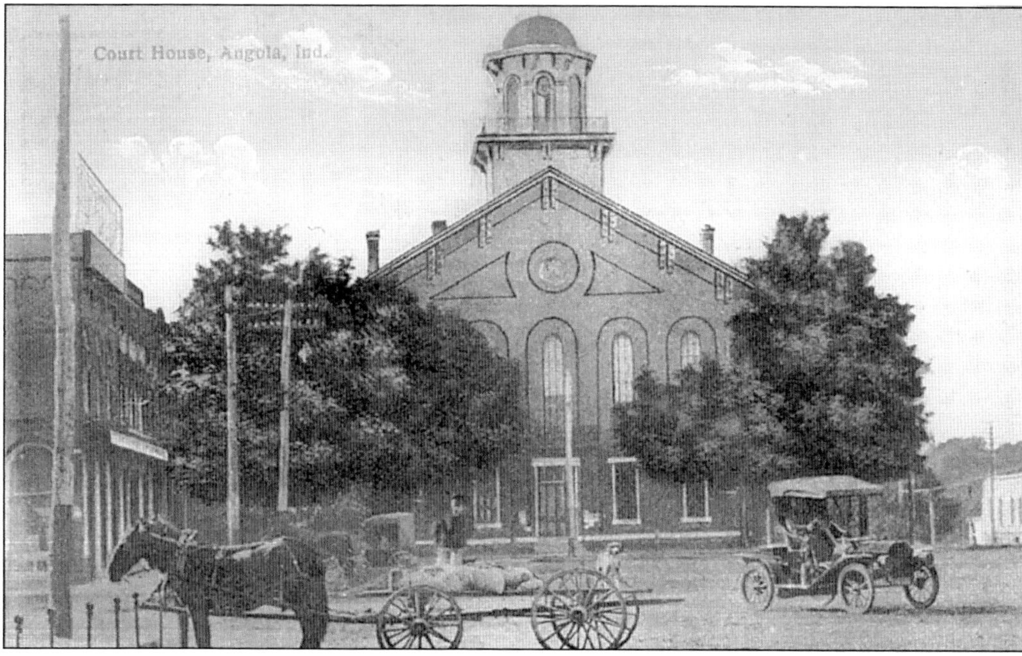

Court House, Angola, Indiana, *c.* 1909. There are burlap bags of animal feed on the wagon.

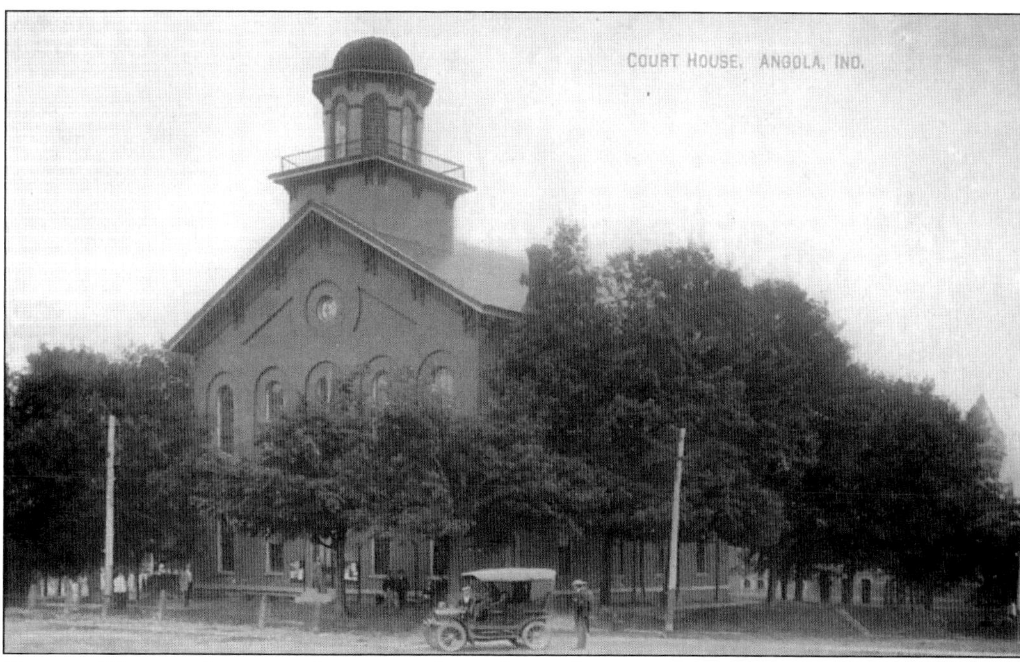

Court House, Angola, Indiana. Several gentlemen are looking over the car. Note the boards either side of the front door of the courthouse. Legal notices were posted on these boards.

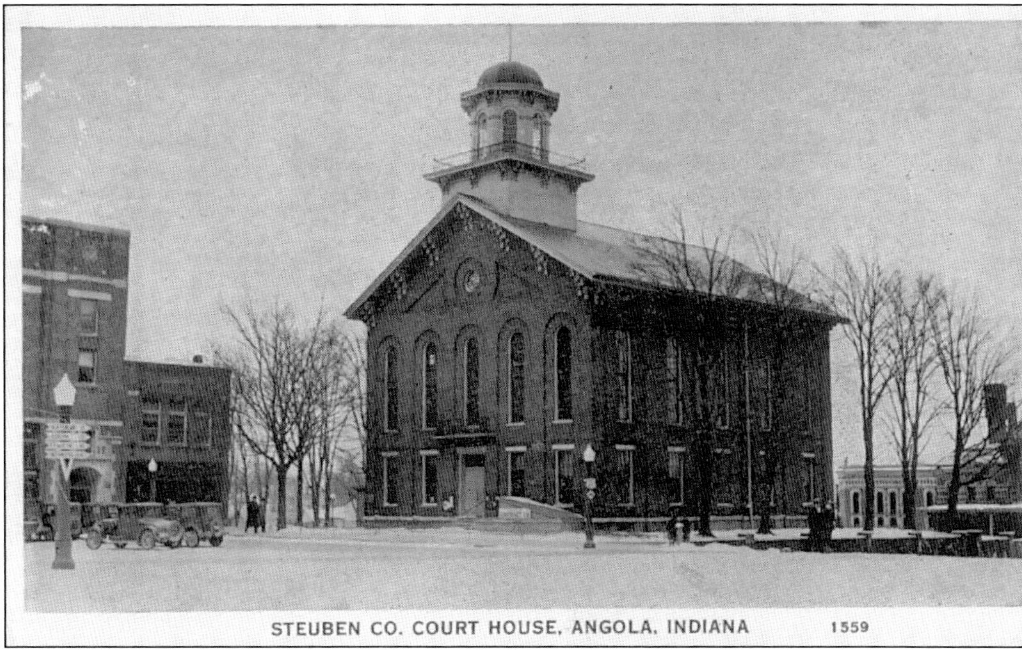

Steuben County Court House, Angola, Indiana, c. 1925. The arrow signs on the left give mileage to Waterloo, Auburn, Fort Wayne, and Indianapolis.

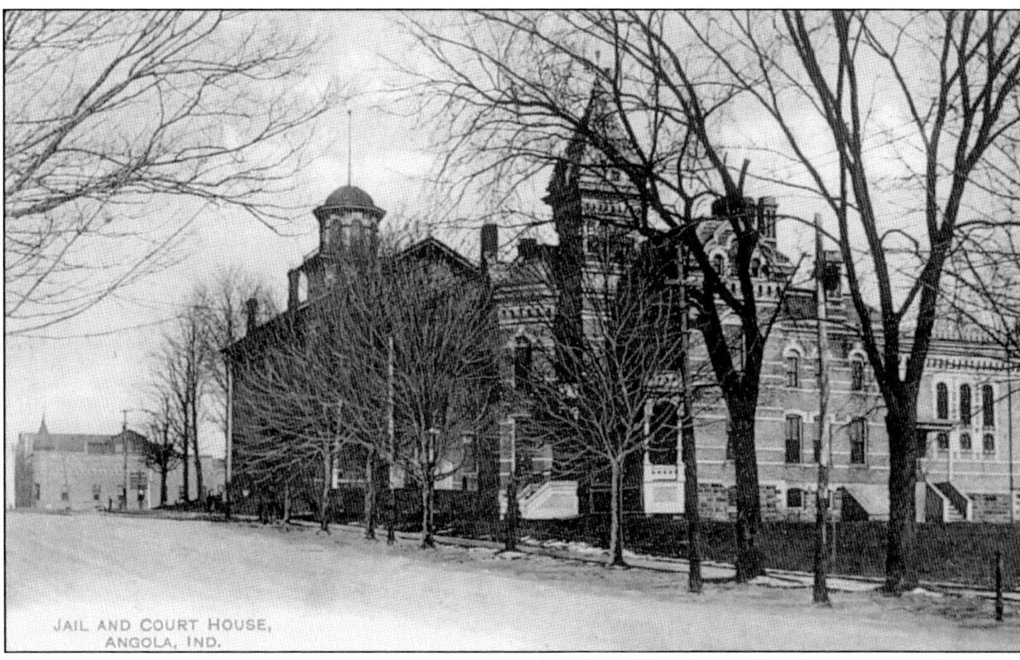

Jail and Court House, Angola, Indiana. The sheriff and his family lived in the front residence. The sheriff's wife usually served as jail matron and provided the meals for the prisoners.

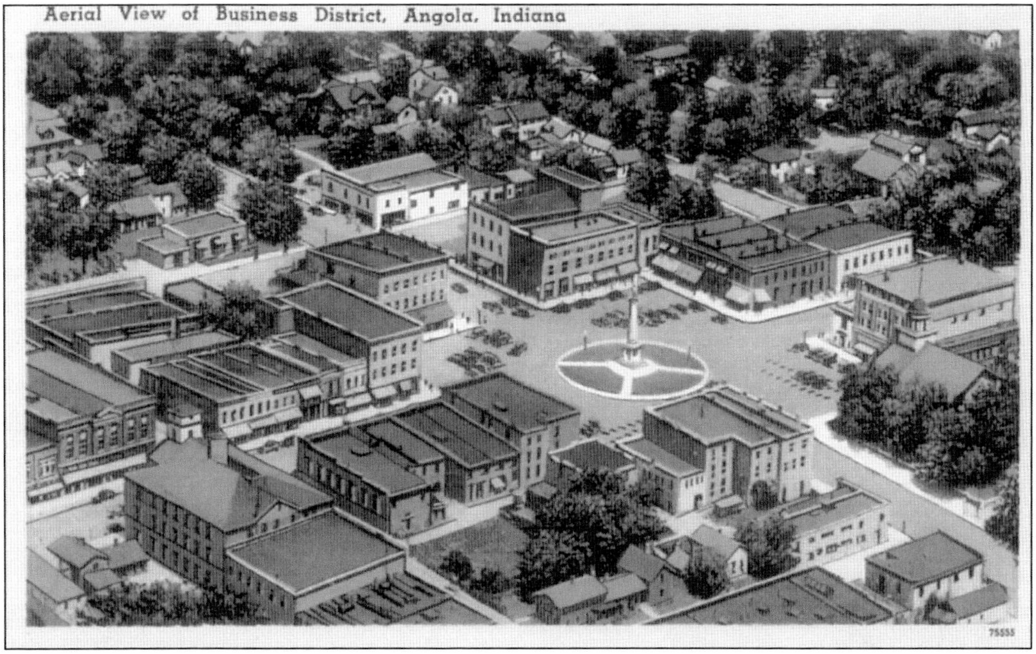

Aerial View of Business District, Angola, Indiana, *c.* 1940. This is a linen card. These views are "sanitized." Trees are removed to show buildings, and unsightly areas are removed. This view is looking northeast.

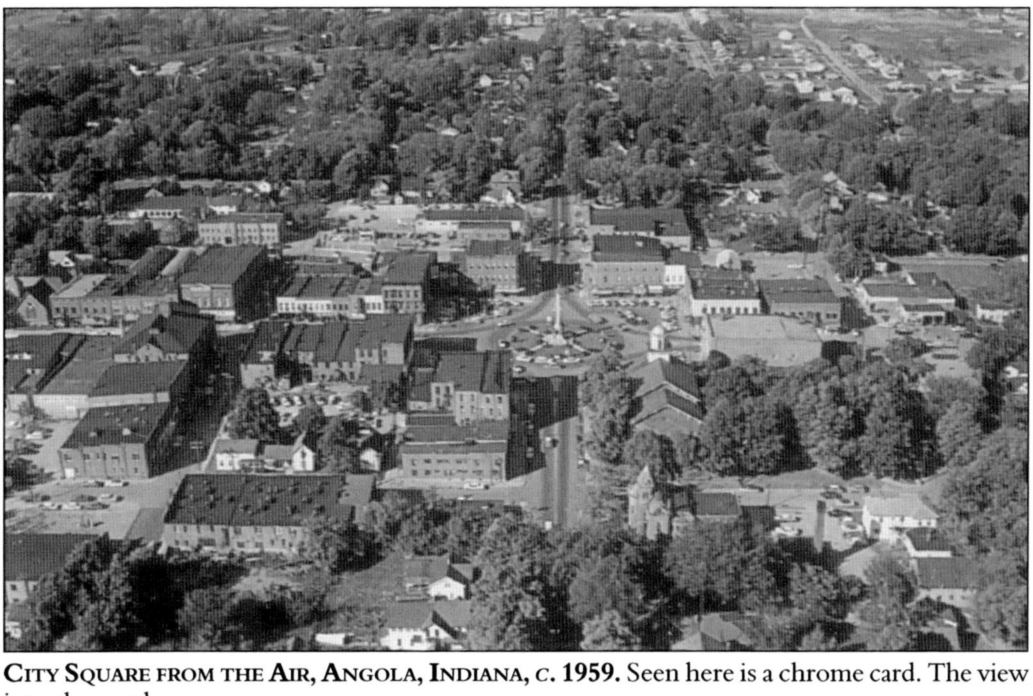

City Square from the Air, Angola, Indiana, *c.* 1959. Seen here is a chrome card. The view is to the north.

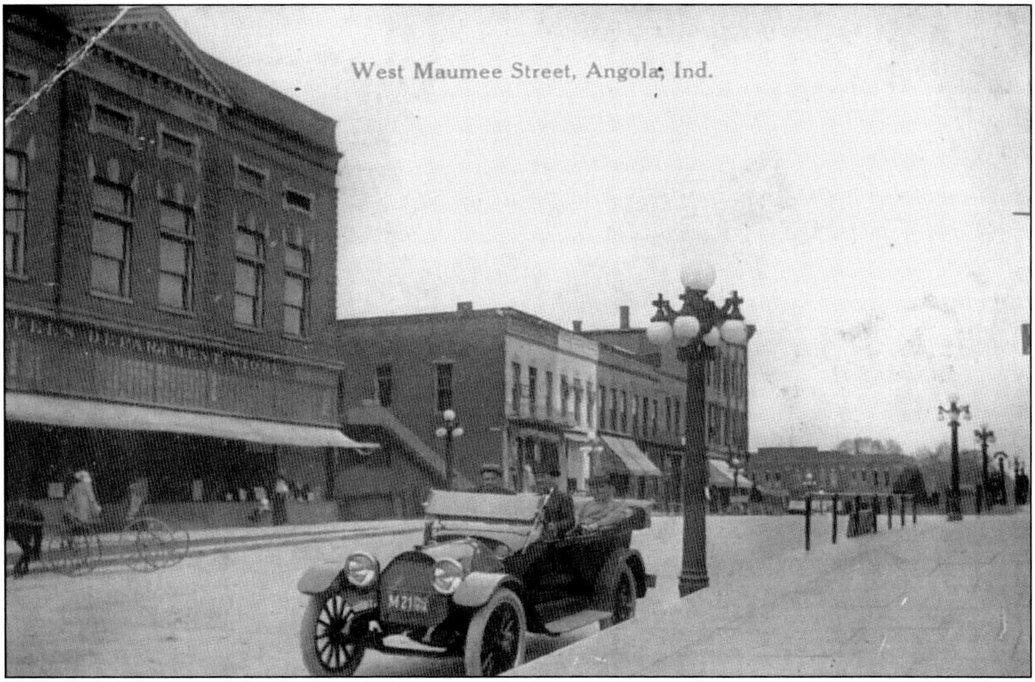

WEST MAUMEE STREET, ANGOLA, INDIANA, *c.* 1914. The card is dated by the 1914 license plate on the touring car. The I.O.O.F. building is on the left. These initials stand for "International Order of Odd Fellows."

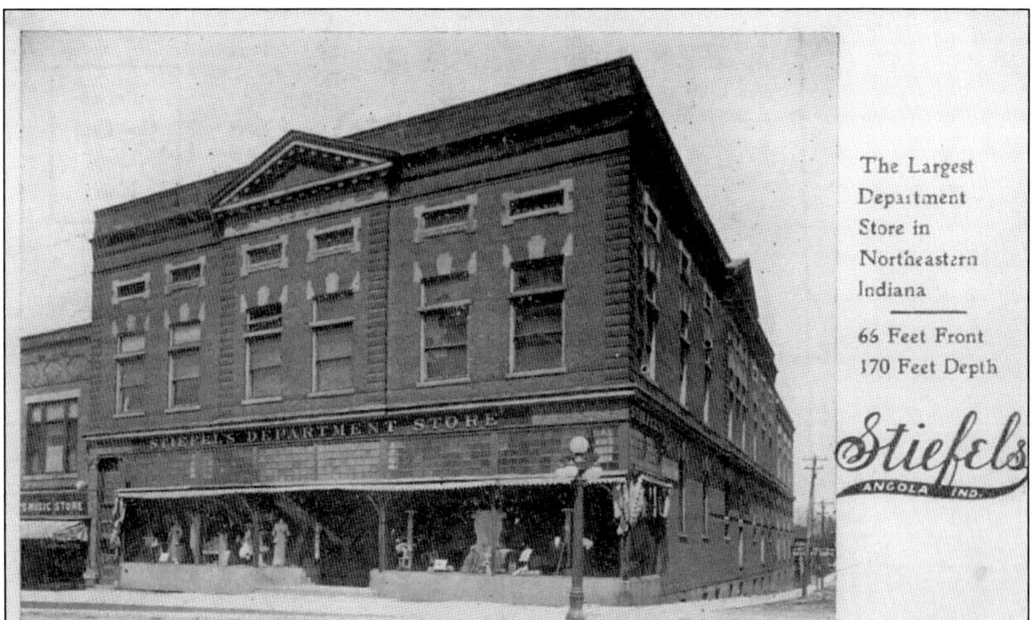

THE LARGEST DEPARTMENT STORE IN NORTHEASTERN INDIANA, 66 FEET, 170 DEPTH. STIEFELS, ANGOLA, INDIANA. Postcards were used to advertise the business.

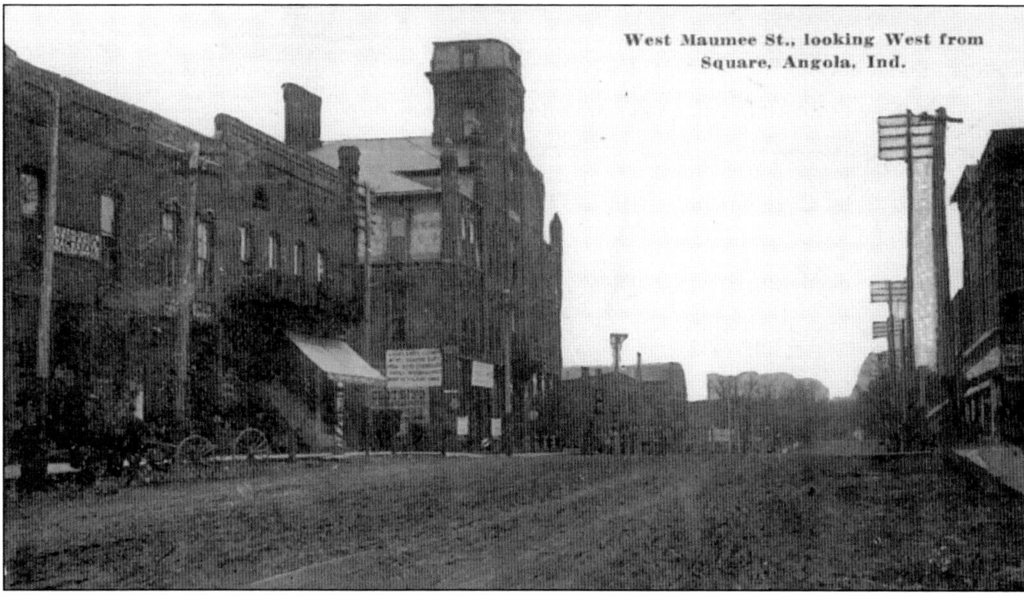

WEST MAUMEE STREET, LOOKING WEST FROM SQUARE, ANGOLA, INDIANA, *c.* 1911. The back message states: "Dear Amy. I have been going to ans your card for a long time but havent had time. Am all o.k. I washed today am writing lots of card and letters tonight. I haven't bee to church at night for a coons age. I was to church sun p.m." The view shows the dirt streets and board sidewalks.

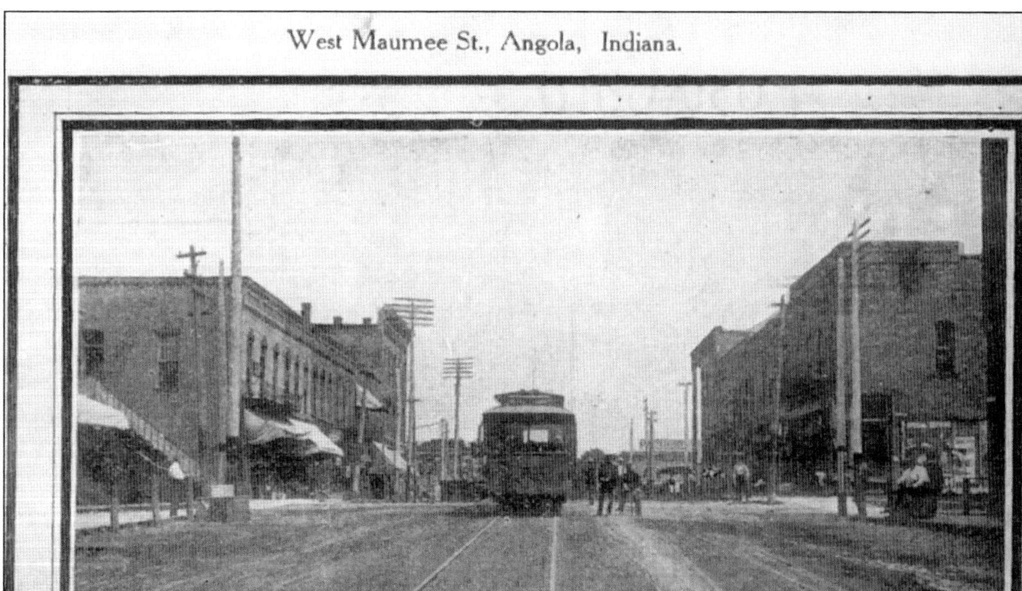

WEST MAUMEE STREET, ANGOLA, INDIANA, *c.* 1911. The back message states: "Dear Friend: Rec'd your card today am glad to know you have recovered from the measles. I was out to Pleasant Lake last sun. It certainly is a nice place. I am not feeling very good tonight guess I will have to get some med. in the morn. Theron." The view shows the tracks and trolley in the center of the street.

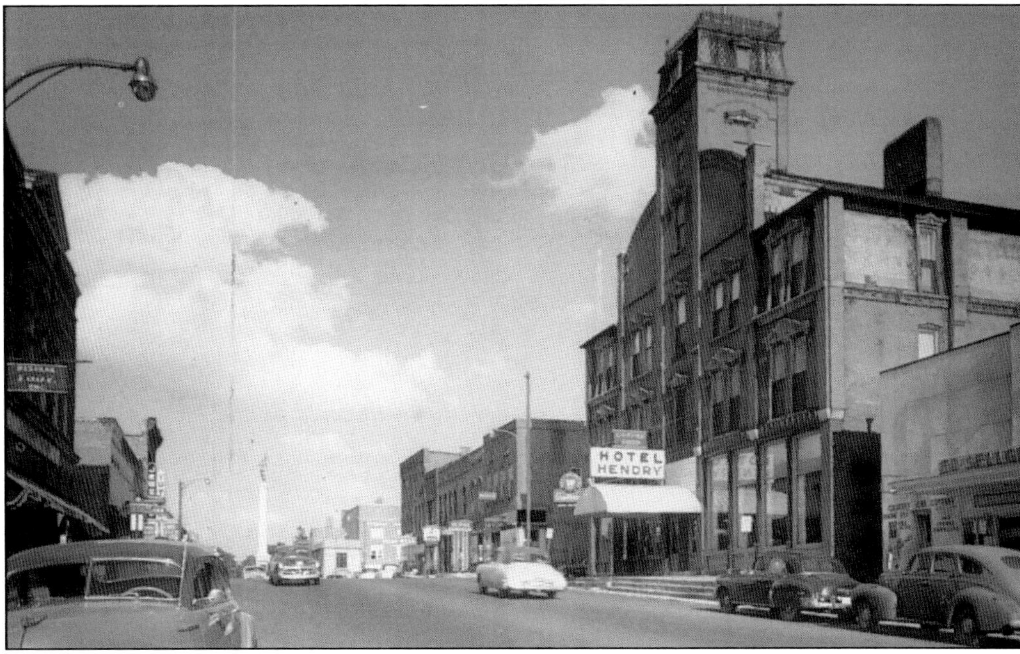

Hotel Hendry—Looking East, Angola, Indiana, c. 1952. This view looks towards the east.

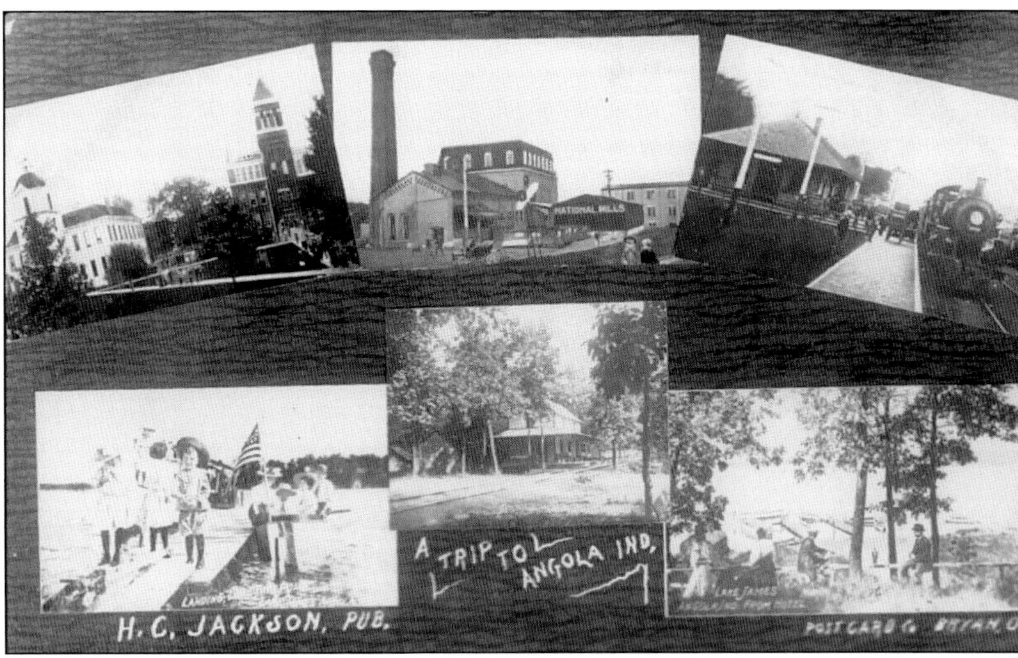

A Trip to Angola, Indiana. The views shown are Tri-State College, National Mills, Angola Depot, and three Lake James scenes. These same views were also used for full-size postcards, one of which appears on the next page.

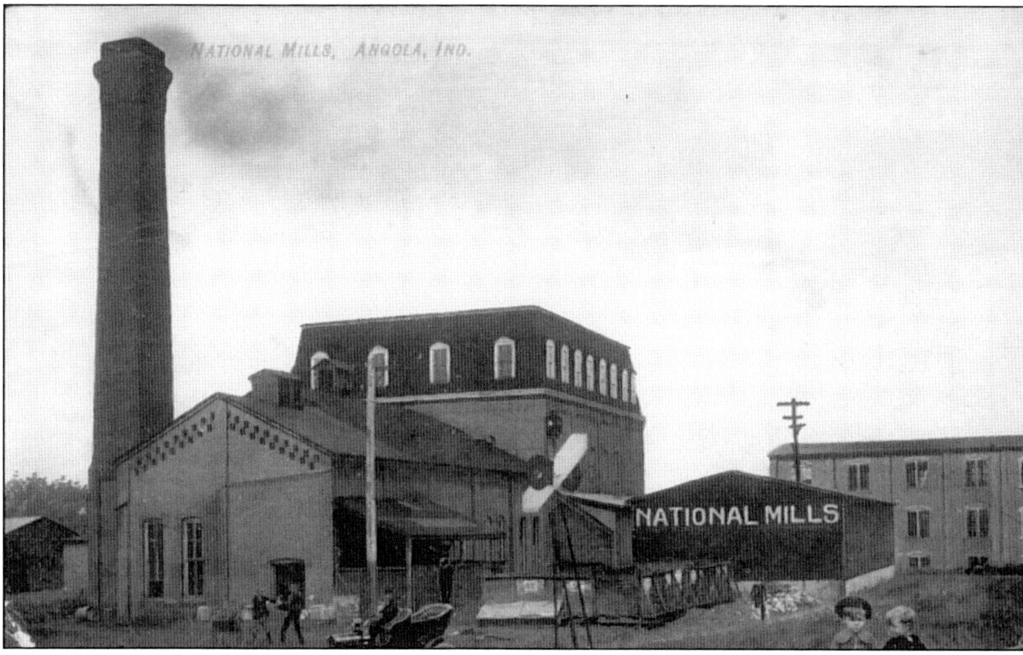

NATIONAL MILLS, ANGOLA, INDIANA, *c.* 1908. With a car in the foreground and smoke belching from the chimney, the factory looks industrious.

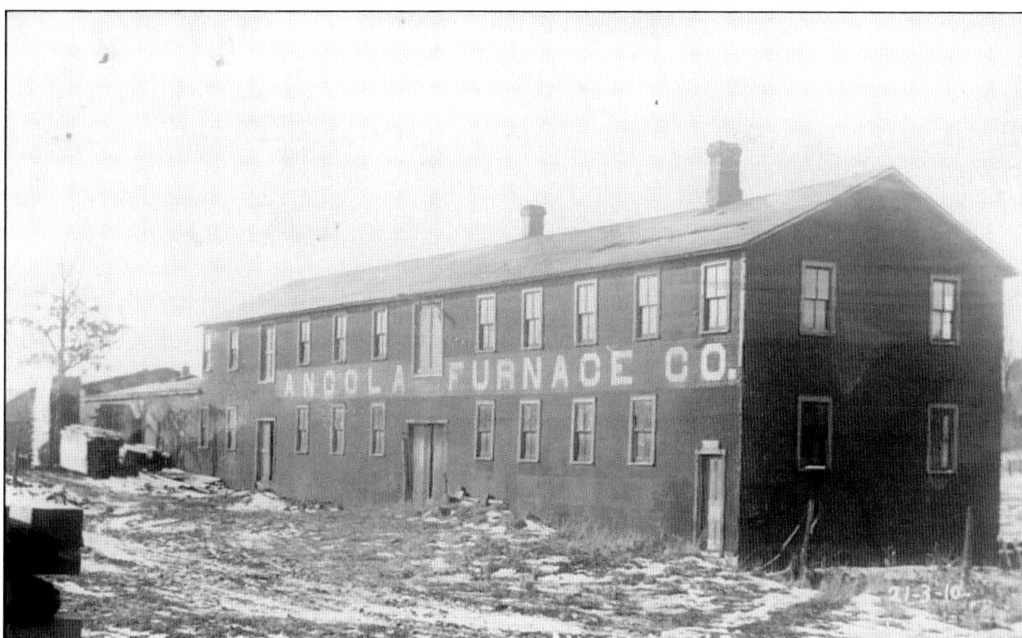

ANGOLA FURNACE, ANGOLA, INDIANA. Buildings of this era had ample windows to provide maximum daylight.

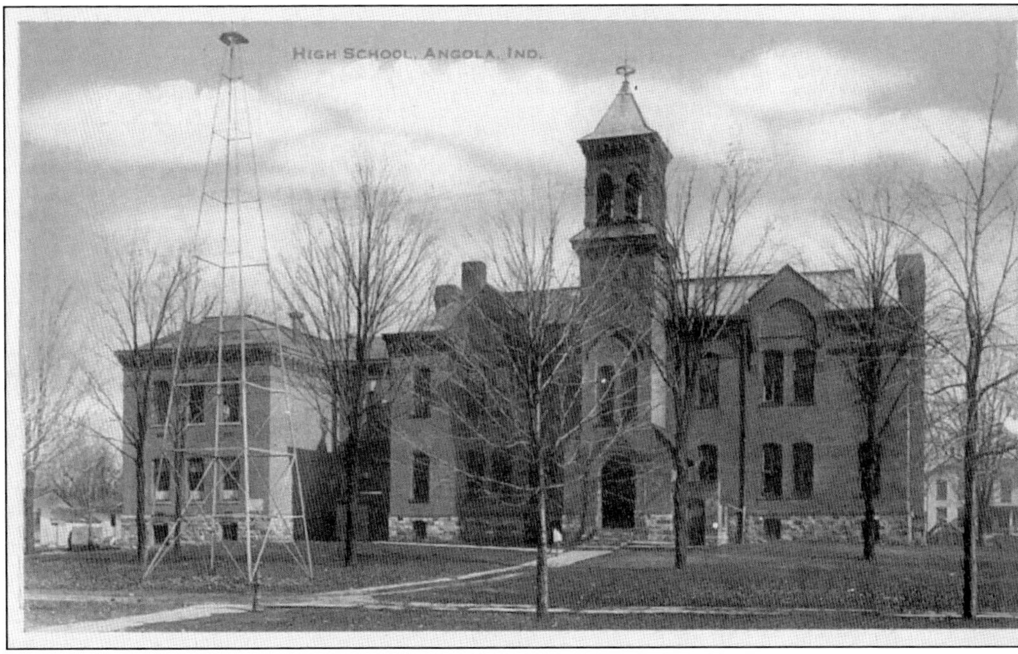

HIGH SCHOOL, ANGOLA, INDIANA. This is a winter view.

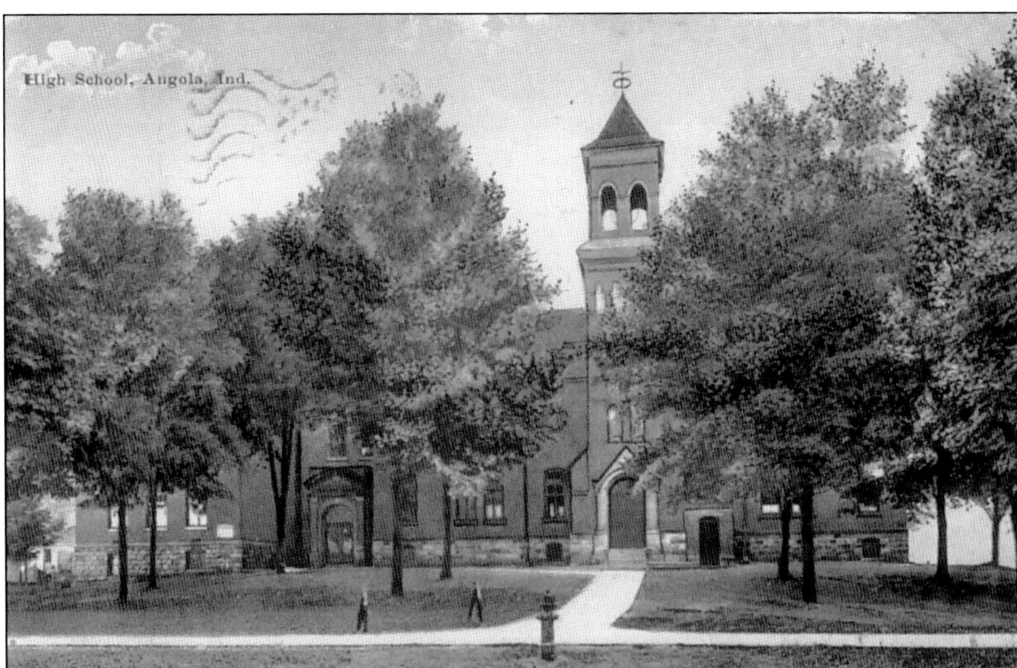

HIGH SCHOOL, ANGOLA, INDIANA. This is a summer view.

HIGH SCHOOL, ANGOLA, INDIANA. This was probably stock artwork with the "A.H.S." and photograph inserted by the publisher.

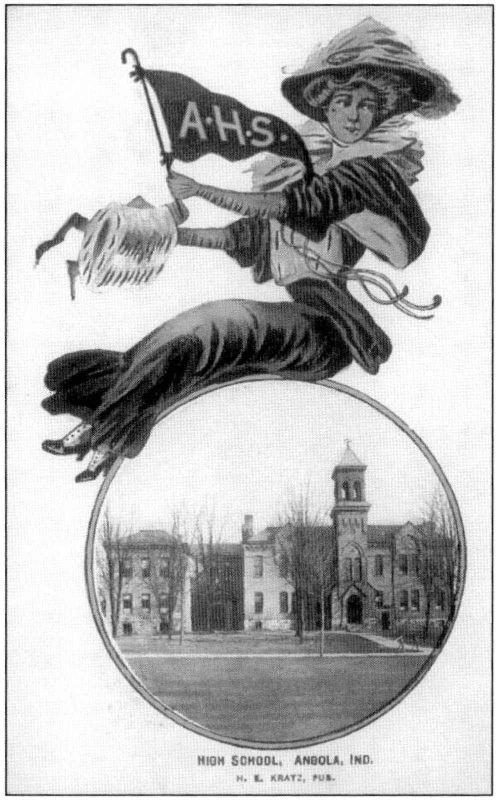

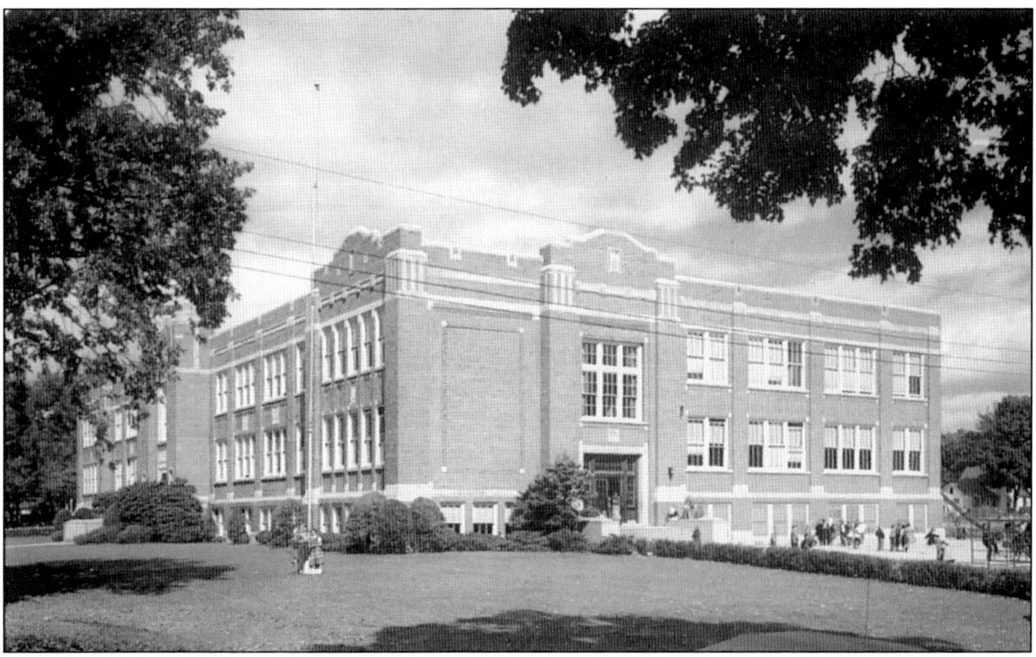

PUBLIC SCHOOL, ANGOLA, INDIANA, *c.* 1952. This is a chrome postcard. The building is now used as the Steuben County Courthouse Annex.

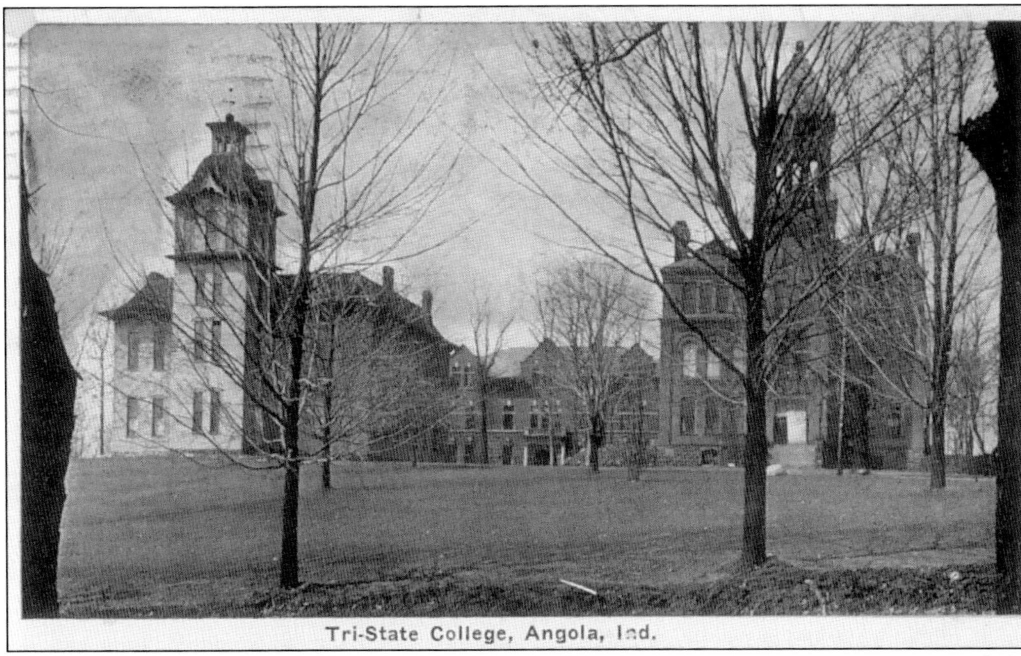

Tri-State College, Angola, Indiana, *c.* 1925. There are many postcard views of the college. Students probably used them for brief correspondence.

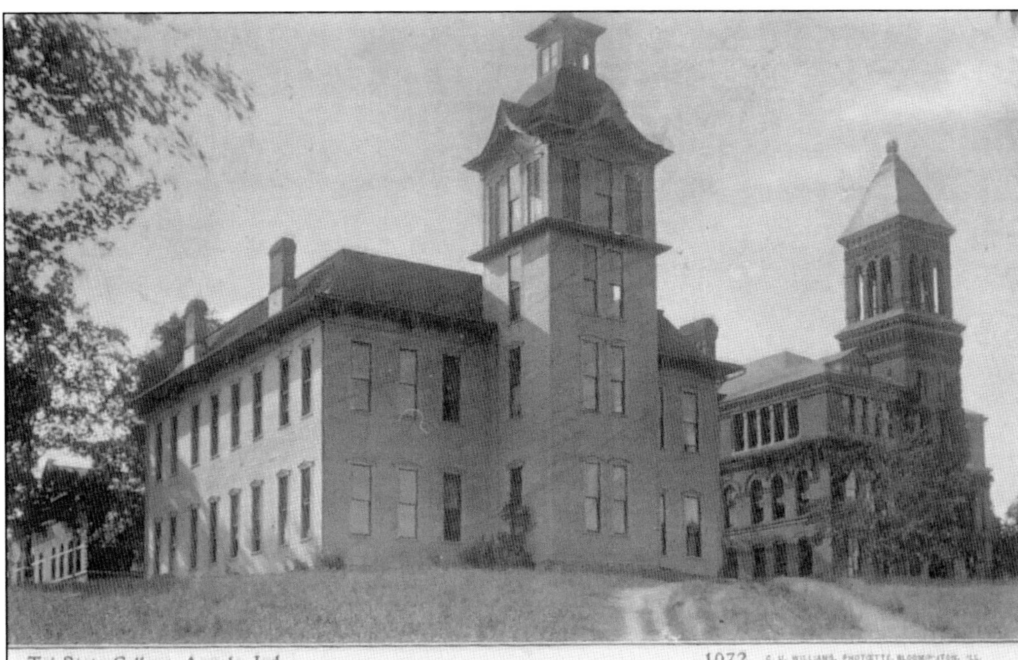

Tri-State College, Angola, Indiana, *c.* 1910. The message states: "I tried to reach you by phone but could not so will send you a card. I have been sick just so I can drag around and do the work. The Dr. says it is nervousness. I didn't set up any all day a week ago today—Mag."

Main Building, Tri-State College, Angola, Indiana, c. 1908. Ivy covered halls of learning are shown here.

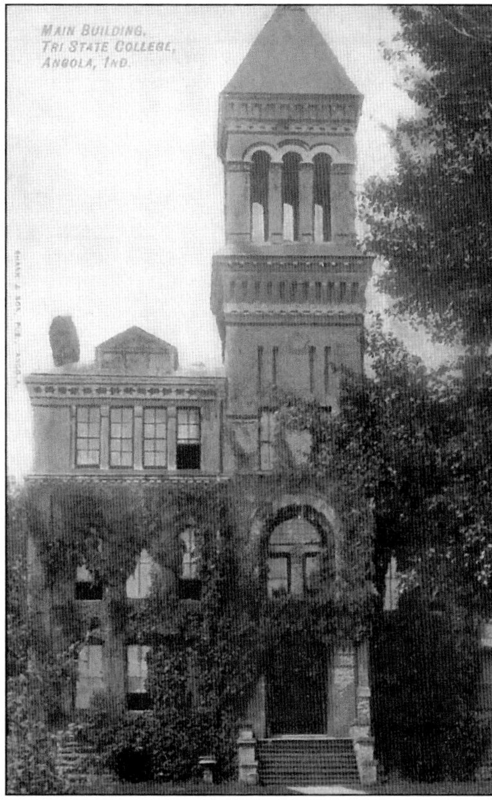

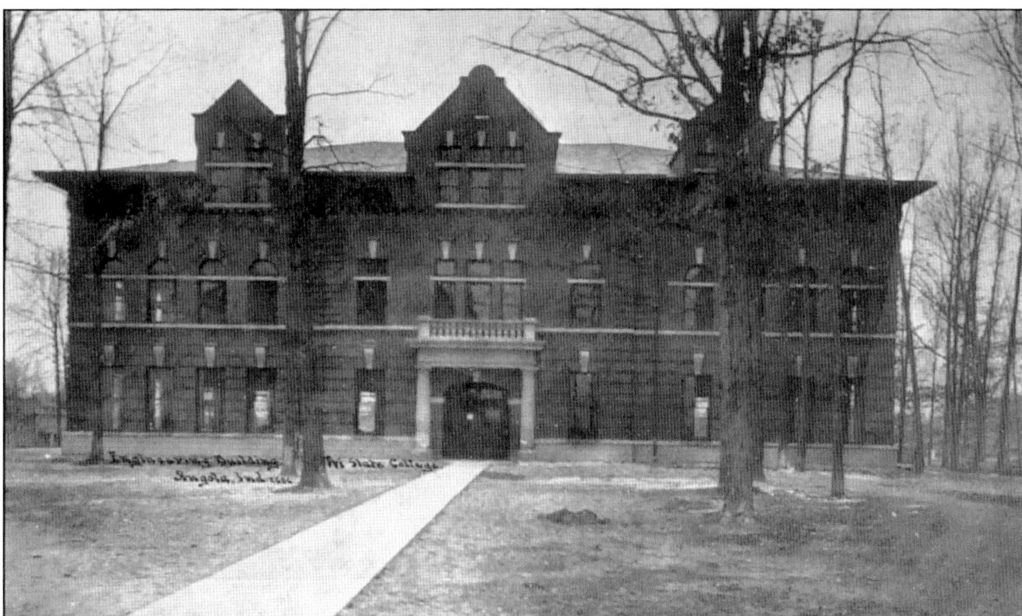

Engineering Building, Tri-State College, Angola, Indiana. Tri-State College has long been noted for its Engineering Department.

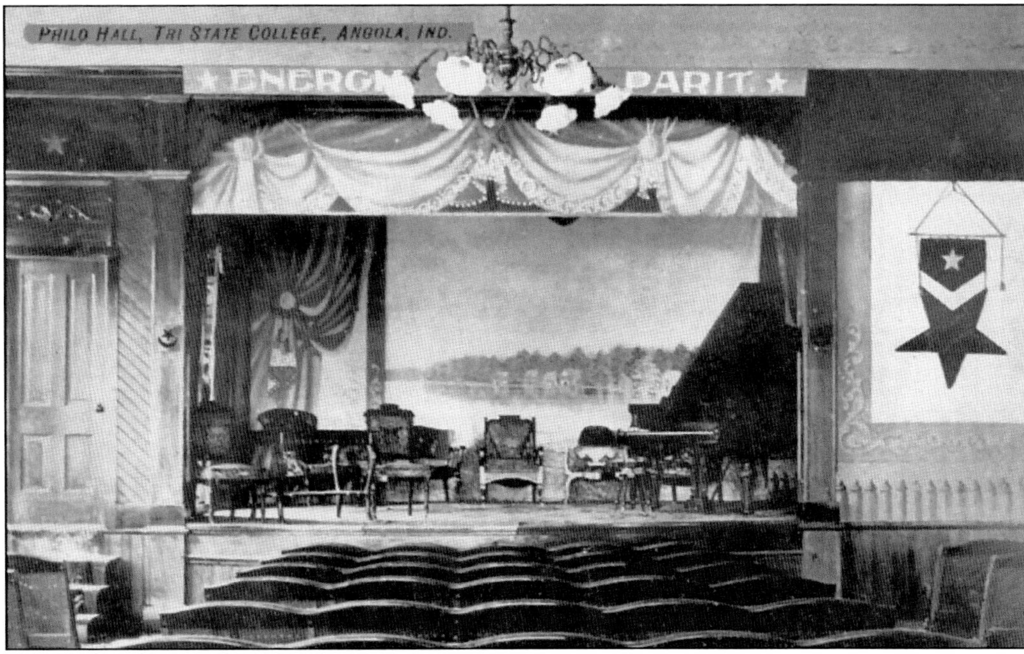

PHILO HALL, TRI STATE COLLEGE, ANGOLA, INDIANA. The Philo Hall was very ornate.

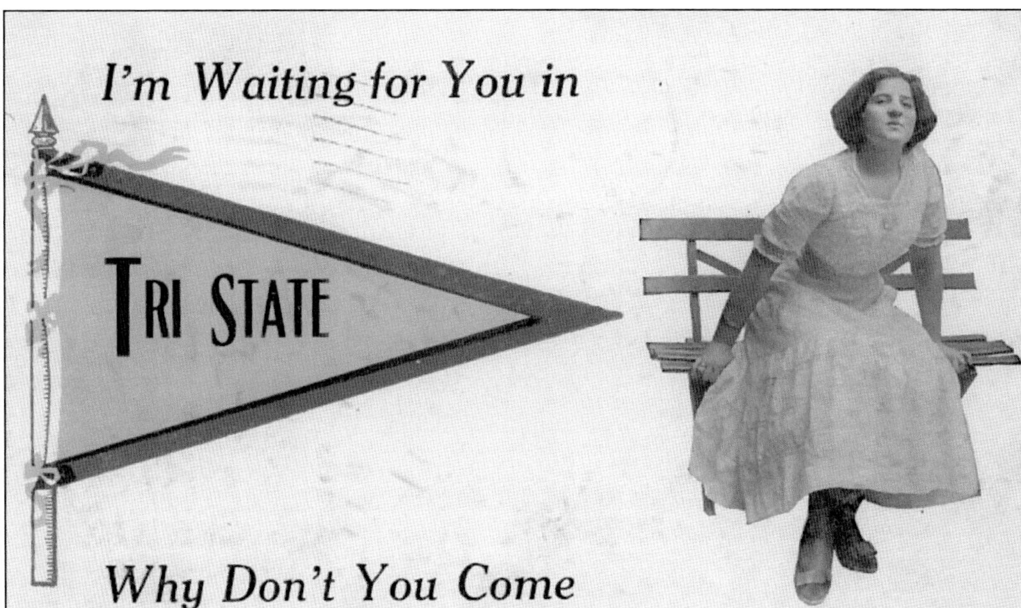

I'M WAITING FOR YOU IN TRI STATE WHY DON'T YOU COME, *C.* 1913. This is a novelty card with a Tri-State Imprint.

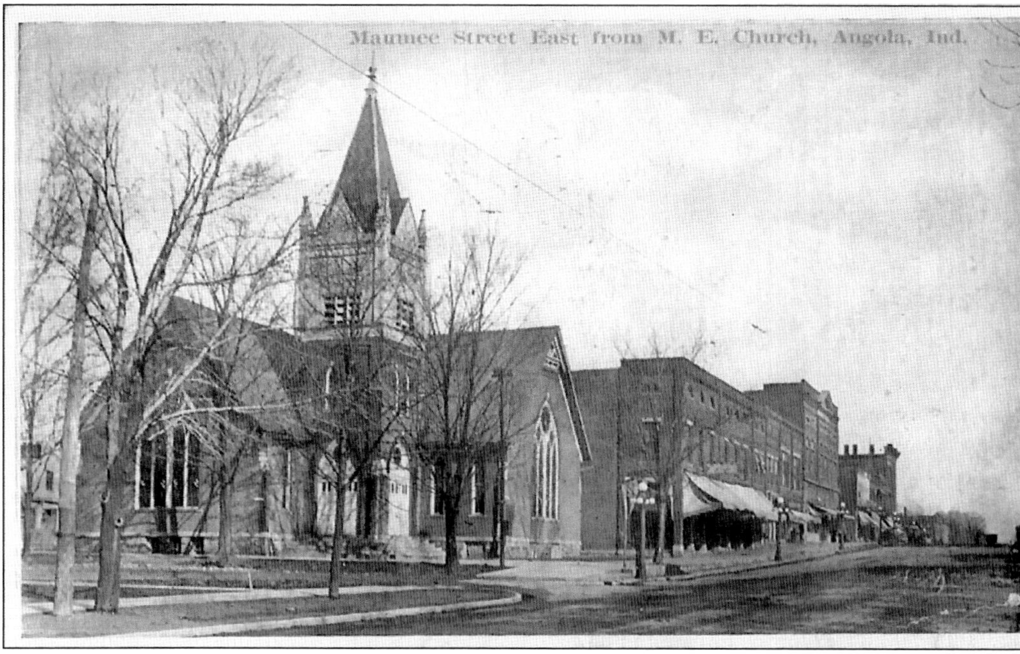

MAUMEE STREET EAST FROM M.E. CHURCH, ANGOLA, INDIANA, *c.* 1925. The Methodist Episcopal Church is now the United Methodist Church.

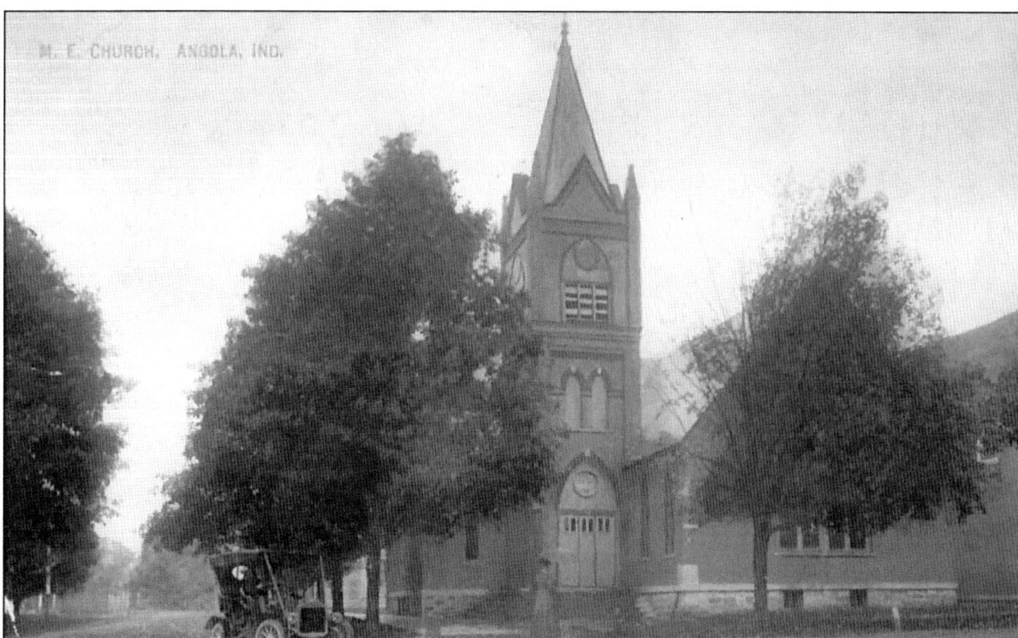

M.E. CHURCH, ANGOLA, INDIANA, *c.* 1908. Another view with an early touring car is shown.

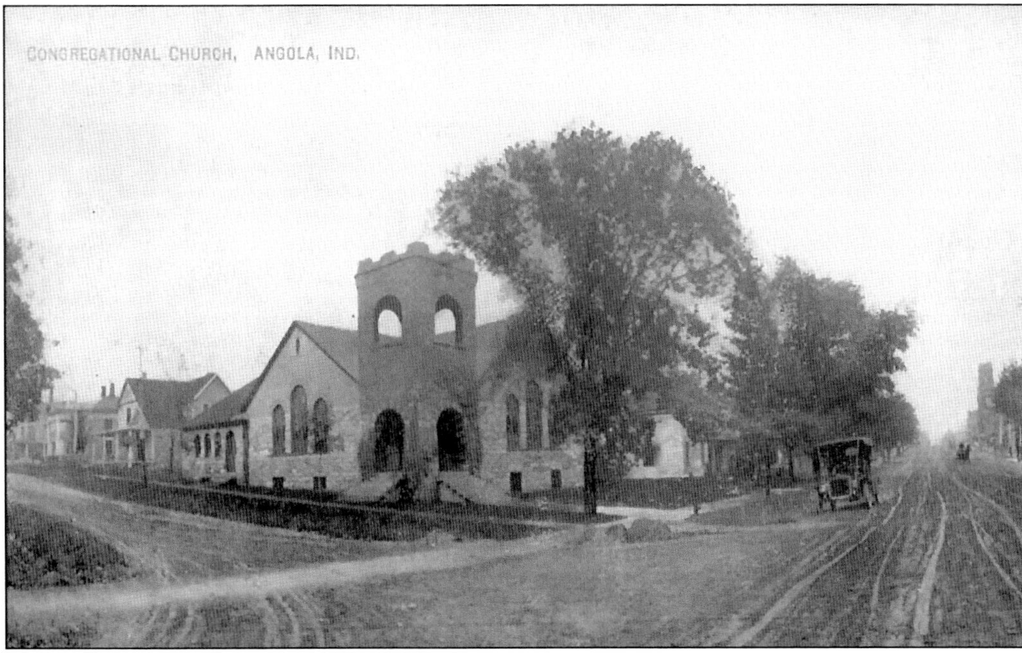

CONGREGATIONAL CHURCH, ANGOLA, INDIANA, *c.* 1909. Dirt streets complete with ruts were commonplace.

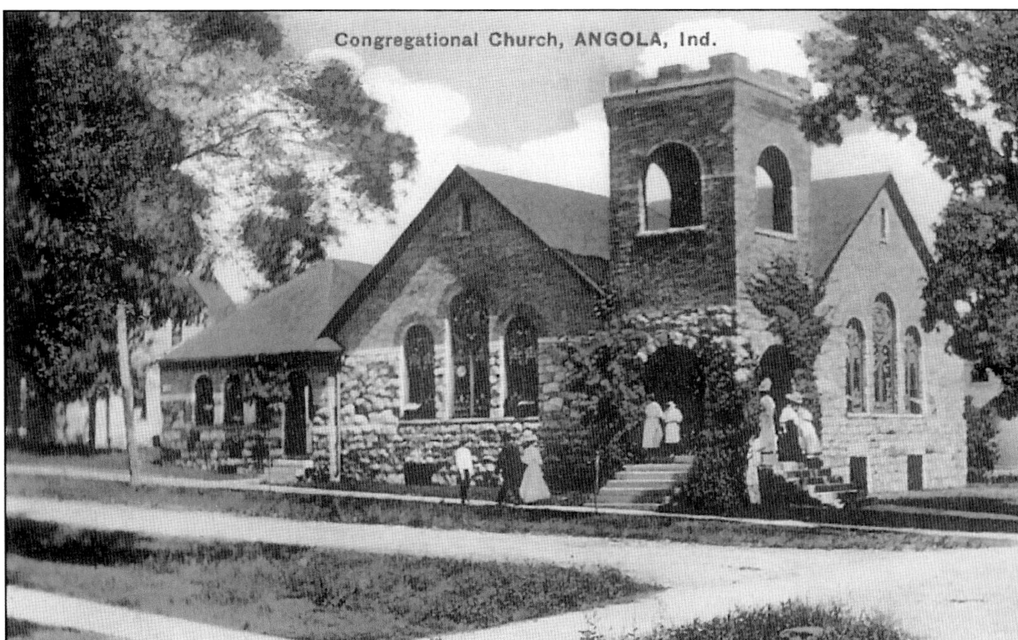

CONGREGATIONAL CHURCH, ANGOLA, INDIANA, *c.* 1909. This is another view with ladies entering the church in their "Sunday Best."

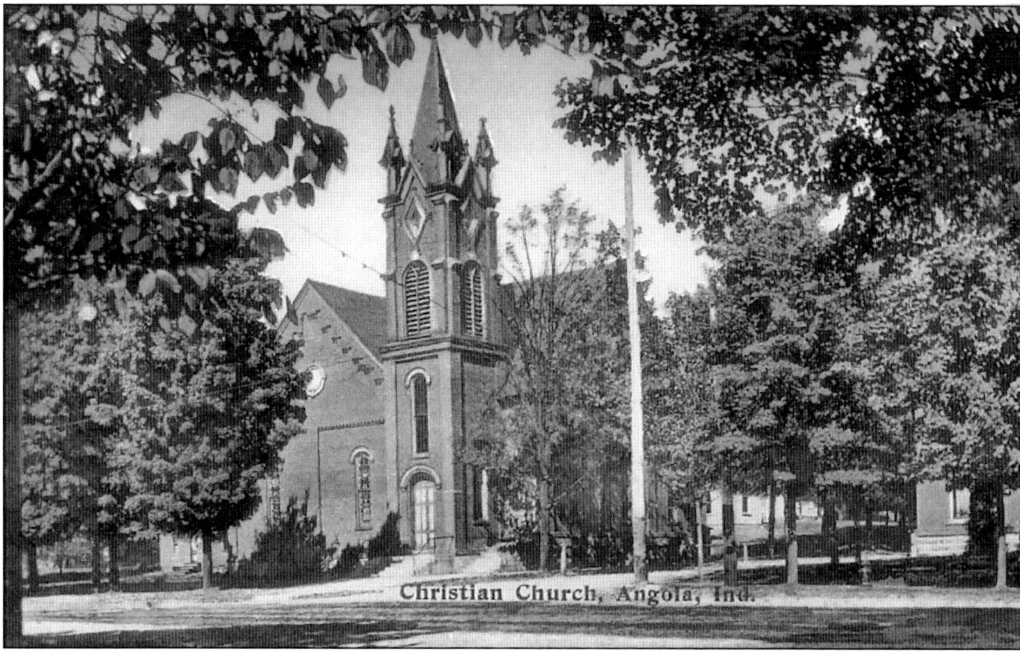

CHRISTIAN CHURCH, ANGOLA, INDIANA. The bell in the tower called parishioners to worship.

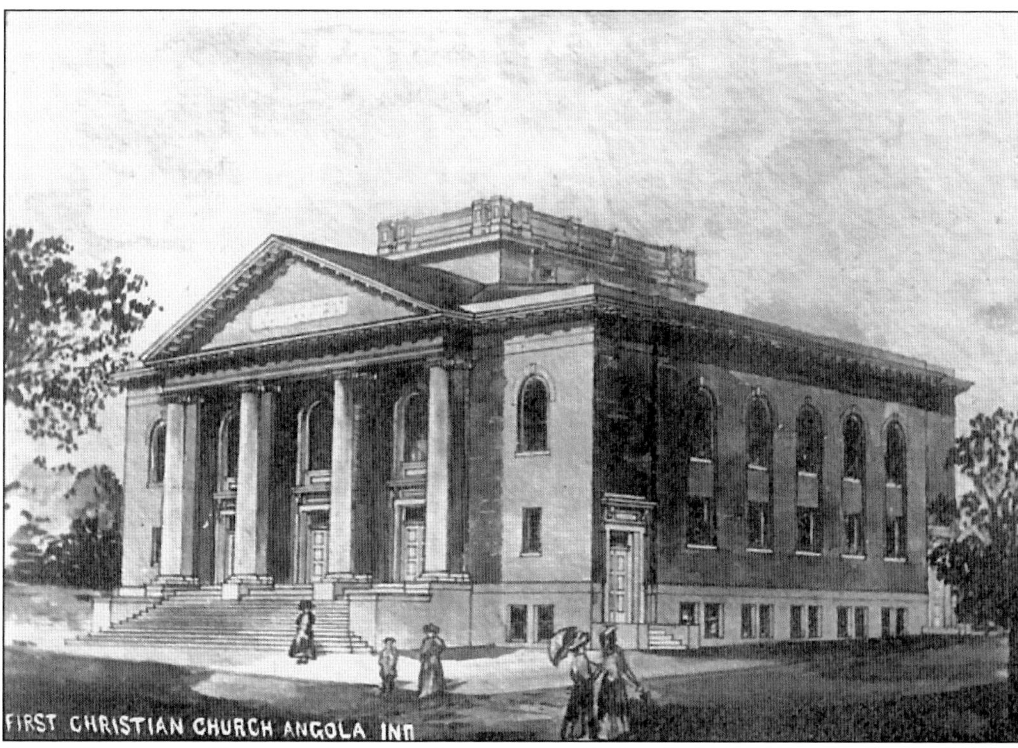

FIRST CHRISTIAN CHURCH, ANGOLA, INDIANA, *C.* 1910. This view is an artist conception, probably prepared by the architect before the building was actually built.

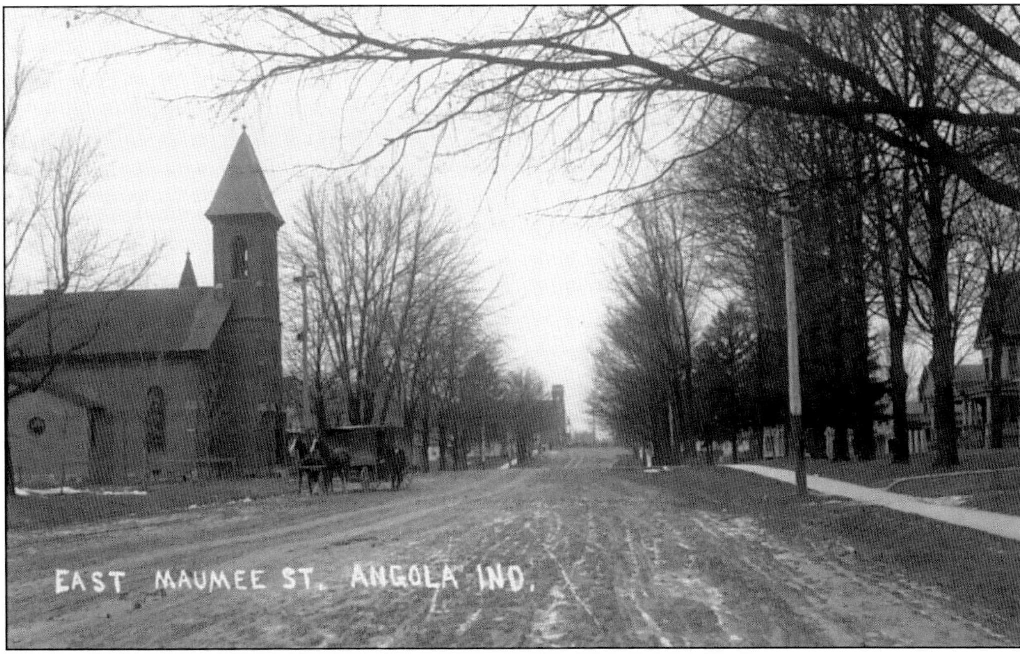

East Maumee Street, Angola, Indiana. The view is looking west. The square and large buildings can be seen in the distant background.

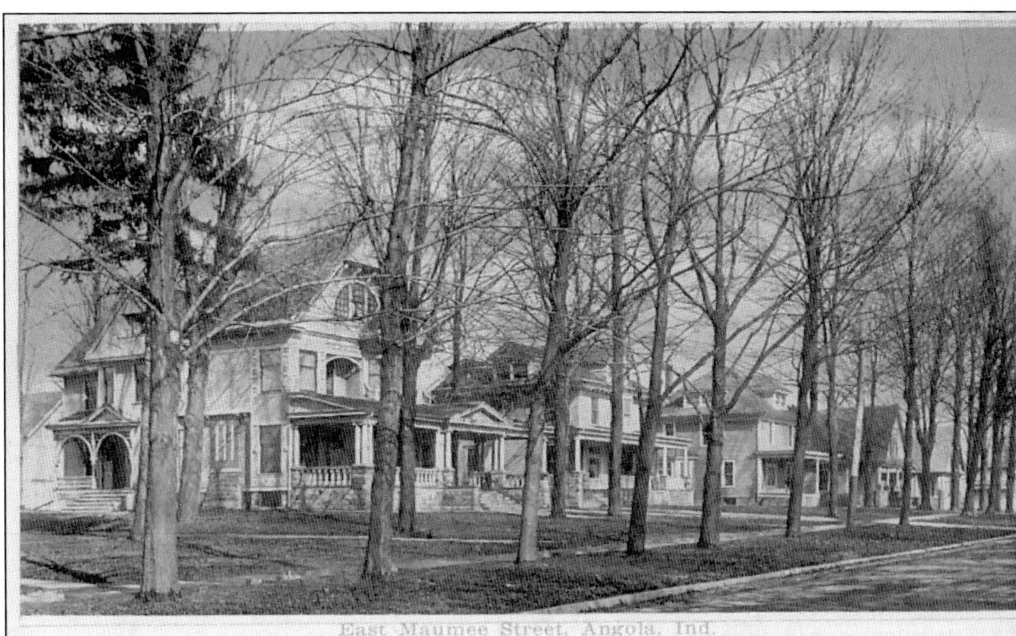

East Maumee Street, Angola, Indiana. Large "Queen Ann" houses with multiple porches were the prevailing style for the wealthy.

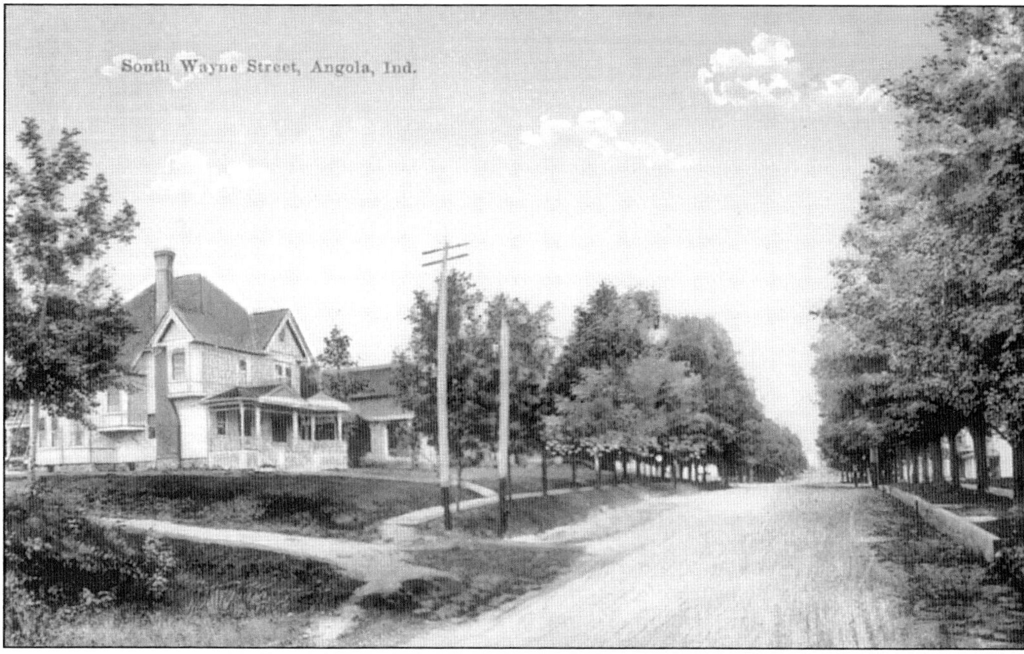

South Wayne Street, Angola, Indiana. The elaborate house appears to be out of place on the dirt path.

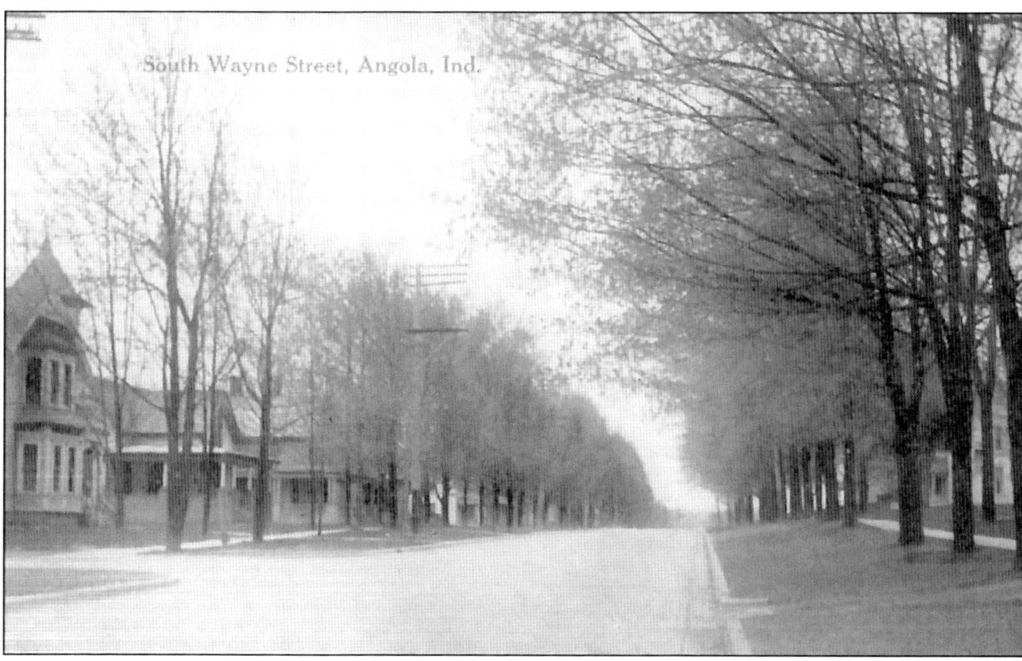

South Wayne Street, Angola, Indiana. Now streets are paved complete with curbs.

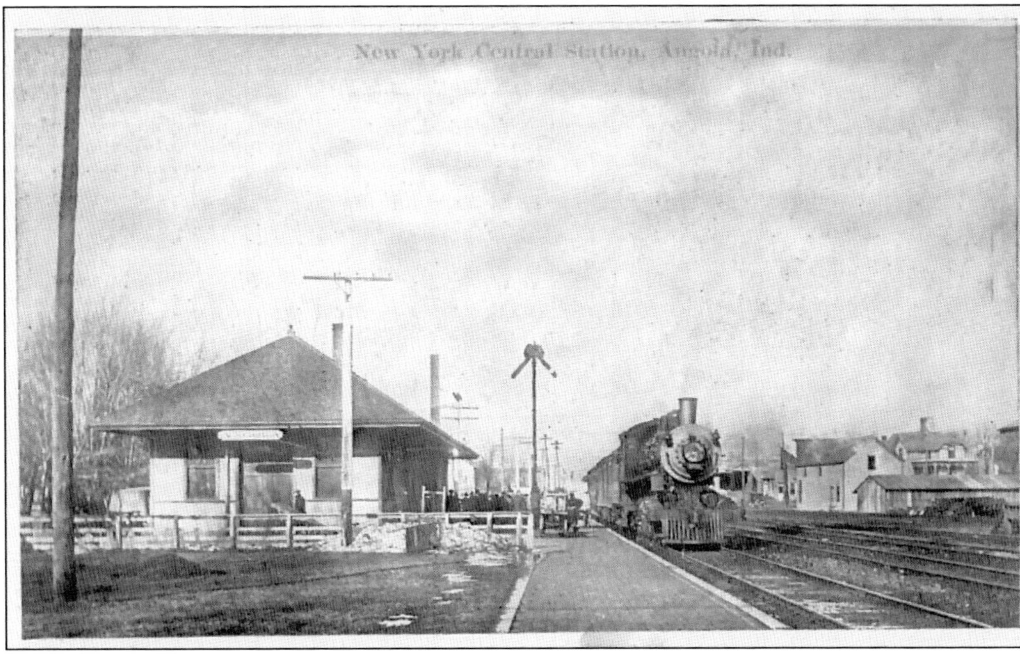

NEW YORK CENTRAL STATION, ANGOLA, INDIANA. The depot was an important place in Angola. The railroad was originally the Fort Wayne, Jackson & Saginaw, which was later acquired by the New York Central.

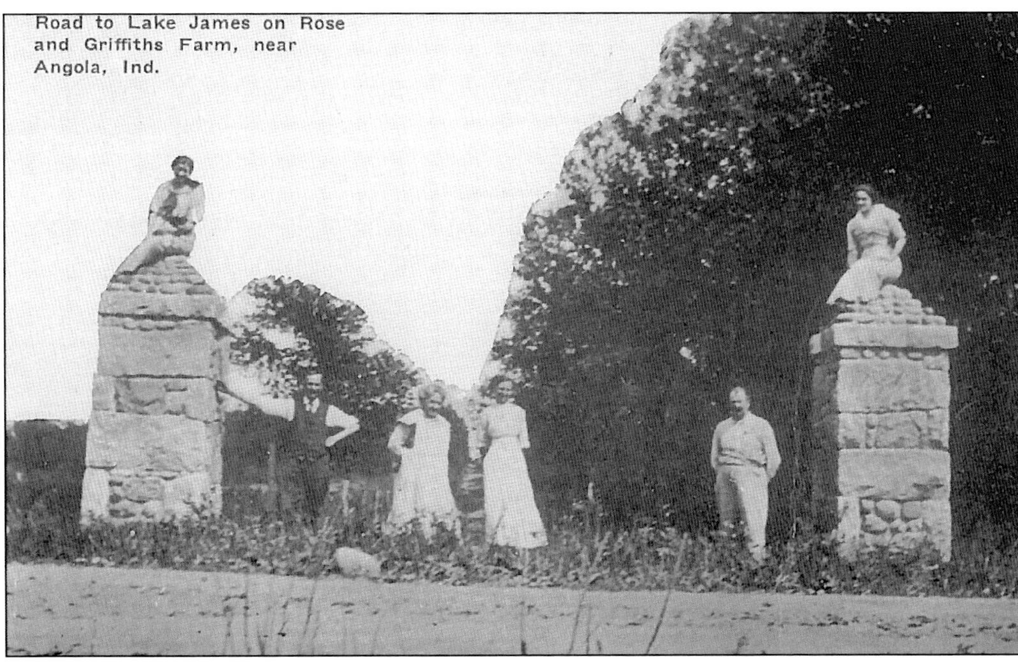

ROAD TO LAKE JAMES ON ROSE AND GRIFFITHS FARM, NEAR ANGOLA, INDIANA. A proud family poses on the corner parts of the farm.

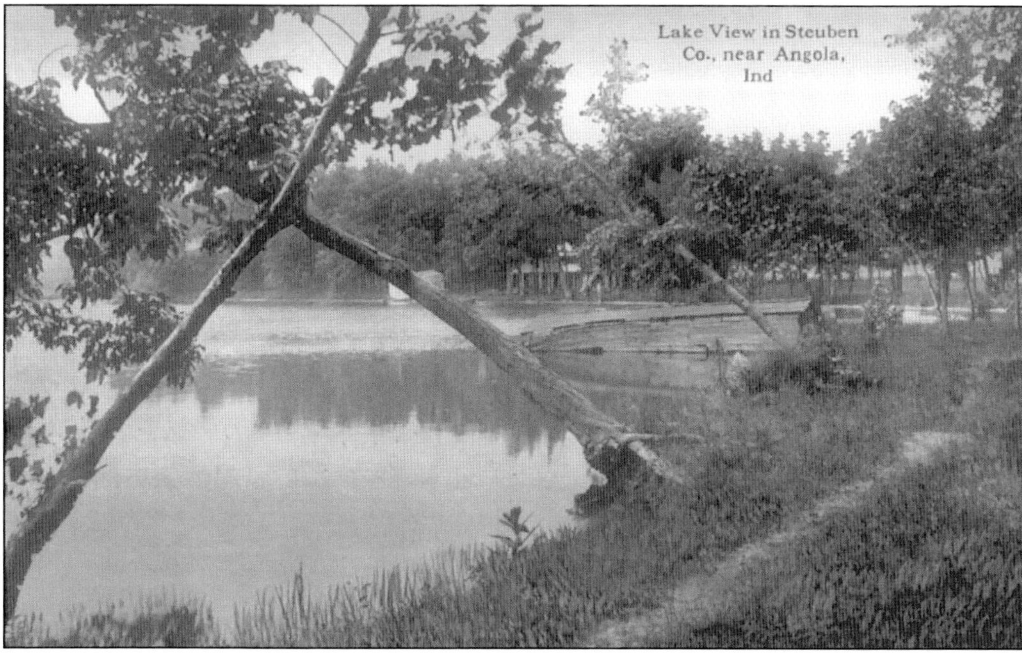

LAKE VIEW IN STEUBEN COUNTY, NEAR ANGOLA, INDIANA. An idyllic scene with an unusual tree is pictured here.

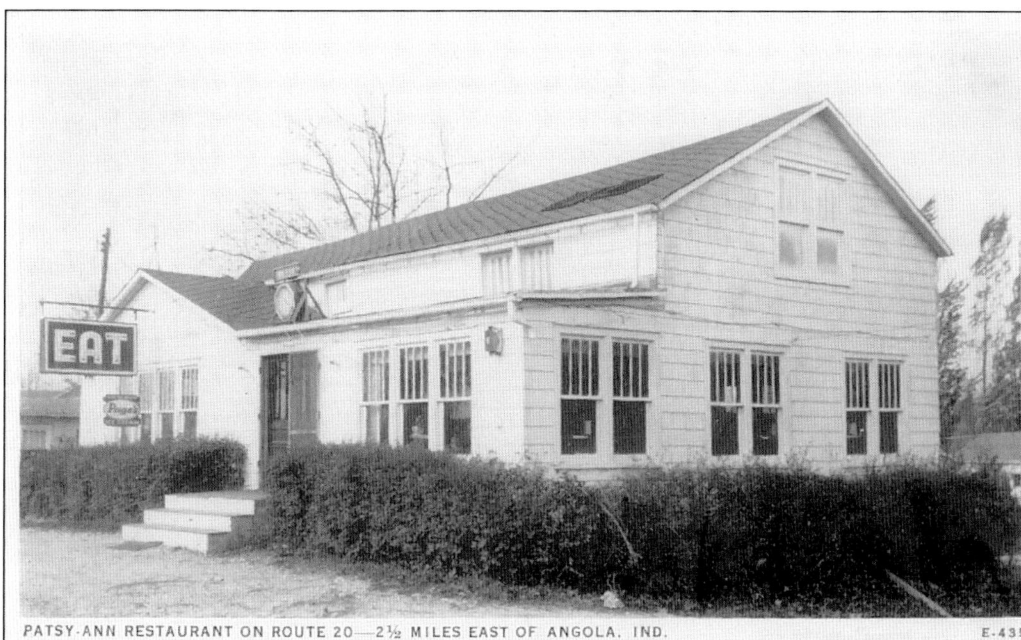

PATSY-ANN RESTAURANT ON ROUTE 20, 2.5 MILES EAST OF ANGOLA, INDIANA. This restaurant is a popular place for tourists to dine.

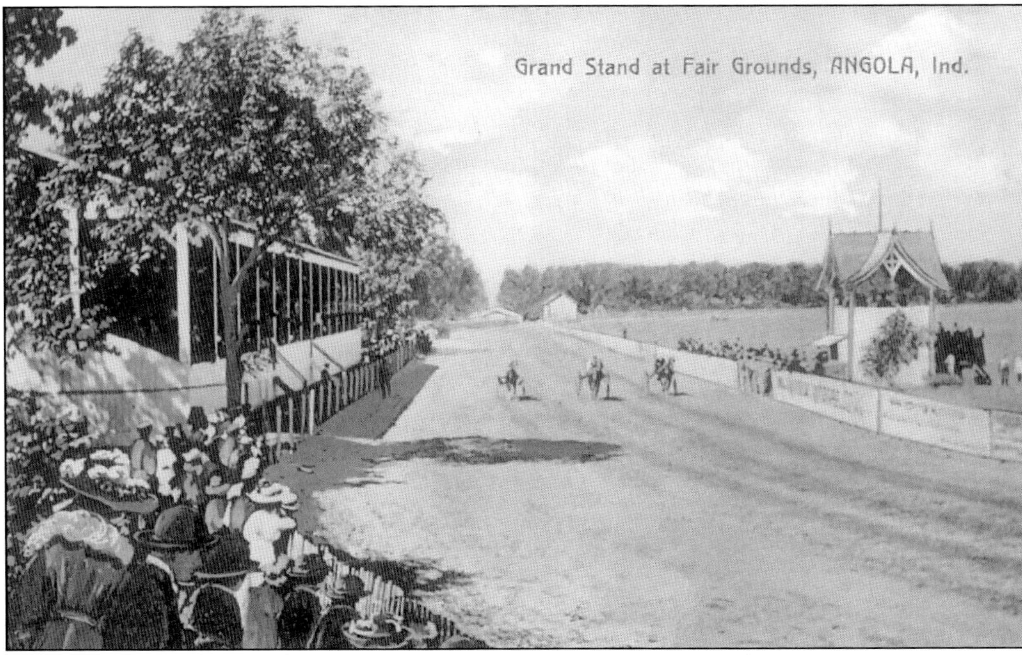

GRAND STAND AT FAIR GROUNDS, ANGOLA, INDIANA. The fair grounds were located on the north edge of Angola. The area is now developed into commercial sites.

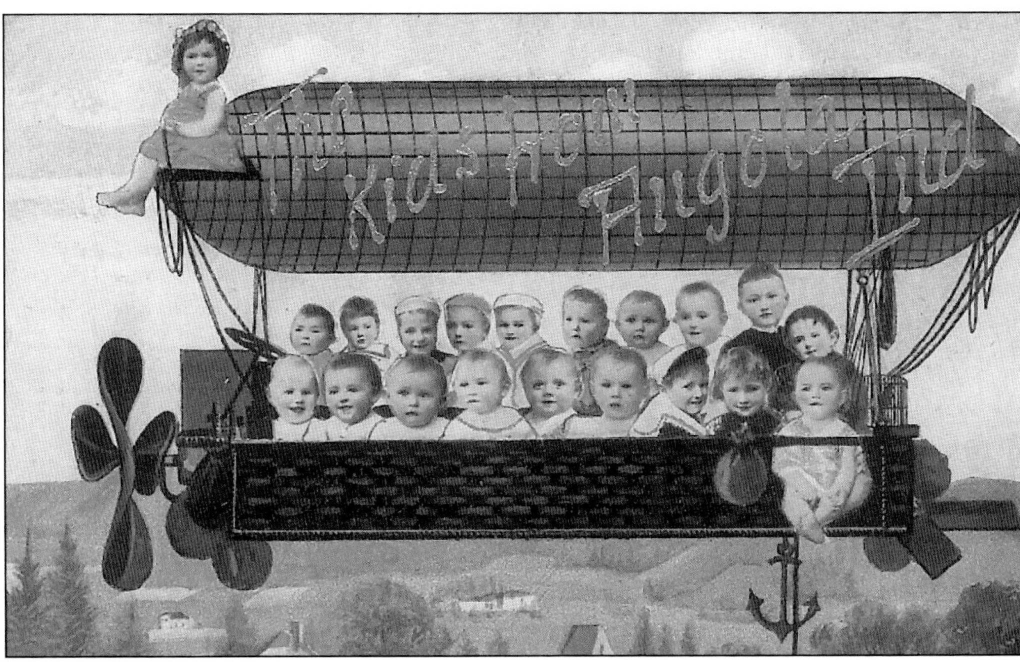

THE KIDS FROM ANGOLA, INDIANA, *c.* 1908. This was stock art work with the Angola reference individually applied.

Two

Fremont

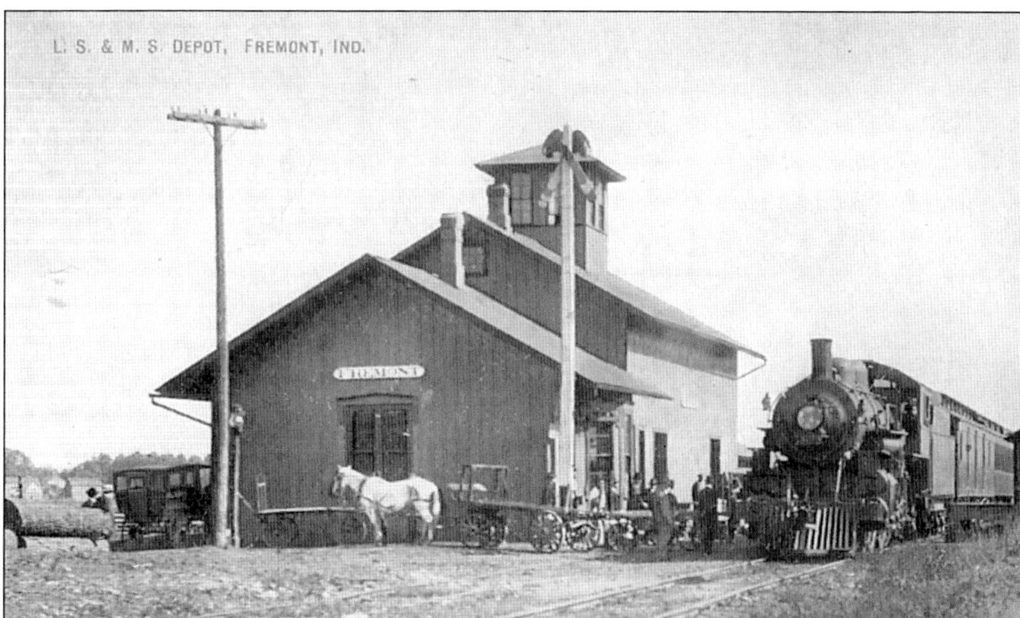

L.S.&M.S. Depot, Fremont, Indiana, *c.* 1916. Horse-drawn vehicles met the train to haul freight and passengers.

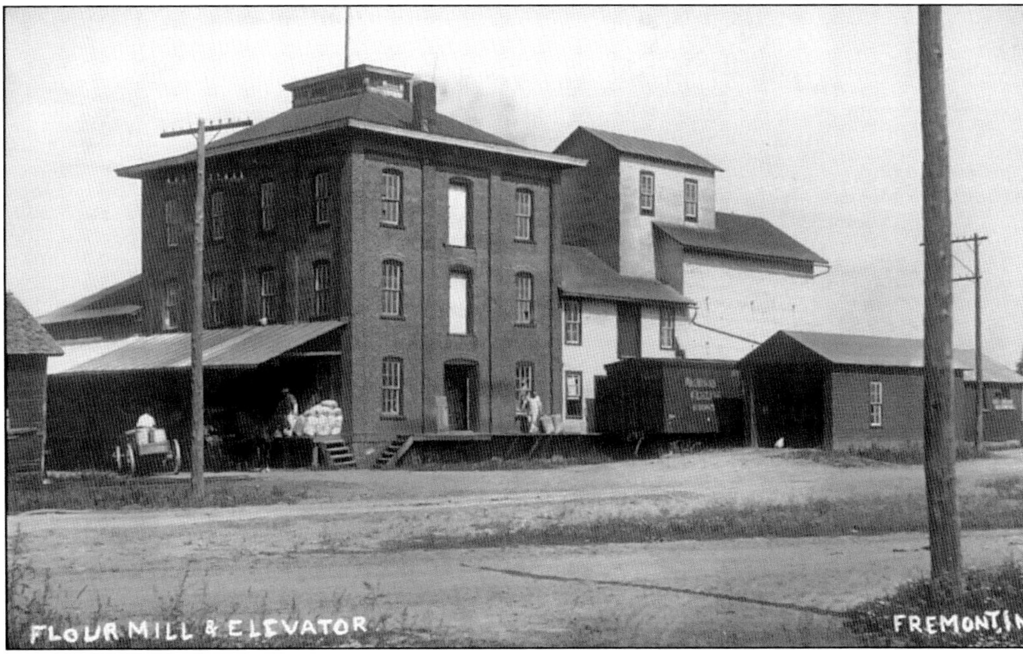

FLOUR MILL & ELEVATOR, FREMONT, INDIANA. Nearly every town had a flour mill to serve its residents.

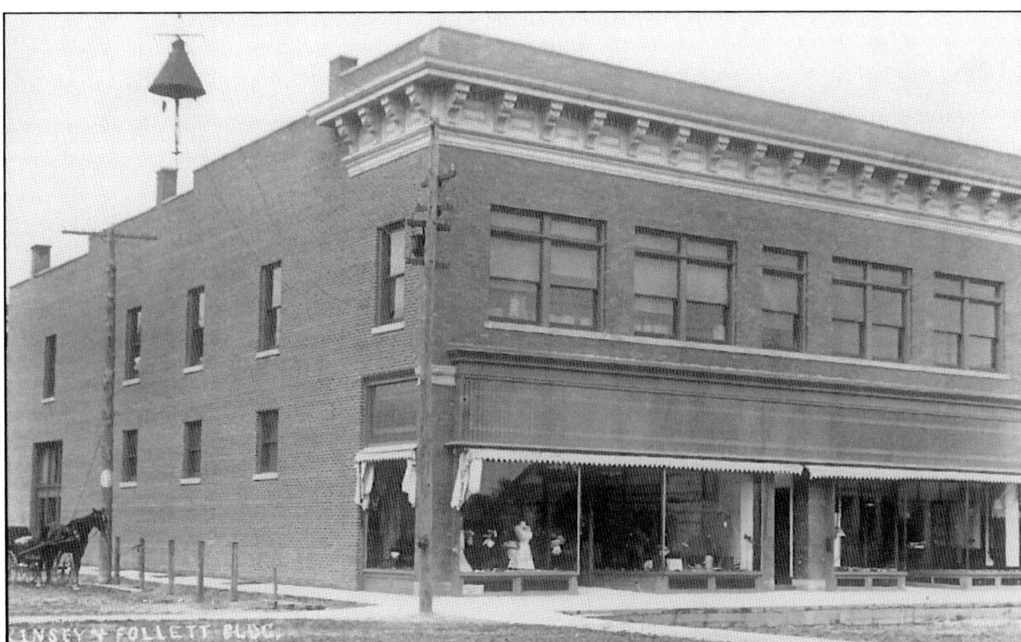

KINSLEY & FOLLETT BUILDING, FREMONT, INDIANA. An elaborate building housed this department store.

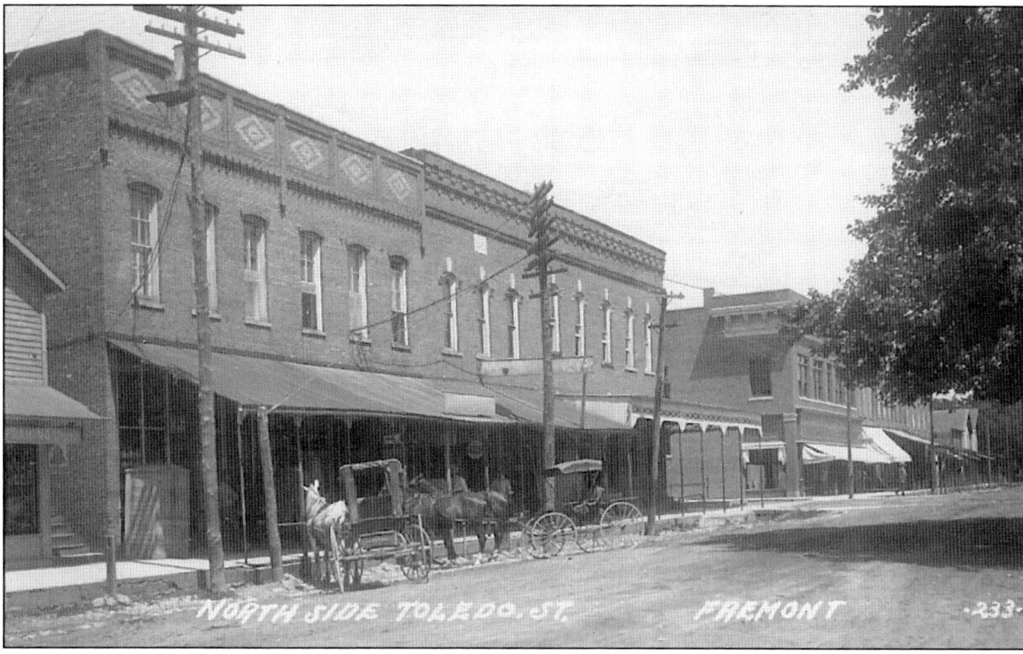

NORTH SIDE TOLEDO STREET, FREMONT, INDIANA, *c.* 1910. The message states: "Will write a few lines and let you know we got home all right, had a dandy sleigh ride did not get very cold Arlene enjoyed it. Good bye. Mrs. Rowan."

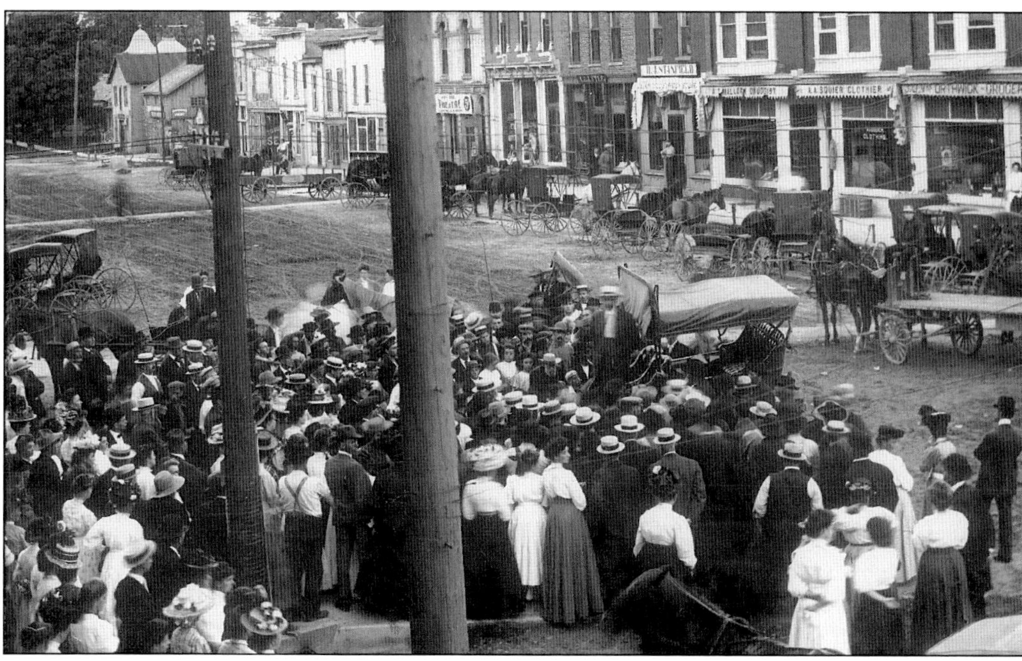

FREMONT, INDIANA. A crowd has gathered, probably for an auction. Stores in the background include Orthweck Grocer, A.A. Squier Clother, A.T. Mallon Druggist, H.A. Stanfield, A. Little, and Theatre.

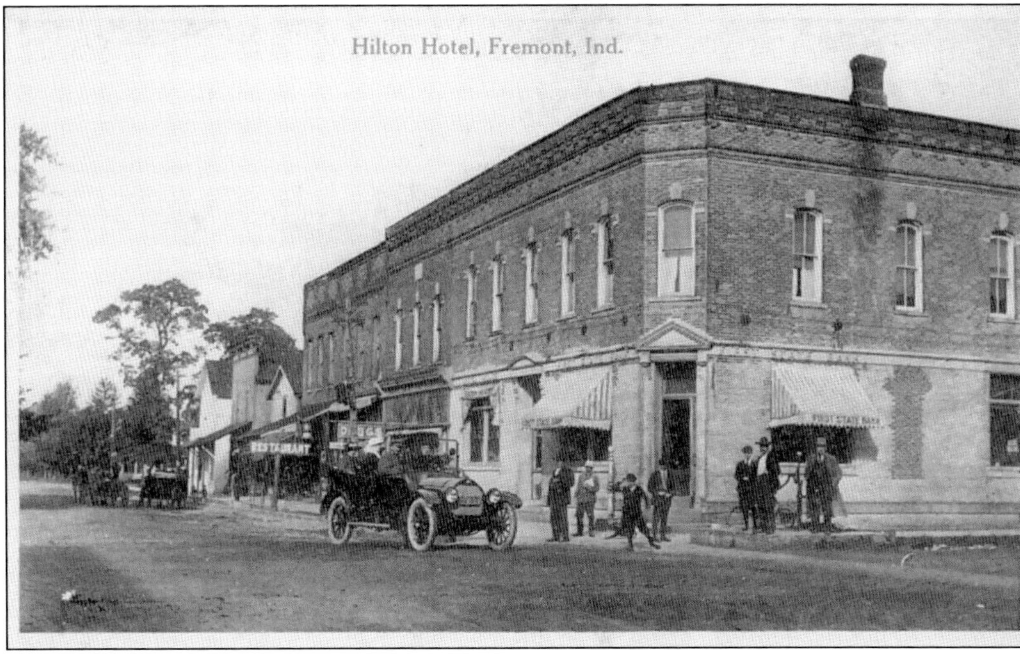

Hilton Hotel, Fremont, Indiana. The First State Bank was located at street level.

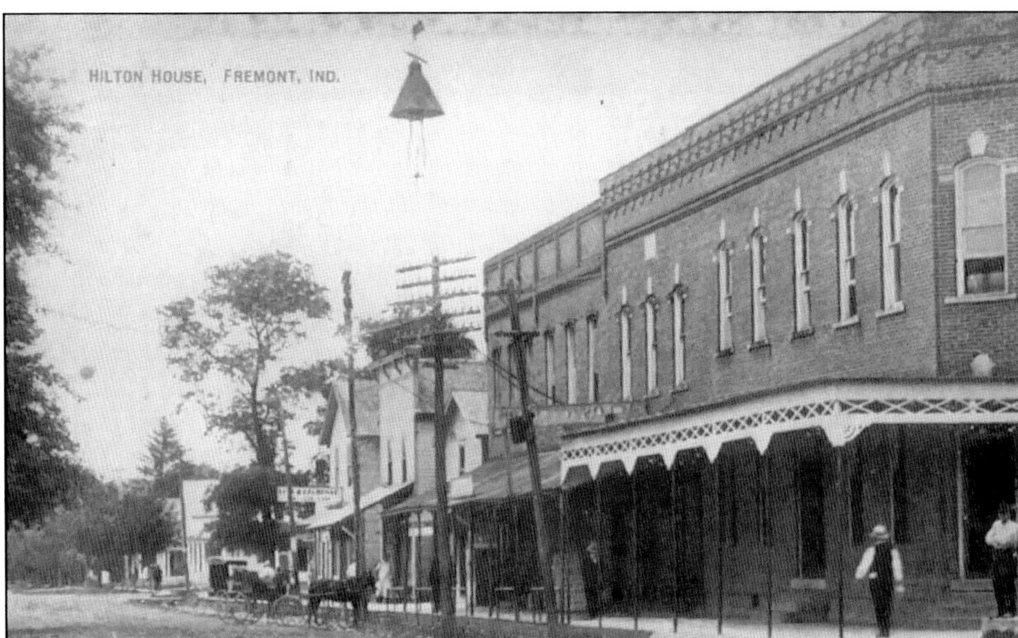

Hilton House, Fremont, Indiana. Every town had a hotel for travelers.

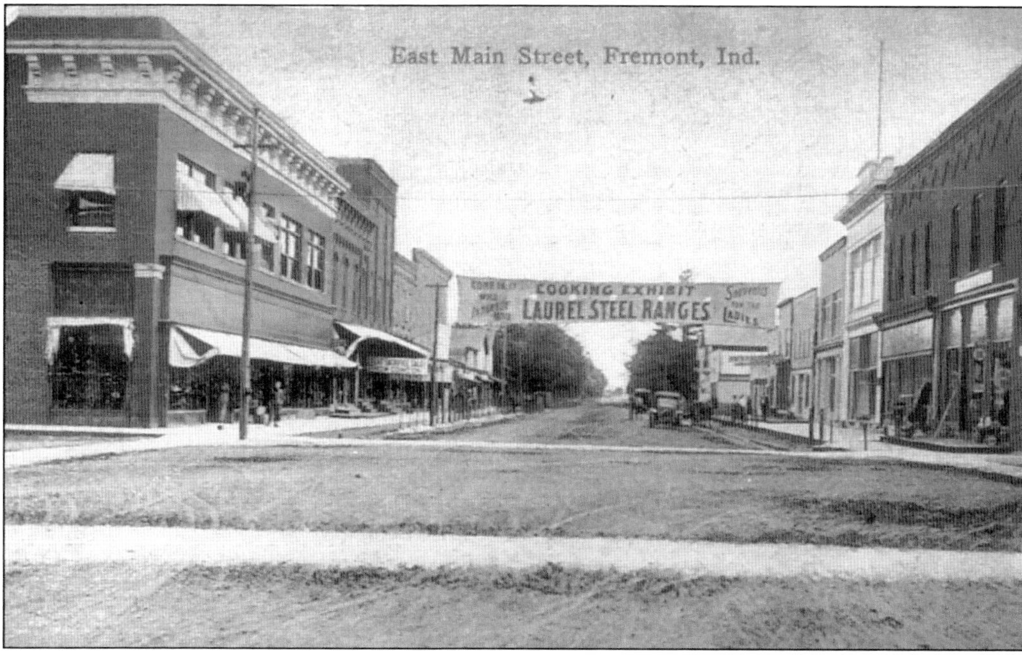

EAST MAIN STREET, FREMONT, INDIANA. A banner across the street advertises: "Cooking Exhibit—Laurel Steel Ranges—Come in, It Will Interest You—Souvenirs for the Ladies."

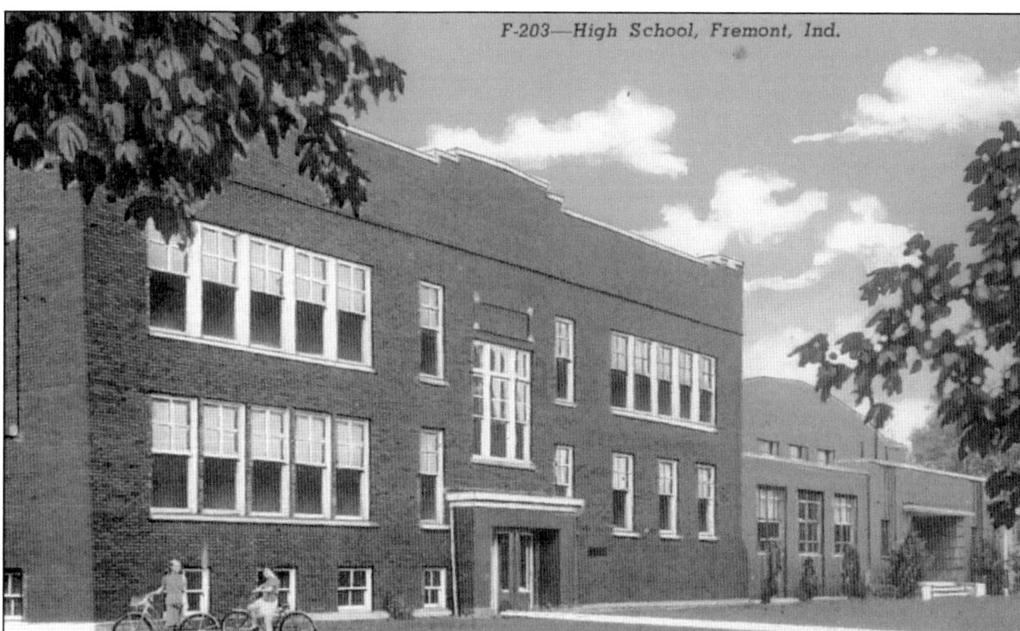

HIGH SCHOOL, FREMONT, INDIANA. This is a linen card showing the school with two children on buggies.

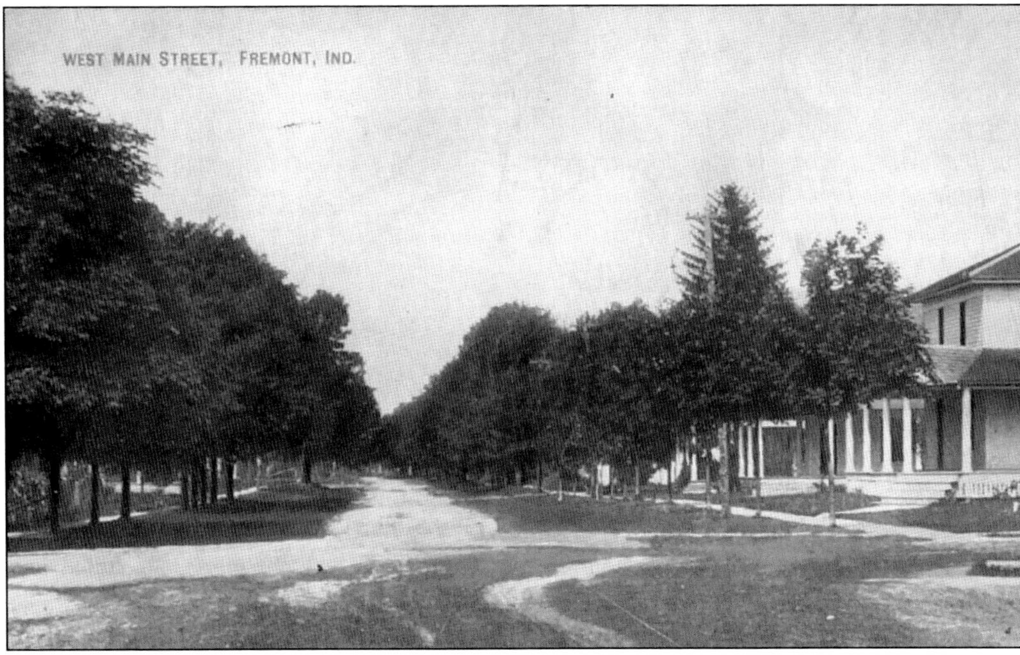

WEST MAIN STREET, FREMONT, INDIANA, *c.* 1910. The message states: "Have you seen my cousins and if you know who this is C.B."

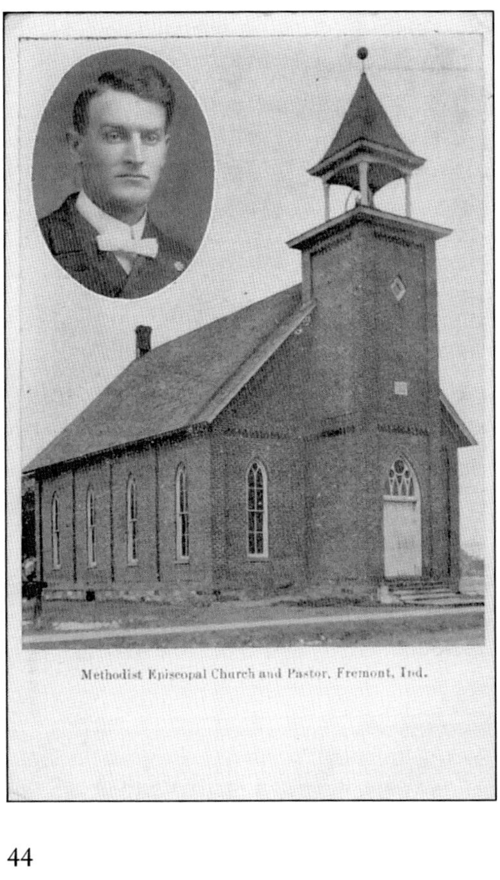

METHODIST EPISCOPAL CHURCH AND PASTOR, FREMONT, INDIANA. Such cards were used for church correspondence.

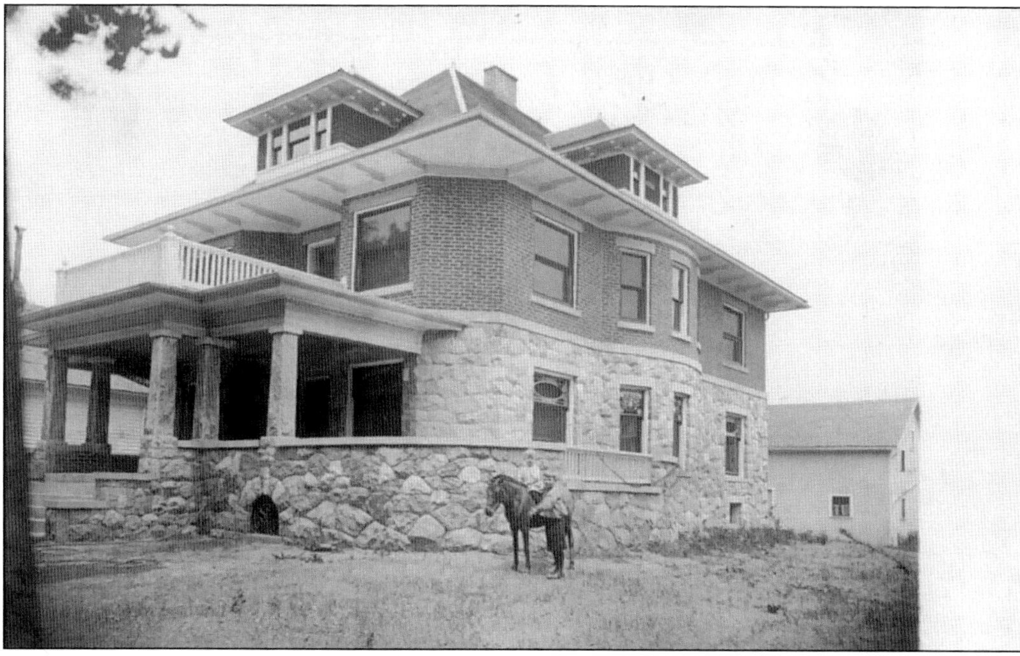

FREMONT, INDIANA. An elaborate late "Queen Ann" style house with a stone foundation with brick above. The house has some Frank Lloyd Wright features such as the wide flat roof overhangs. A boy poses on his pony in the front yard.

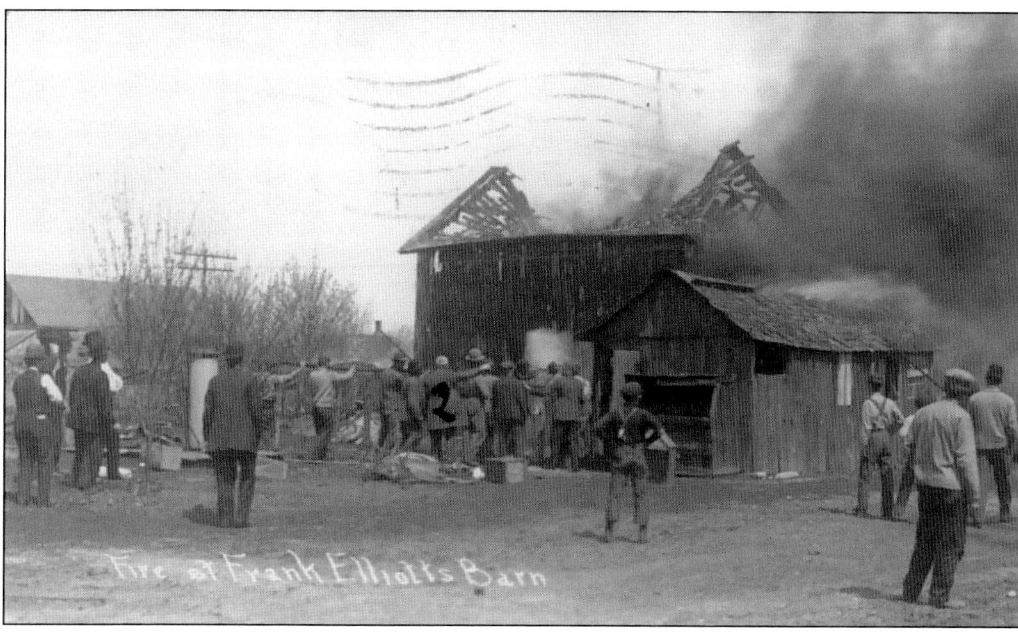

FIRE AT FRANK ELLIOTS BARN, *c.* 1913. The message states: "Just to show you what can be done when you have real fire fighting apparatus. No. 1 (lower right) is the chief trying to get a clue and also to find out what to do when the water runs out. No. 2 (center) is the fat guy who had to ride from the engine house because he was to fat to run and keep even with the other fire fighters."

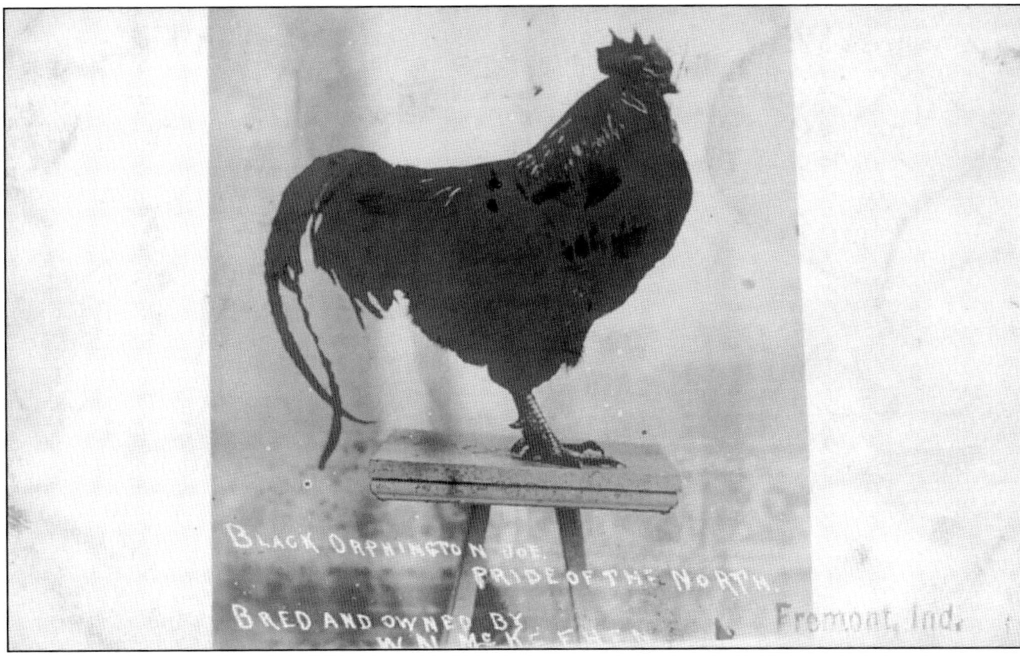

BLACK ORPHINGTON JOE, PRIDE OF THE NORTH, BRED AND OWNED BY W.N. MCKEEHEN, FREMONT, INDIANA. A real photo card showing a prize chicken.

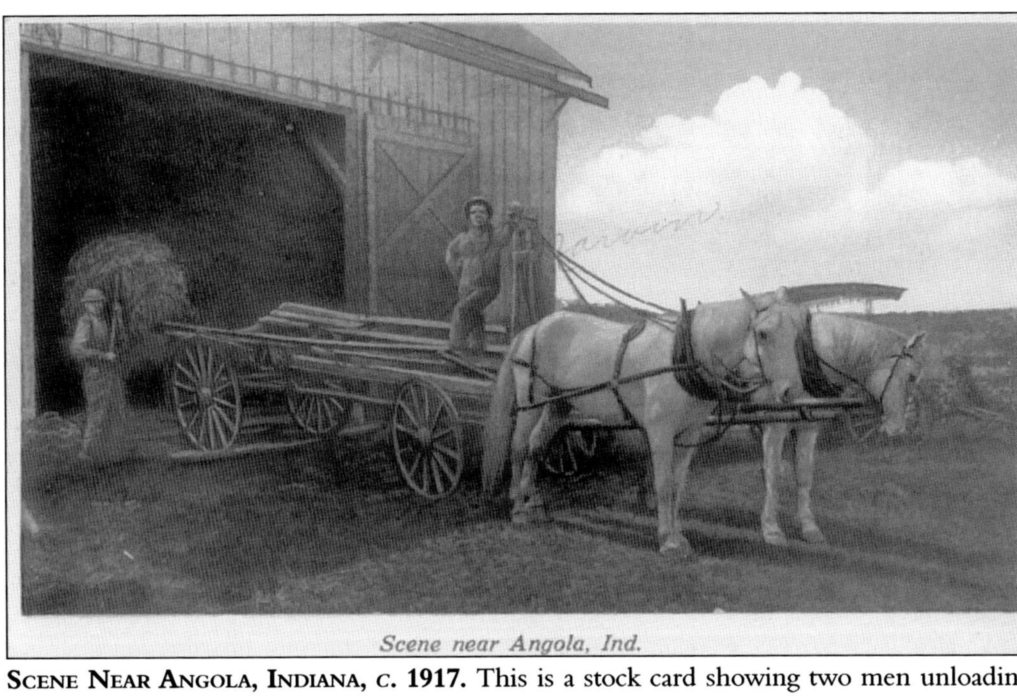

SCENE NEAR ANGOLA, INDIANA, *C.* 1917. This is a stock card showing two men unloading loose hay into the barn.

Three

Hamilton

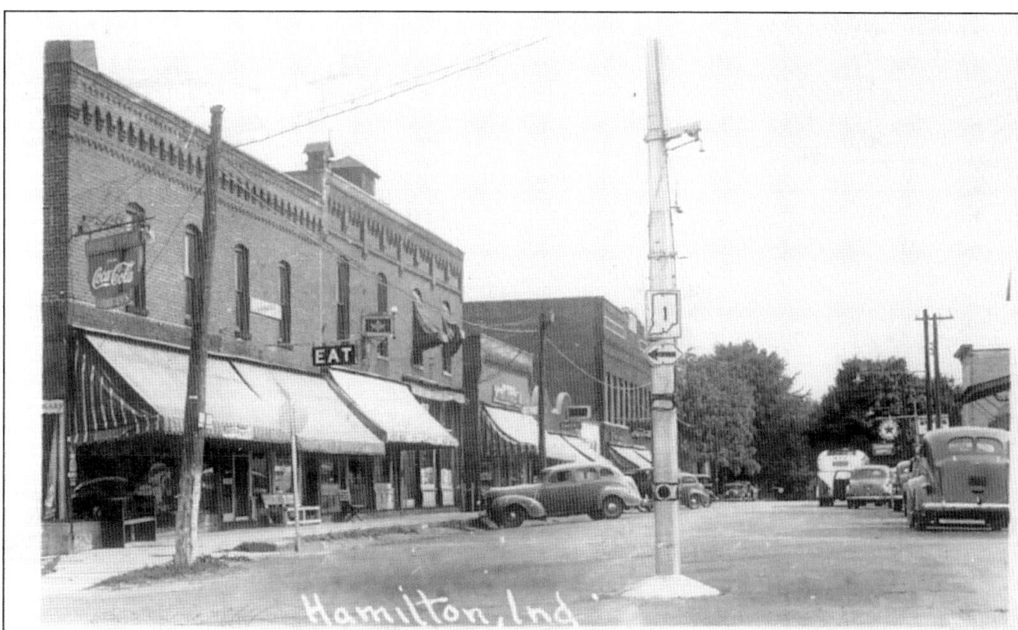

Hamilton, Indiana, c. 1944. The flag pole in the center of the intersection was a longtime landmark at Hamilton.

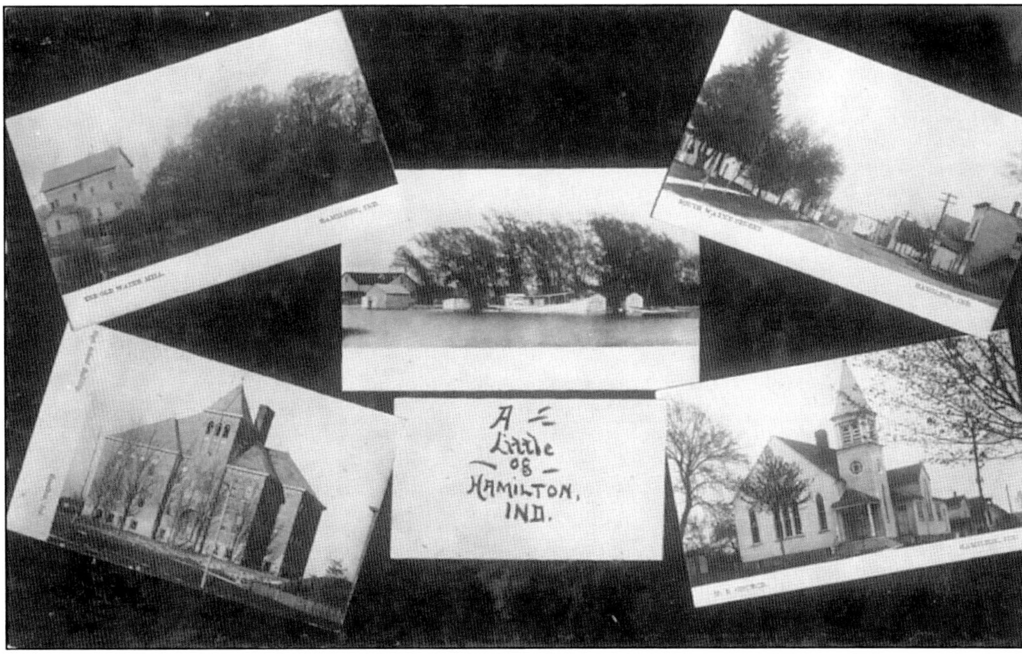

A Little of Hamilton, Indiana. Views including Old Water Mill, South Wayne Street, High School Building, M.E. Church, and a lake scene are depicted here.

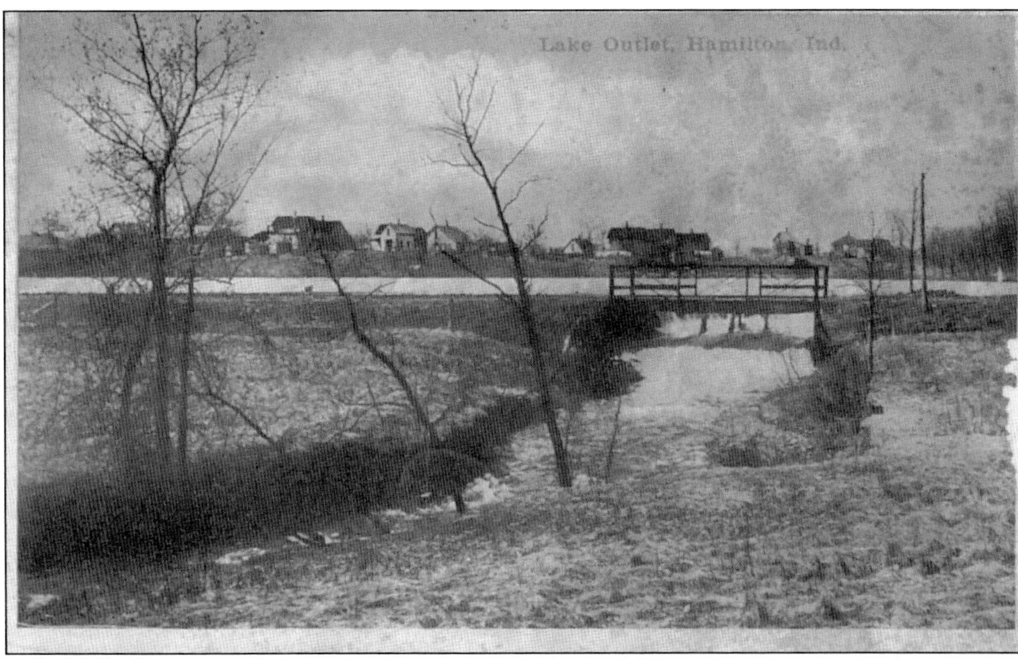

Lake Outlet, Hamilton, Indiana. The lake was created by a dam that was built to provide a mill pond for the water powered mill.

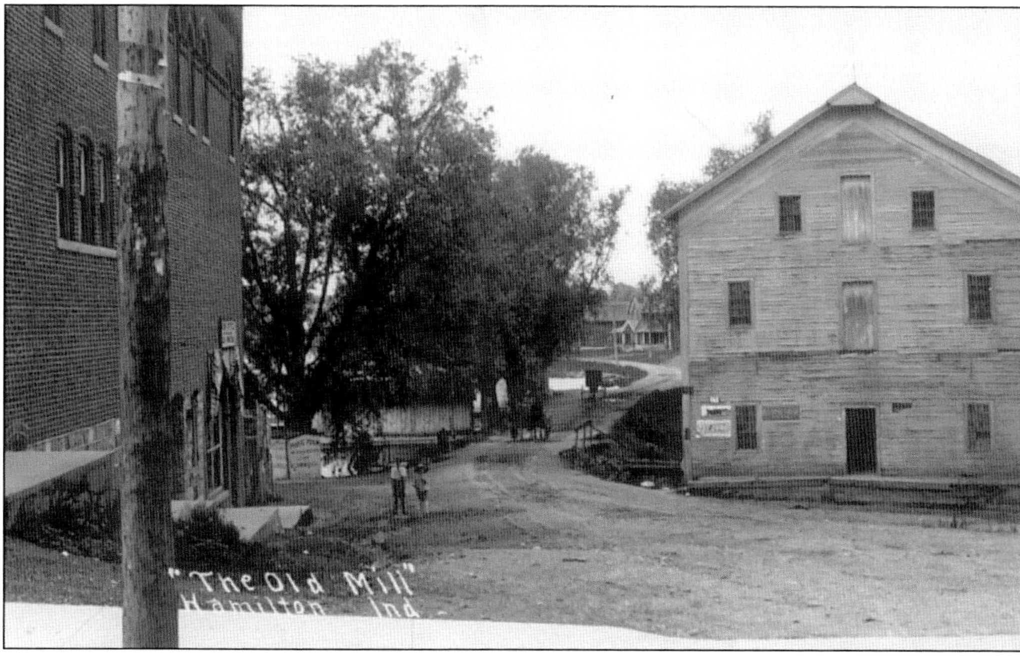

"THE OLD MILL" HAMILTON, INDIANA. The lake provided a steady supply of water to run the mill.

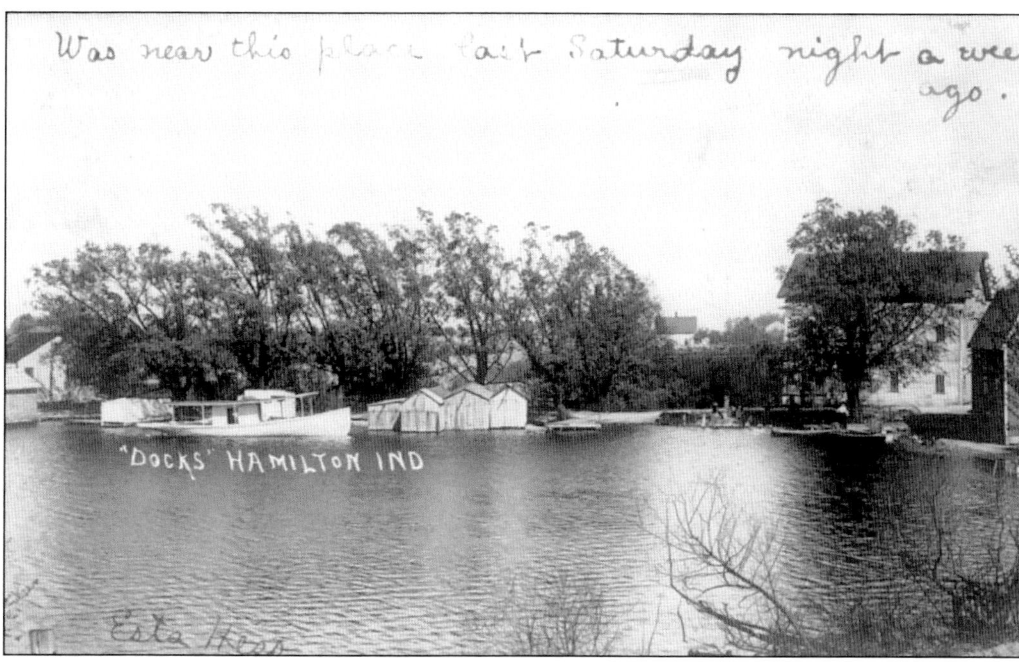

"DOCKS" HAMILTON, INDIANA, *c.* 1908. The message states: "Was near this place last Saturday night a week ago."

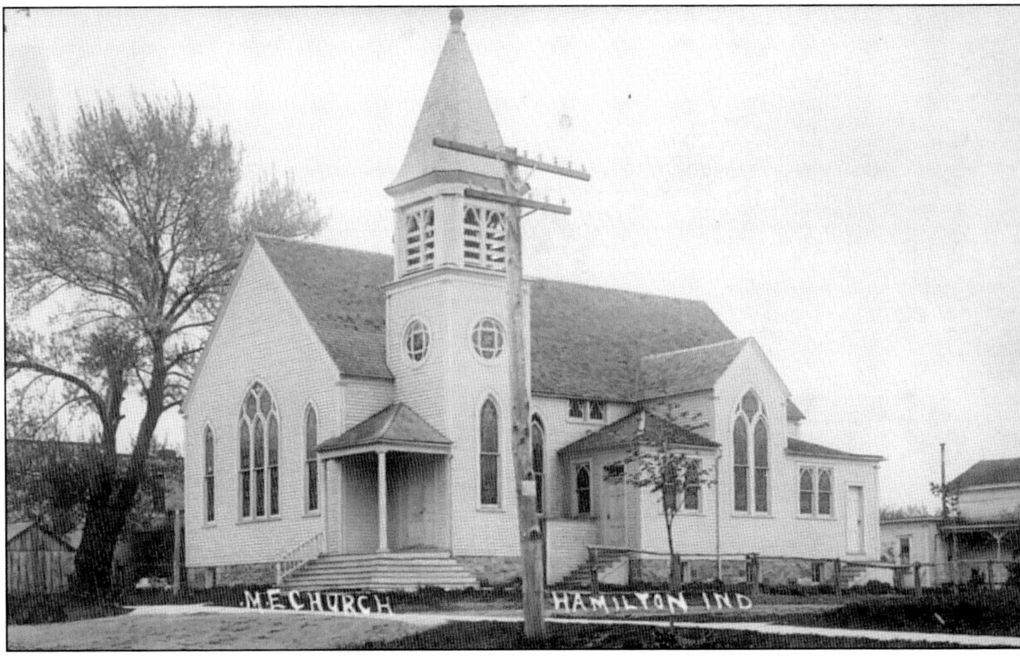

M.E. CHURCH, HAMILTON, INDIANA. Seen here is a handsome building with elaborate stained-glass windows.

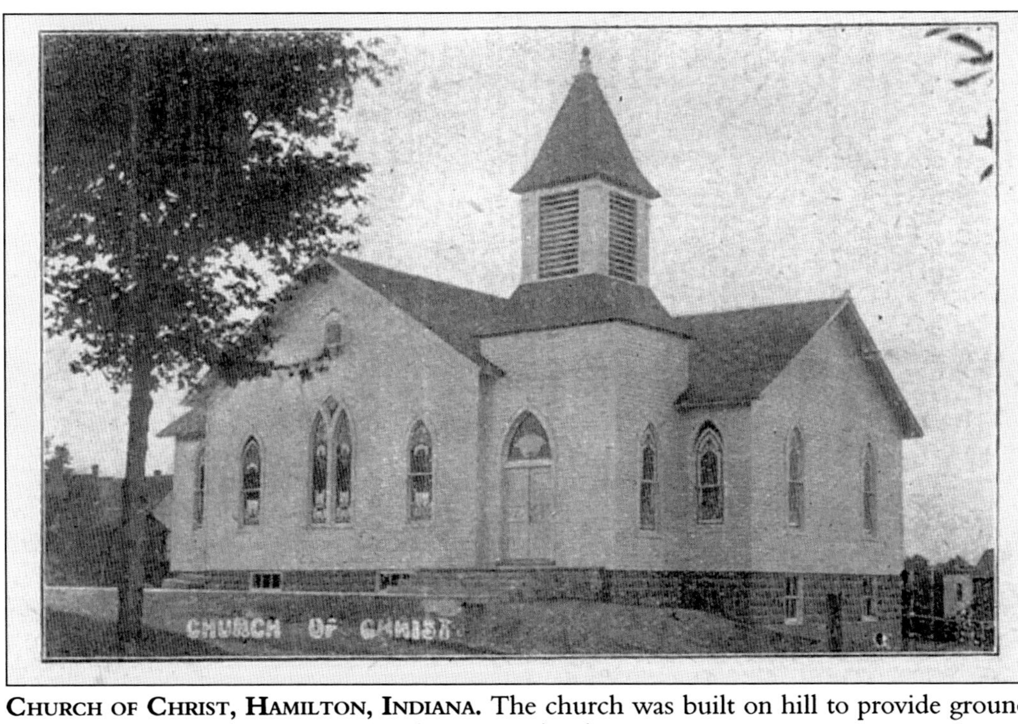

CHURCH OF CHRIST, HAMILTON, INDIANA. The church was built on hill to provide ground level access for both the basement and sanctuary levels.

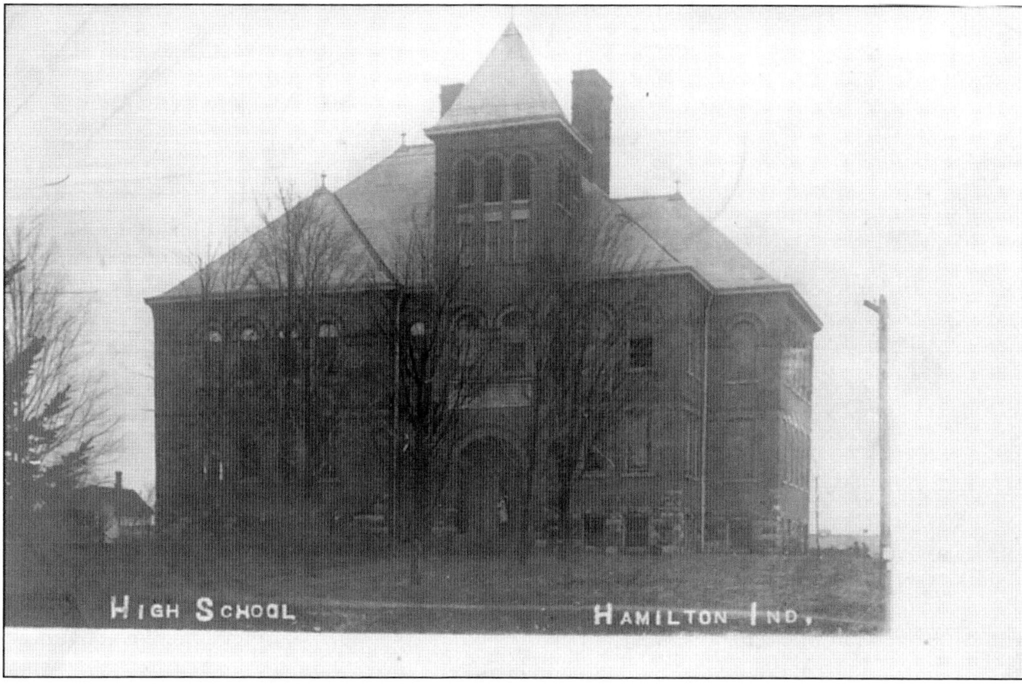

HIGH SCHOOL, HAMILTON, INDIANA, *c.* 1907. The school overlooked Hamilton Lake from its back side.

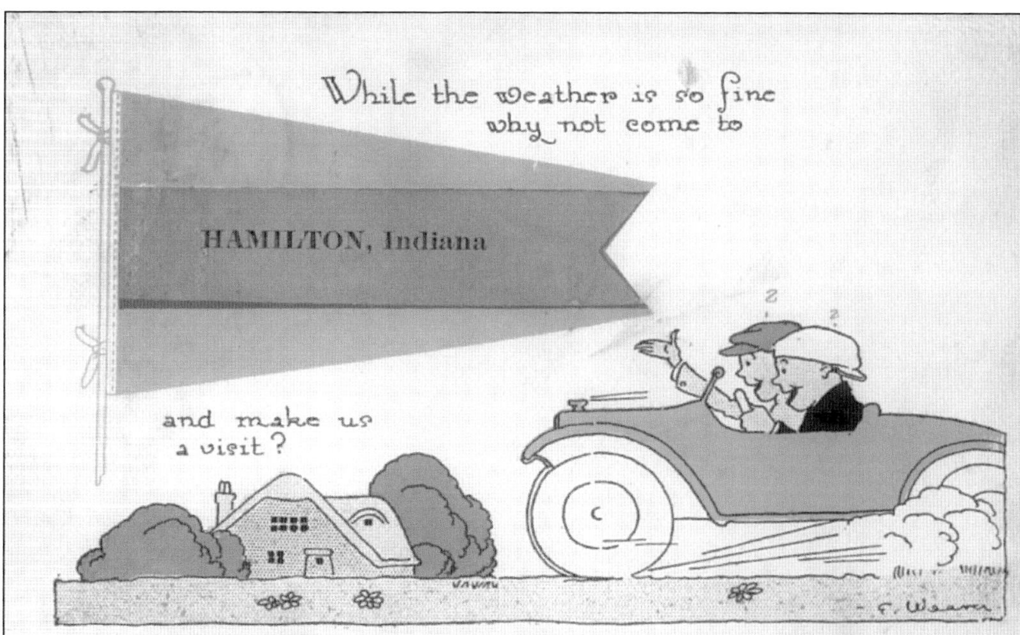

WHILE THE WEATHER IS SO FINE WHY NOT COME TO HAMILTON, INDIANA, AND MAKE US A VISIT? A stock card with a Hamilton imprint is shown here.

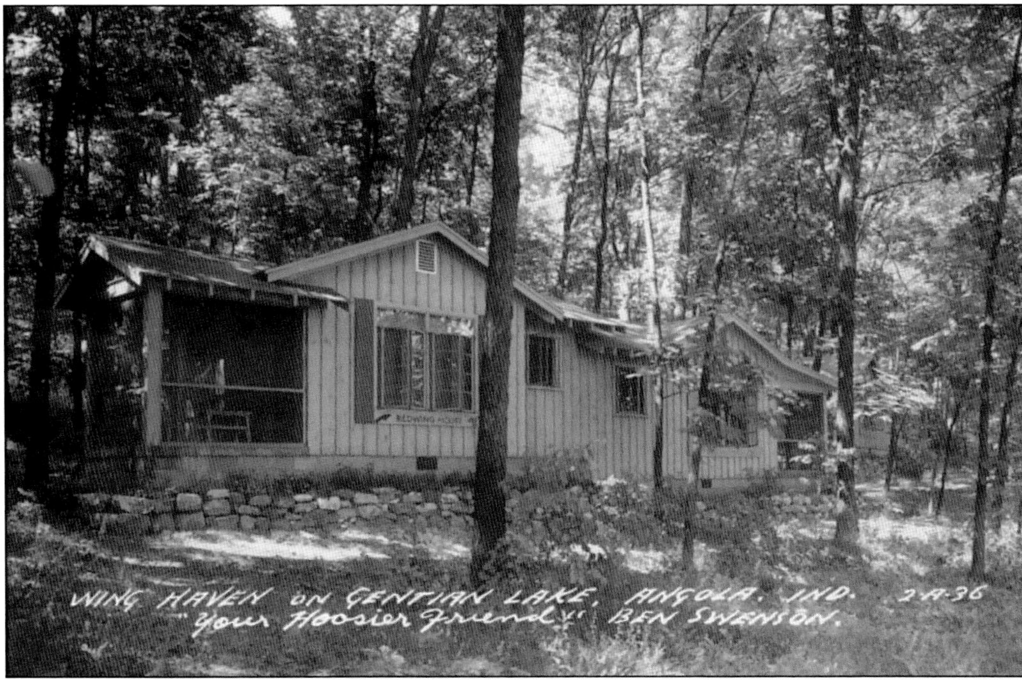

WING HAVEN ON GENTIAN LAKE, ANGOLA, INDIANA, "YOUR HOOSIER FRIEND" BEN SWENSON. This was a popular resort in its era.

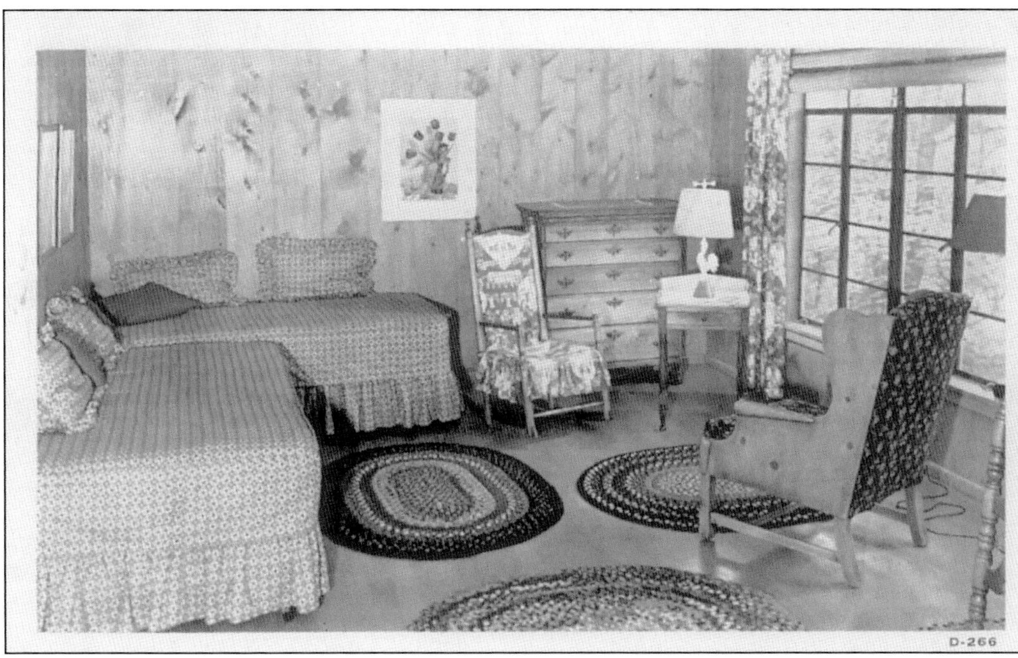

WING HAVEN, GENTIAN LAKE, ANGOLA, INDIANA, *c.* 1951. The message states: "This room is just like ours. We also have a dressing room and bath. Thru this window you can see the lake just a short distance. John has gone in to Angola—but I love the peace and quiet out here. Everything new. Just opened this summer."

Four

Hoosier Hills

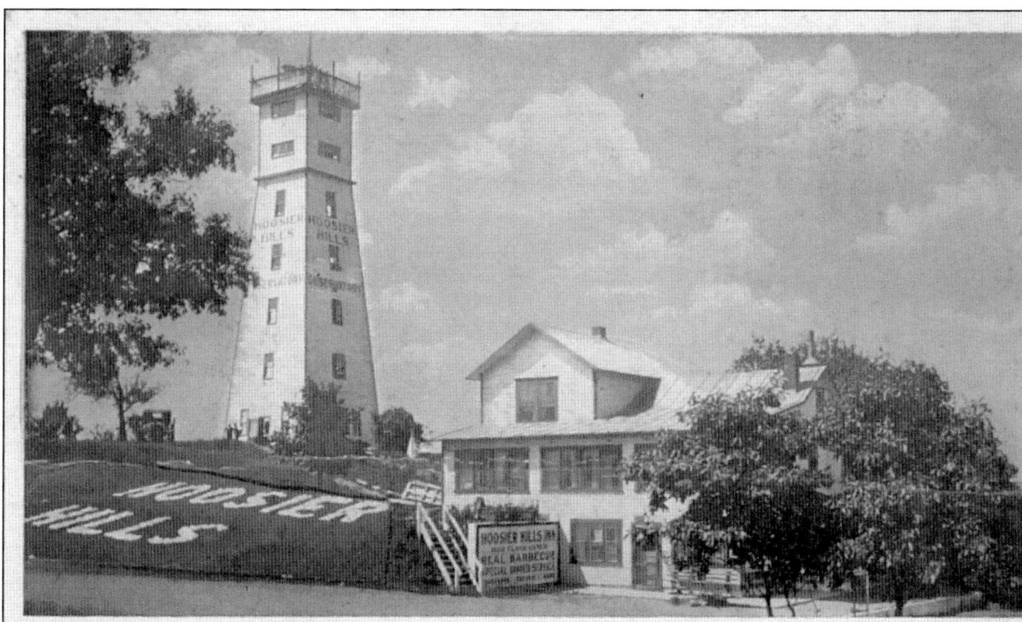

Hoosier Hills, Angola, Indiana, U.S. 27. This was a popular tourist attraction for many years. The sign reads: "Hoosier Hills Inn—High Class Lunch—Real Barbecue—Special Dinner Specials." The "Hoosier Hills" sign was made of rocks that were painted white.

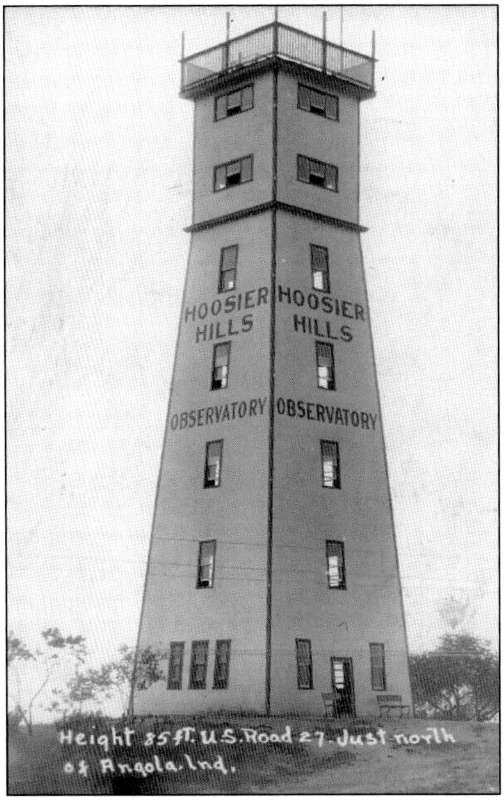

HOOSIER HILLS OBSERVATORY, HEIGHT 85 FEET, U.S. ROAD 27, JUST NORTH OF ANGOLA, INDIANA. The tower purported to be the highest point in Indiana. It provided a great view of the lake country.

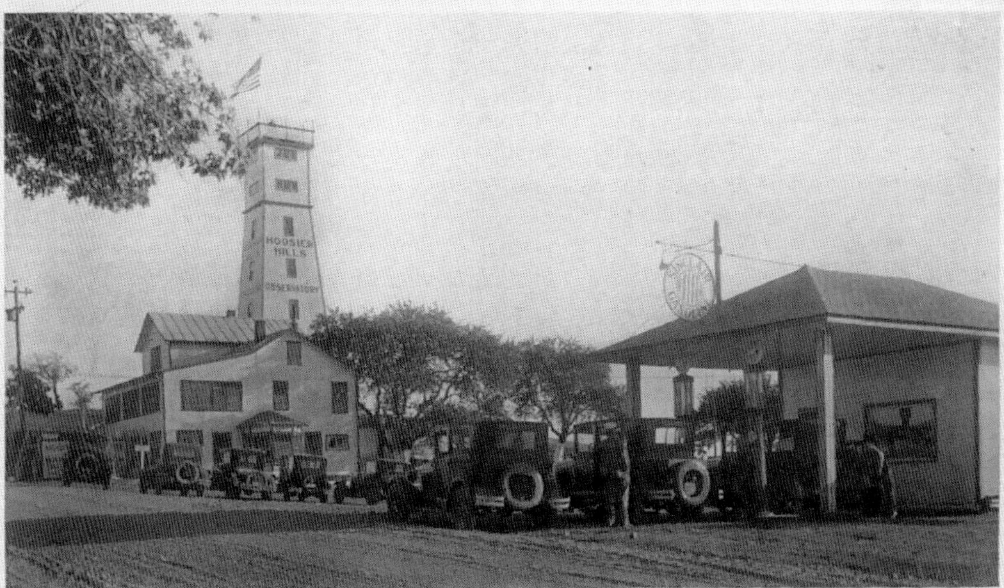

Hoosier Hills, Angola, Ind., U. S. 27

HOOSIER HILLS, ANGOLA, INDIANA, U.S. 27. Cars are lined up in the parking lot. A flag flies from the tower.

Five

HUDSON

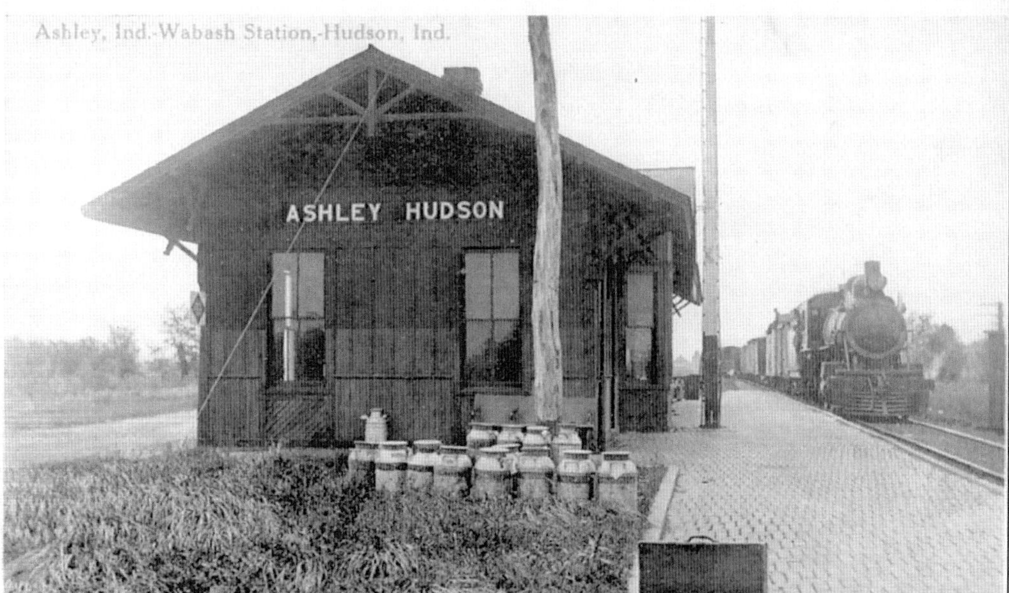

WABASH STATION, HUDSON, INDIANA. A train approaches the station. Milk cans are lined up to be loaded on the train.

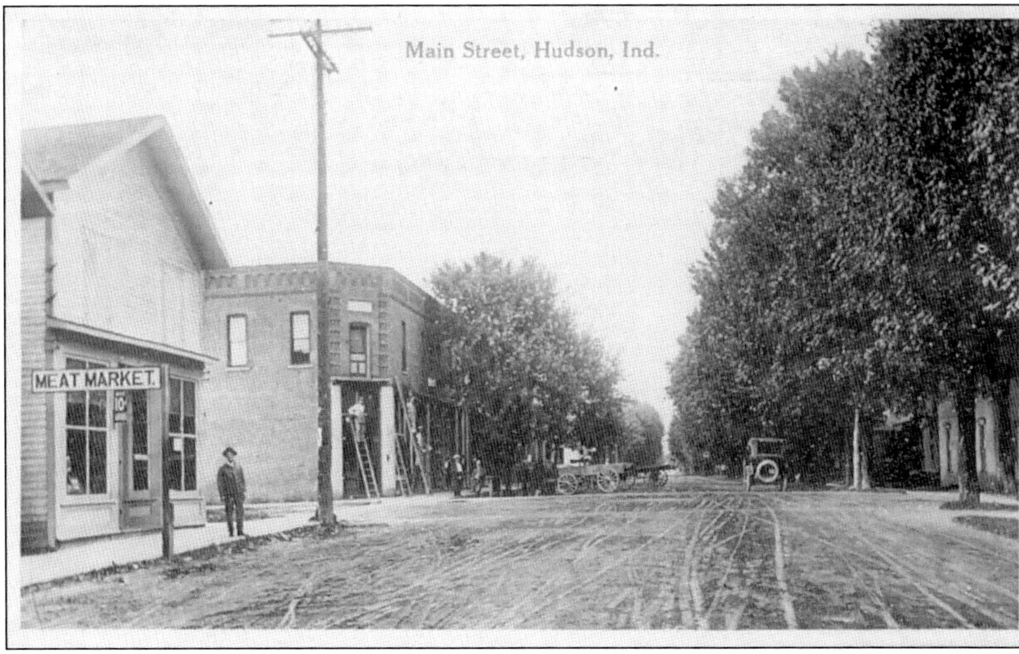

Main Street, Hudson, Indiana. Workers are painting the trim on the bank building, which was once robbed by John Dillinger. It is now the location of Dillinger's Restaurant.

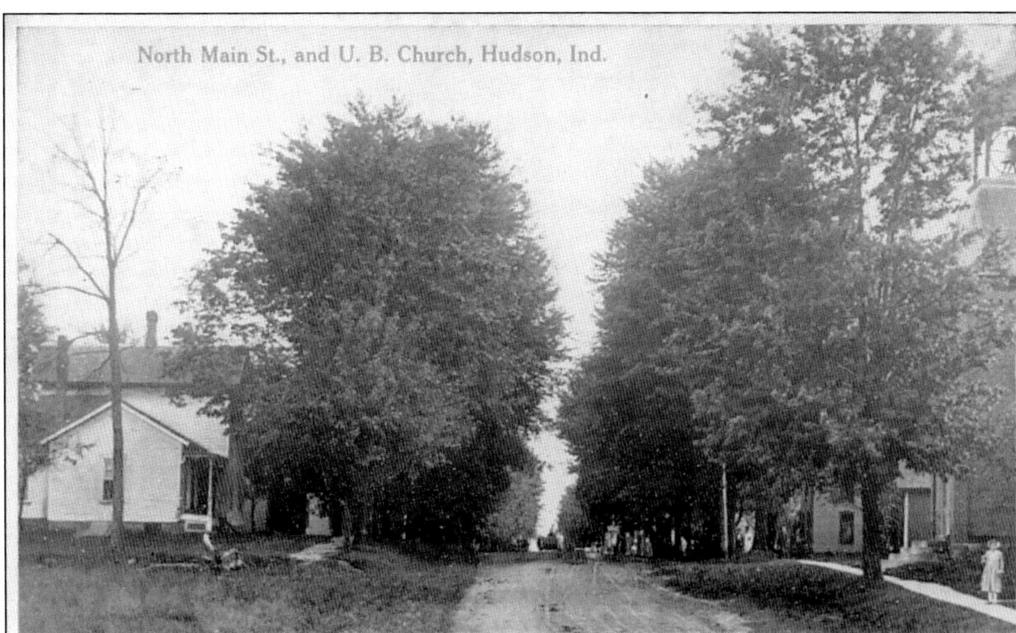

North Main Street, and U.B. Church, Hudson, Indiana. A young girl poses for the photograph.

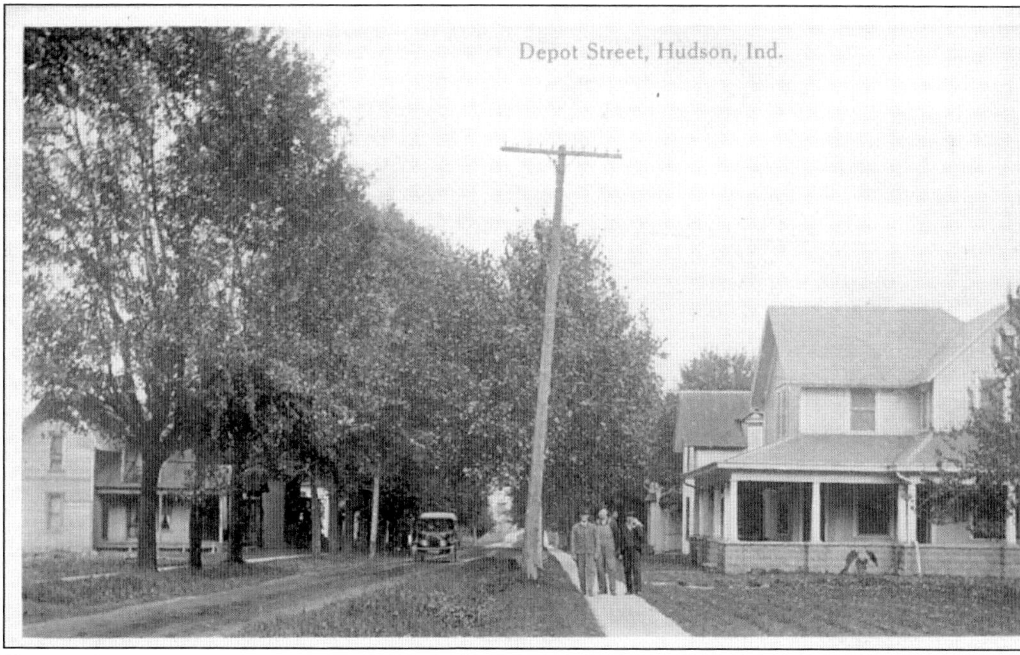

DEPOT STREET, HUDSON, INDIANA. Nearly every town had a "Depot Street."

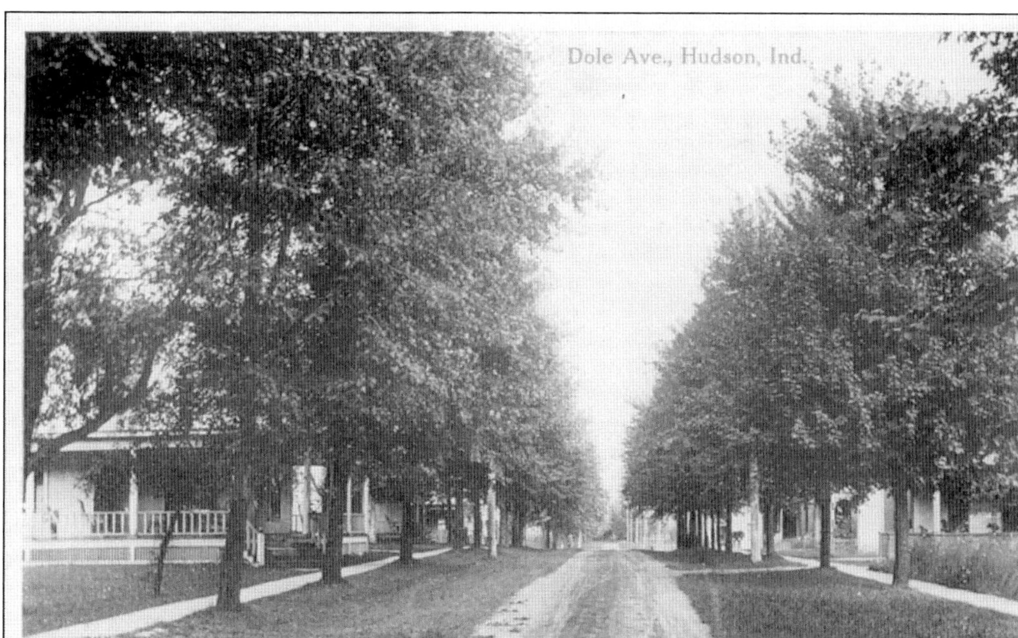

DOLE AVENUE, HUDSON, INDIANA. It was common for farmers to retire and move to the nearest small town and build a nice house.

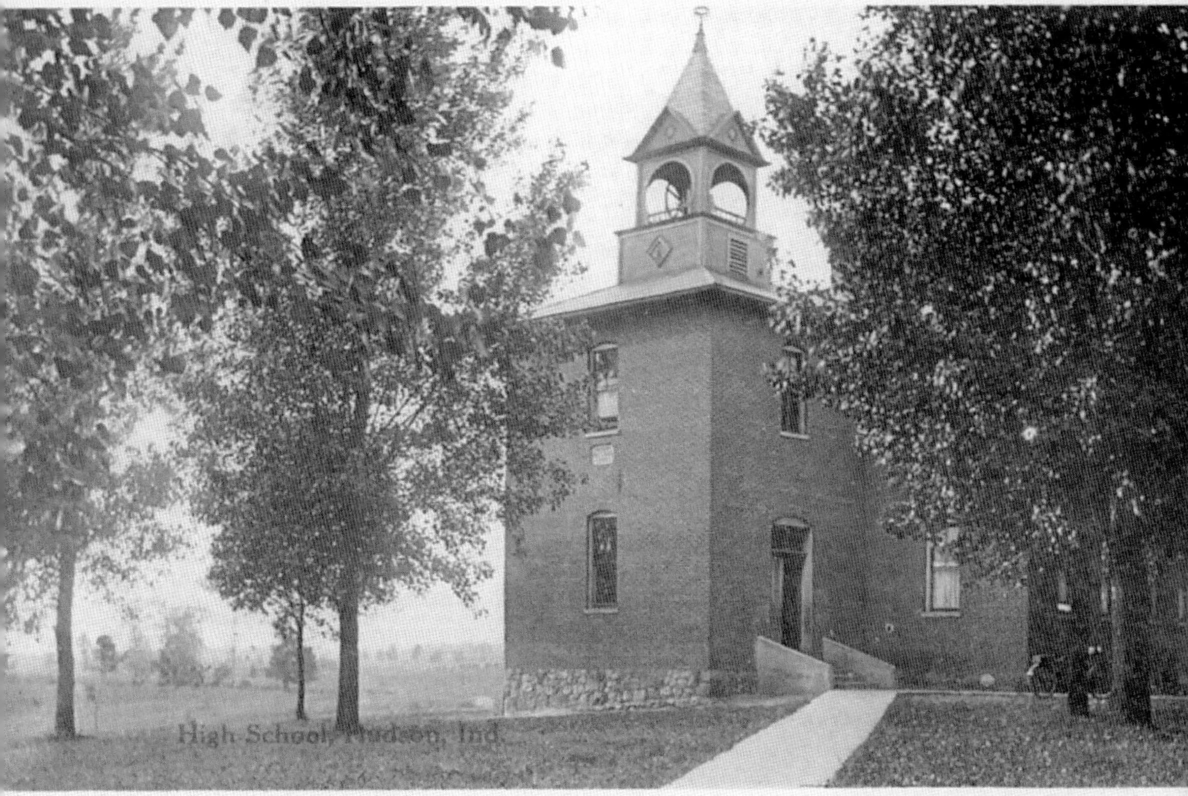

HIGH SCHOOL, HUDSON, INDIANA. The school was small but adequate for this small town.

Six

LAKES

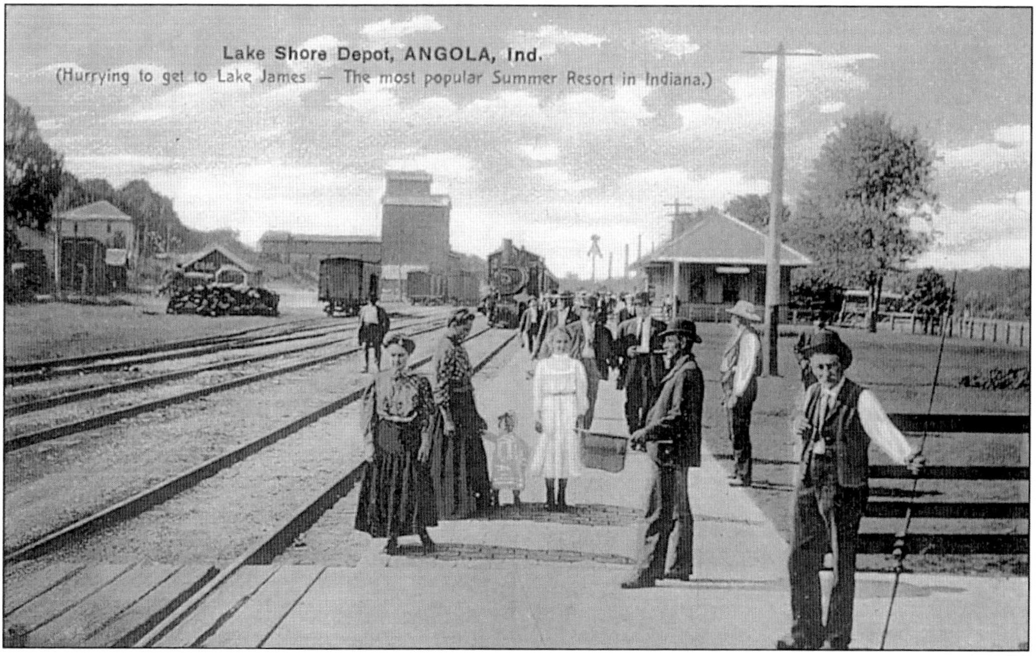

LAKE SHORE DEPOT, ANGOLA, INDIANA. Seen here are vacationers hurrying to get to Lake James—the most popular summer resort in Indiana, *c.* 1911. Known as the "Land of 101 Lakes," Steuben County has long been a tourist destination.

Buck Lake

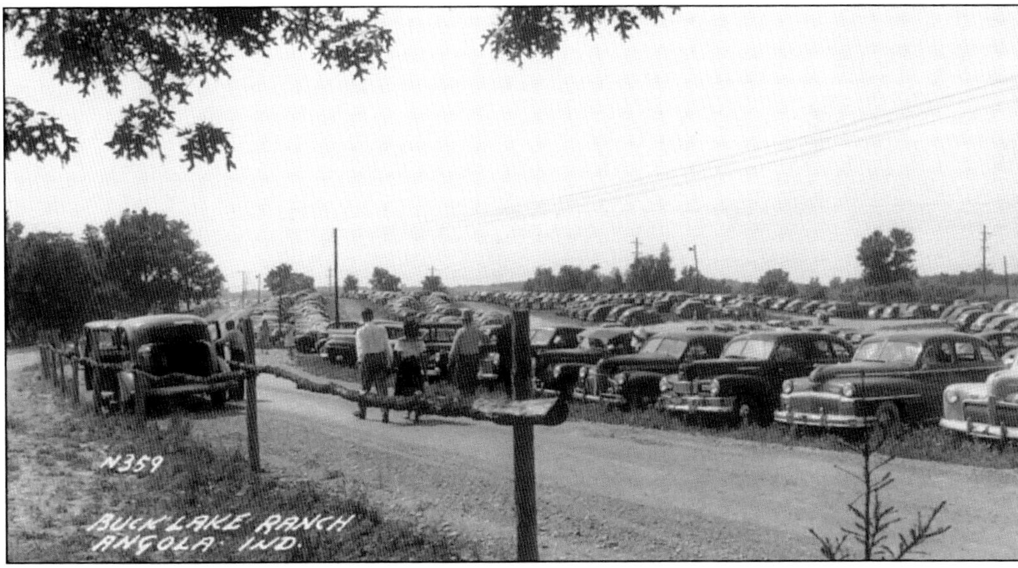

Buck Lake Ranch, Angola, Indiana. Hundreds of cars line the parking area.

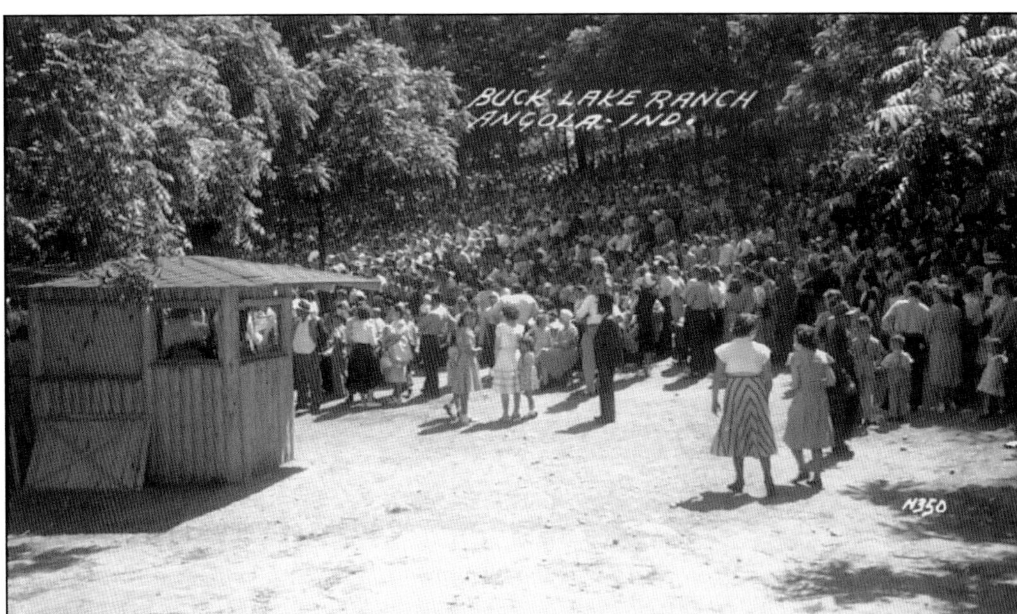

Buck Lake Ranch, Angola, Indiana. Benches were built into the side of a hill overlooking the stage.

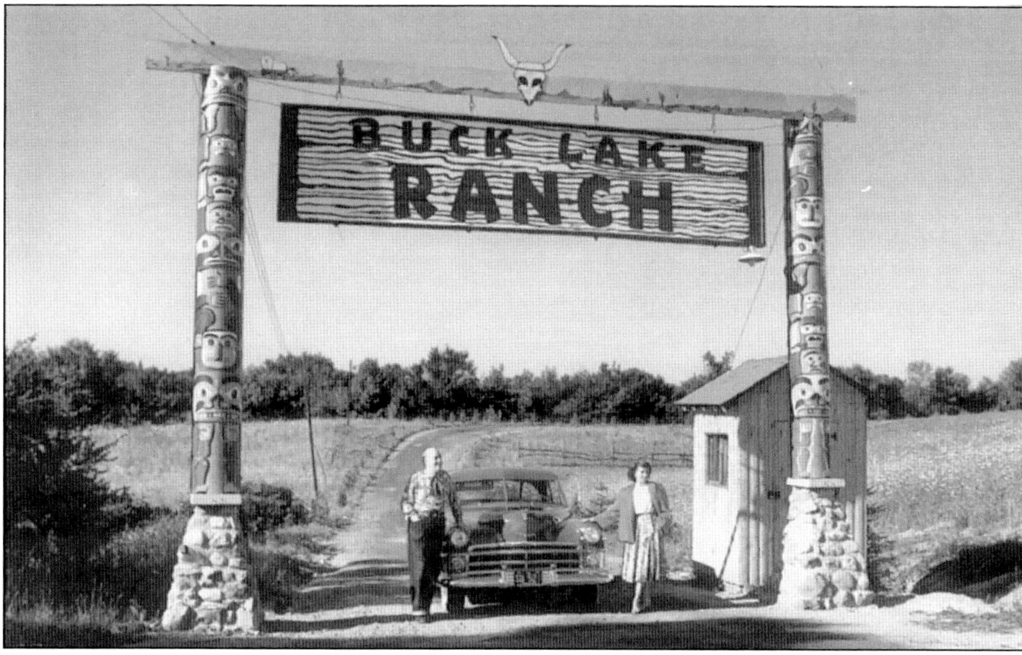

BUCK LAKE RANCH, ANGOLA, INDIANA. Seen here is one of America's greatest amusement parks. Mr. and Mrs. Harry Smythe welcome visitors at the entrance.

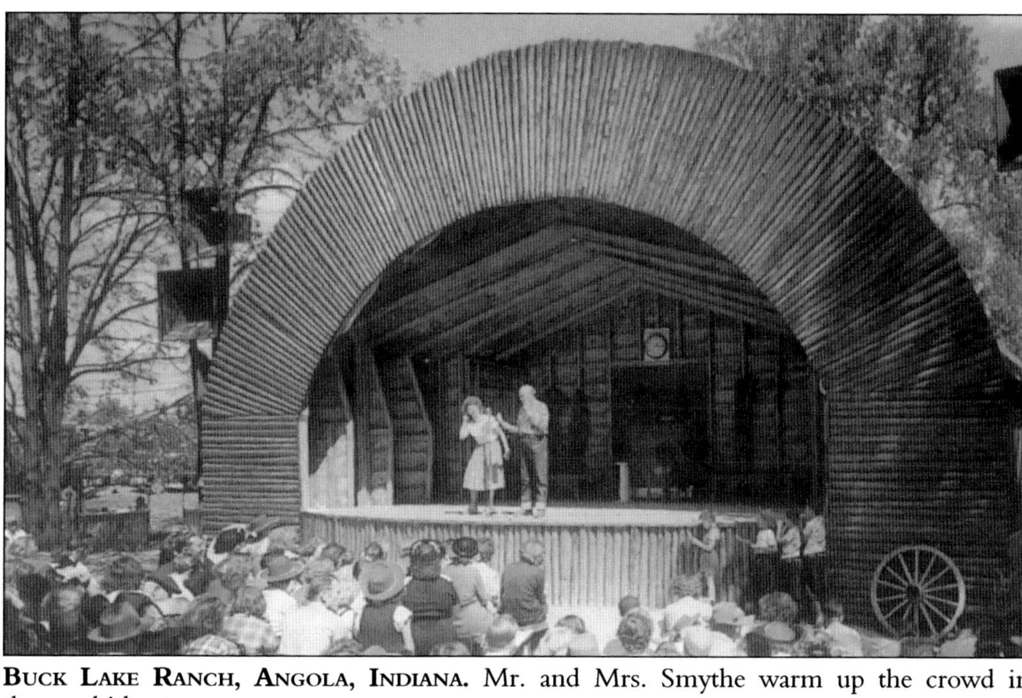

BUCK LAKE RANCH, ANGOLA, INDIANA. Mr. and Mrs. Smythe warm up the crowd in the amphitheater.

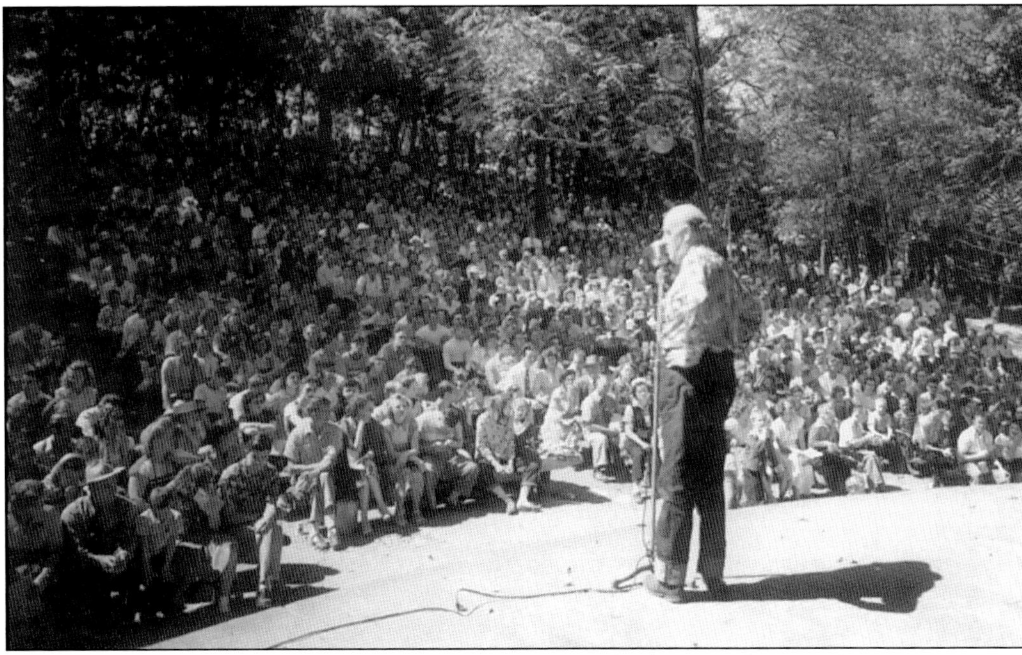

Buck Lake Ranch, Angola, Indiana. Harry Smythe looks over the crowd.

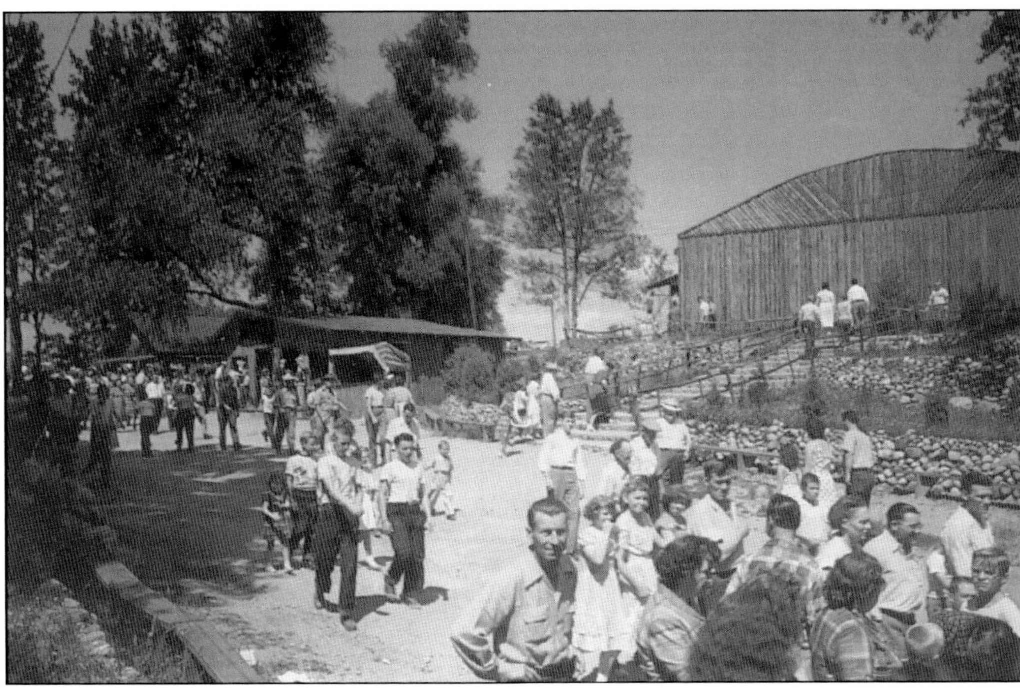

Buck Lake Ranch, Angola, Indiana. Visitors came from the surrounding area to hear top country and pop entertainers. All of the buildings were made from pine logs with a natural finish.

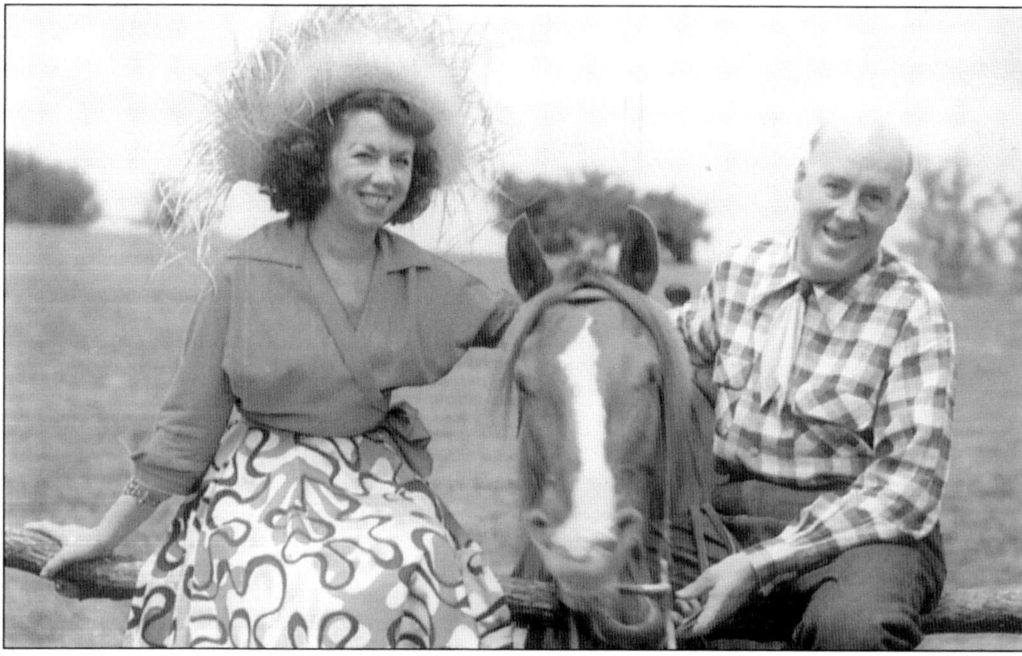

Buck Lake Ranch, Angola, Indiana. Mr. and Mrs. Harry Smythe were the owners and promoters of one of the Midwest's premier attractions.

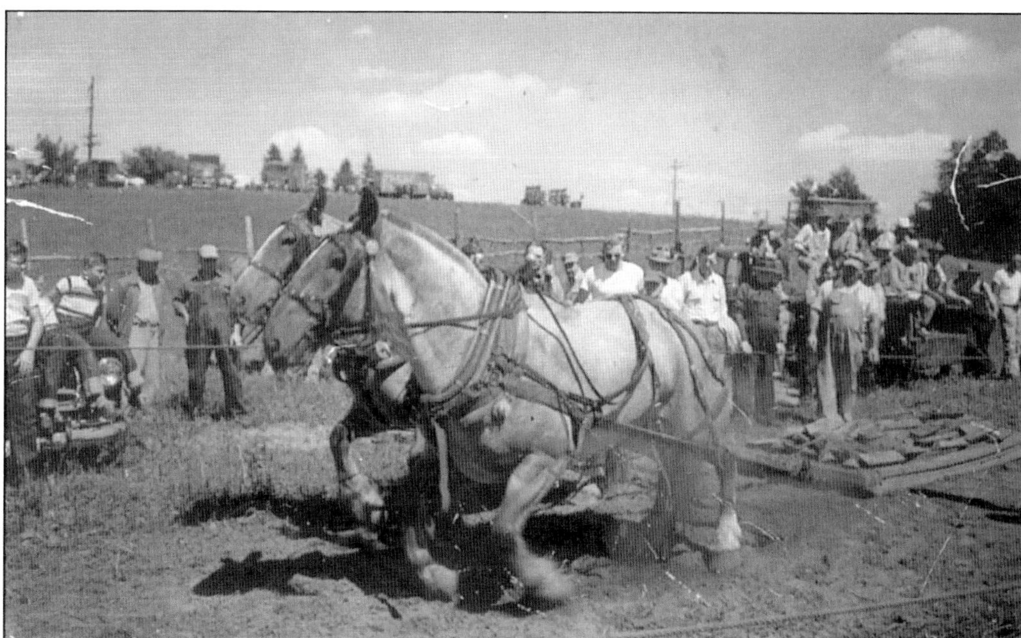

Buck Lake Ranch, Angola, Indiana. Horse pulling contests were popular.

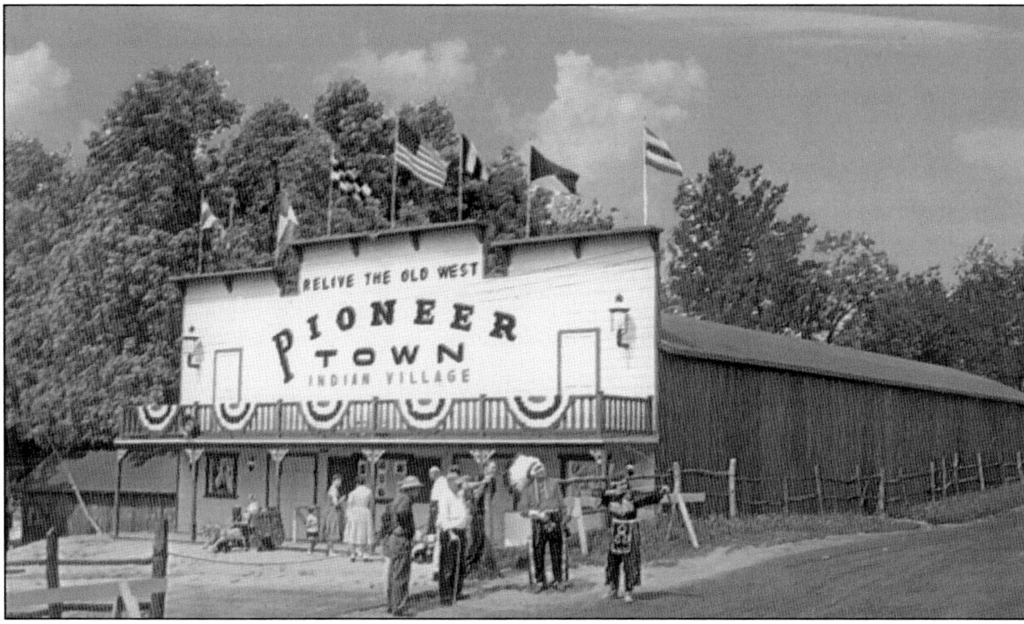

PIONEER TOWN, ANGOLA, INDIANA. The Early American Museum and Indian Village at Buck Lake Ranch, Angola is shown here. Annie Oakley, Buffalo Bill, Wyatt Earp, and Sitting Bull, in lifelike figures, are beautifully staged in western settings. The murals are by Hollywood artist George Diestel.

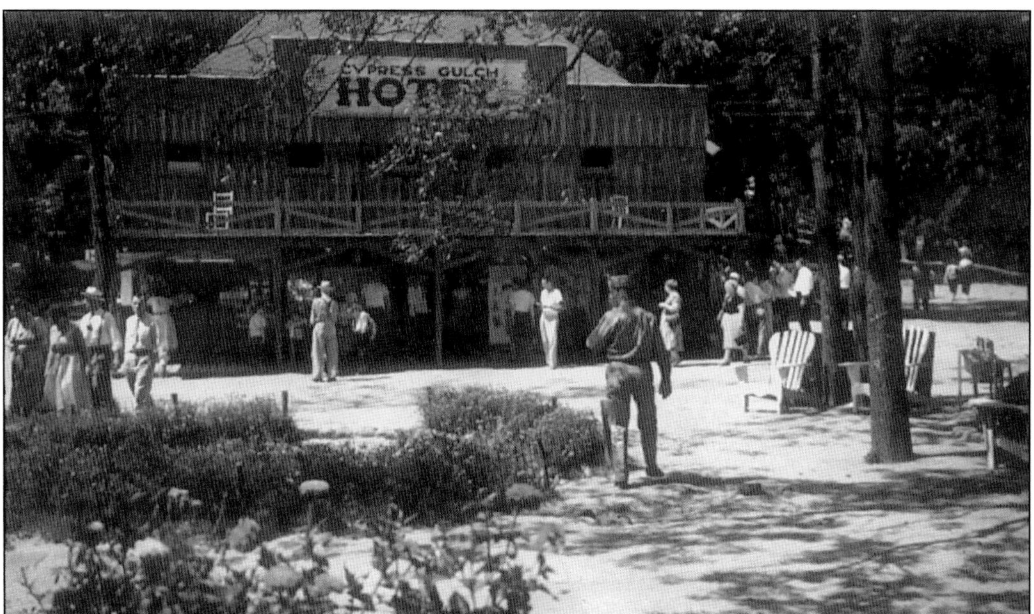

BUCK LAKE RANG, ANGOLA, INDIANA. The Old West is brought back to life at the Cypress Gulch Hotel, Buck Lake Ranch, Angola, Indiana.

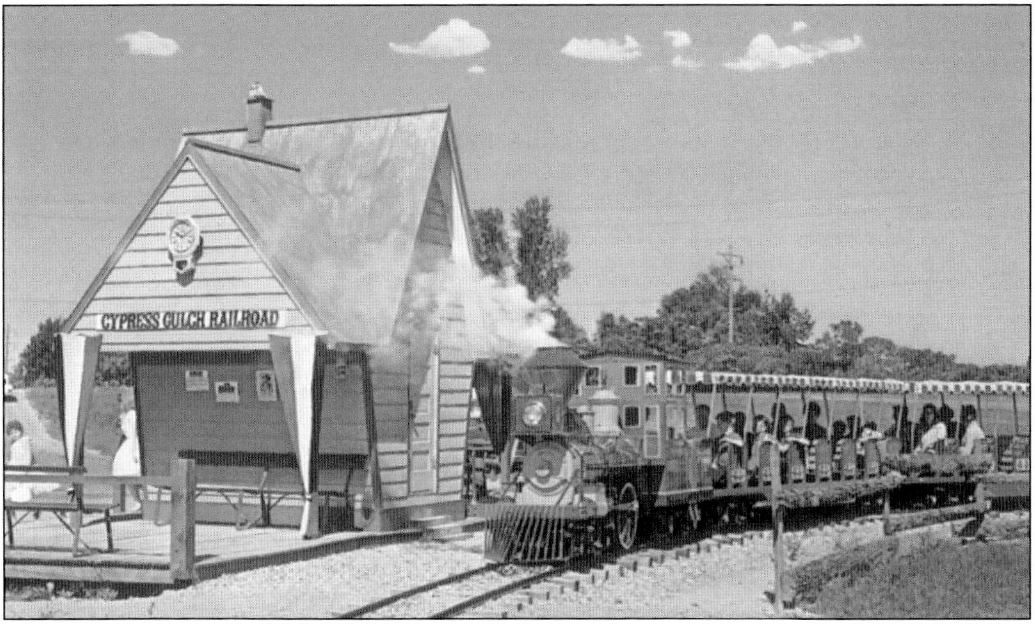

FRONTIER TRAIN RIDE, BUCK LAKE RANCH, 1863. The Old 1863 Train at Buck Lake Ranch, Angola, Indiana, covers a mile ride around the park, lurching past the old depot, passing the train signals, and catching a view of Old Fort Laramie before traveling under a tunnel. Passengers enjoy the beautiful wooded wonderland and a thrilling ride while recapturing memories of olden days.

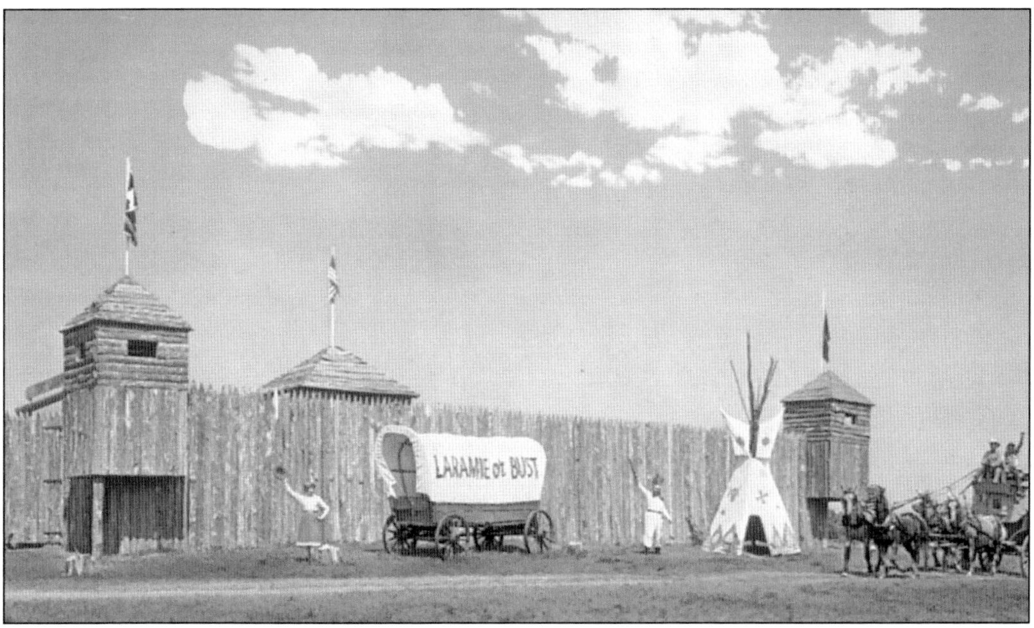

OLD FORT LARAMIE. This is a replica of the famous historical Fort Laramie where much of the early western history was made with Buffalo Bill, General Custer,and Sitting Bull. Fort Laramie was a Trading Post in 1837, two years before the Treaty of Horse Creek in 1839, and then became an Army post.

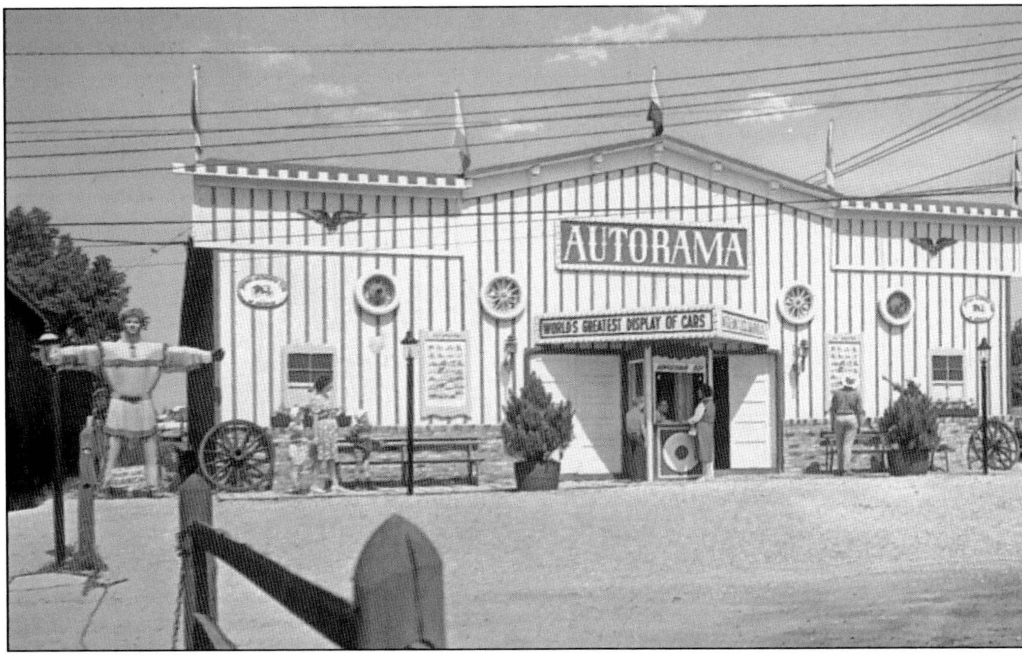

THE AUTORAMA. The Buck Lake Autorama is an exhibit of 32 historic automobiles with Tom Mix's custom built car, the King and Queens' Rolls Royce, and many other classic and antique cars worth a half-million dollars, in a beautiful setting at Buck Lake Ranch, Angola, Indiana.

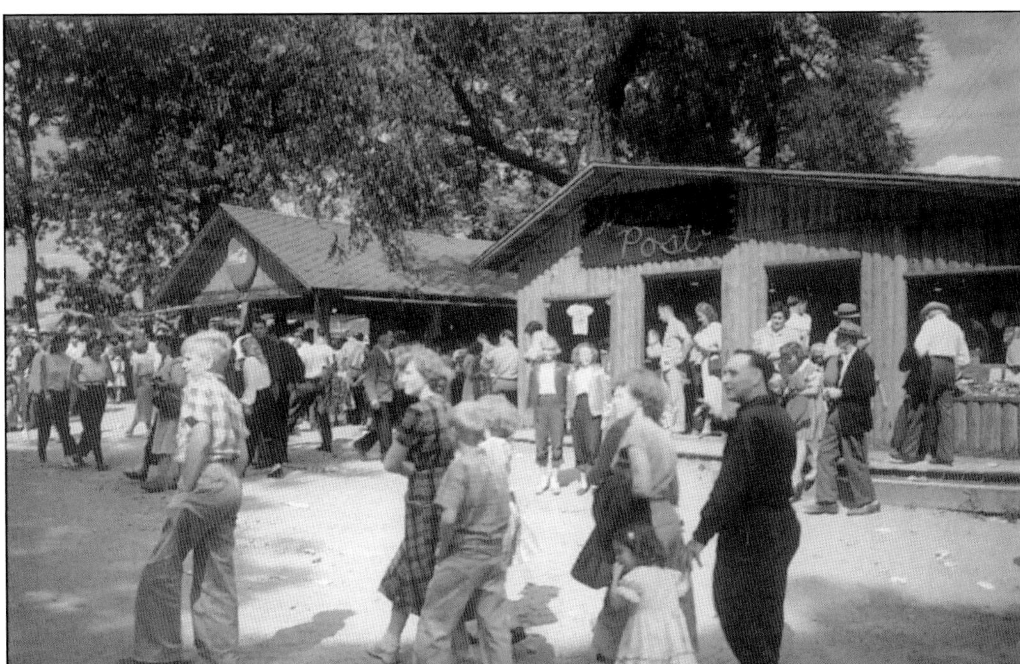

BUCK LAKE RANCH, ANGOLA, INDIANA. The Post sold souvenirs and other merchandise.

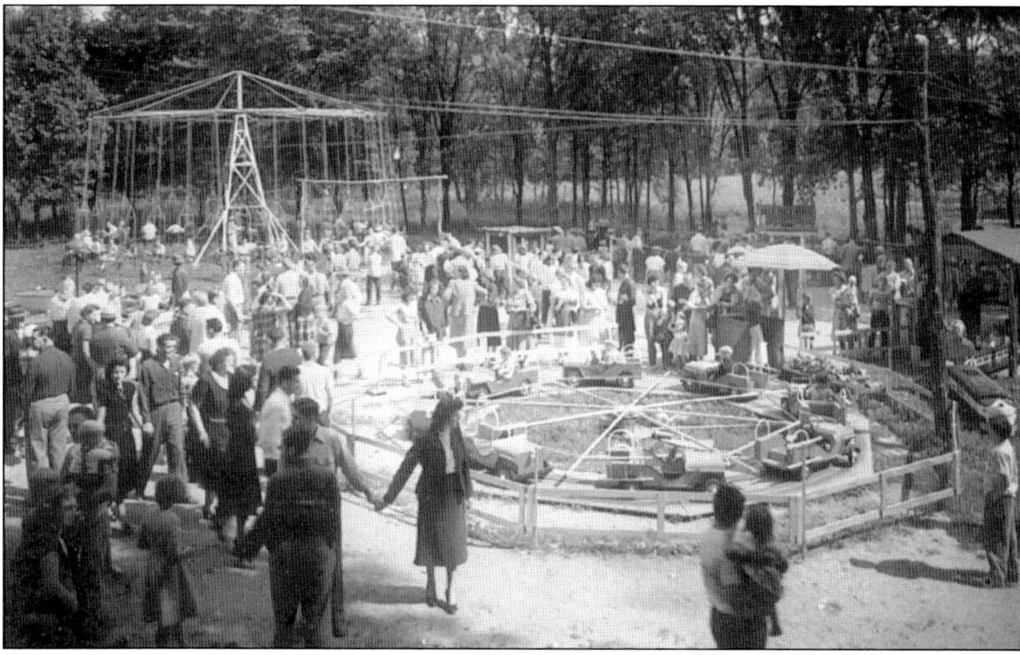

BUCK LAKE RANCH, ANGOLA, INDIANA. Kiddie rides provided an amusement park atmosphere.

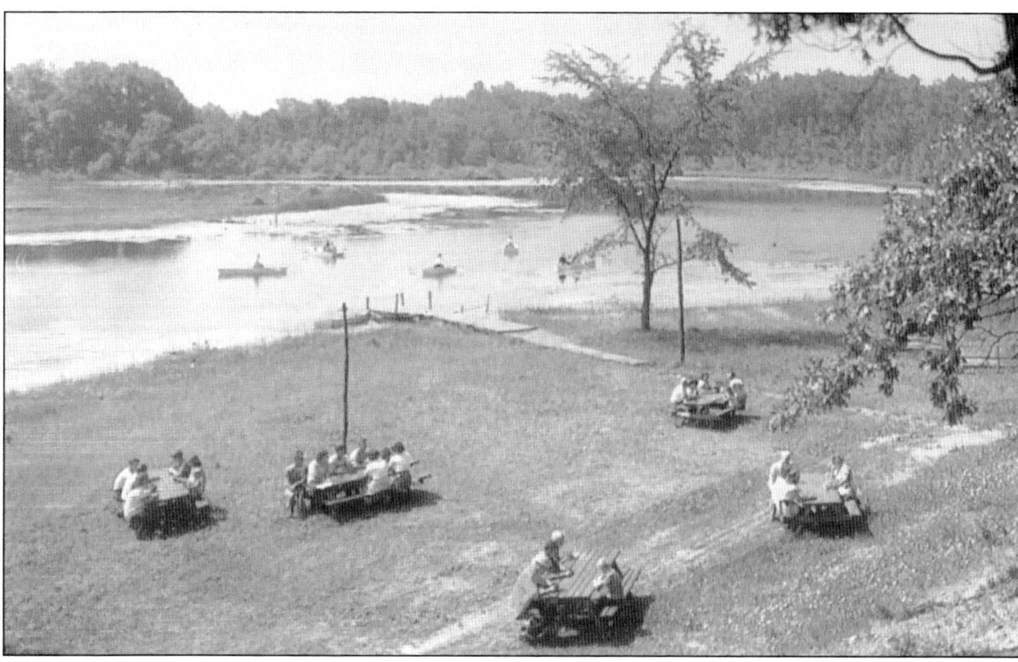

BUCK LAKE RANCH, ANGOLA, INDIANA. Some brought picnics which were consumed overlooking Buck Lake.

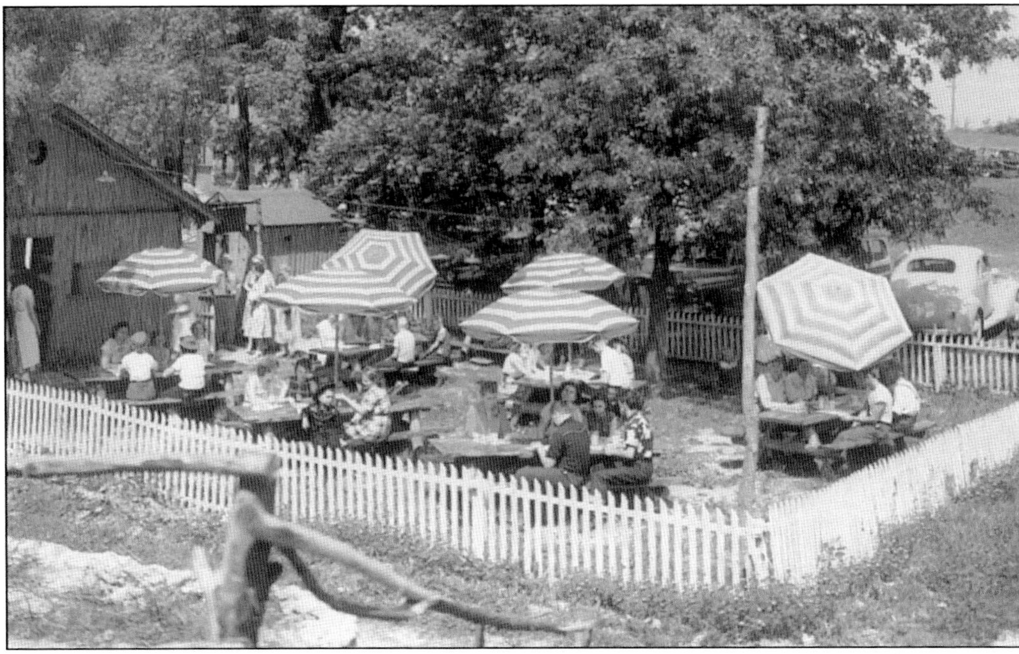

Buck Lake Ranch, Angola, Indiana. The restaurant provided outdoor tables for diners.

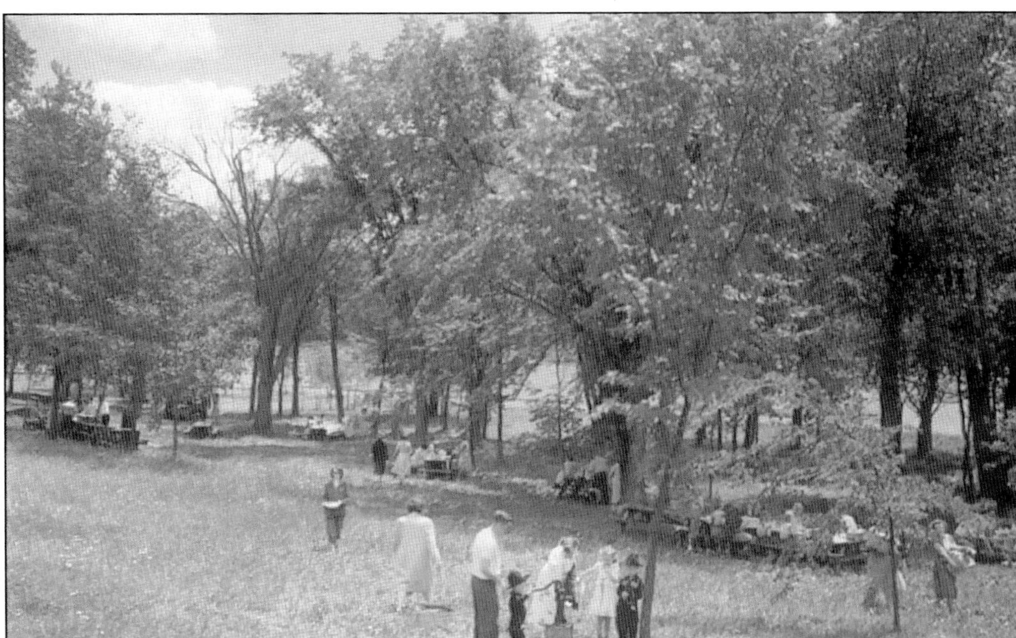

Buck Lake Ranch, Angola, Indiana. The old pump was a popular place for little cowboys to get a drink of water.

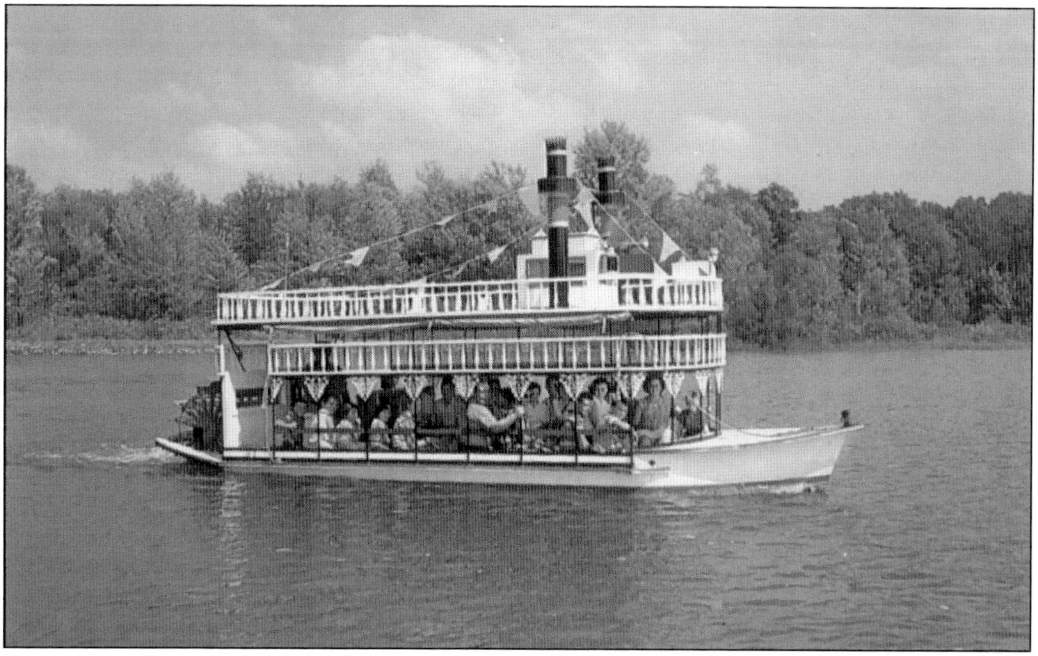

Show Boat Ride. *The Little Show Boat* is a replica of *The Mississippi Show Boat* that holds 30 passengers. Pictured here is a cool ride on beautiful Buck Lake showing the scenic view of the wooded Buck Lake Ranch.

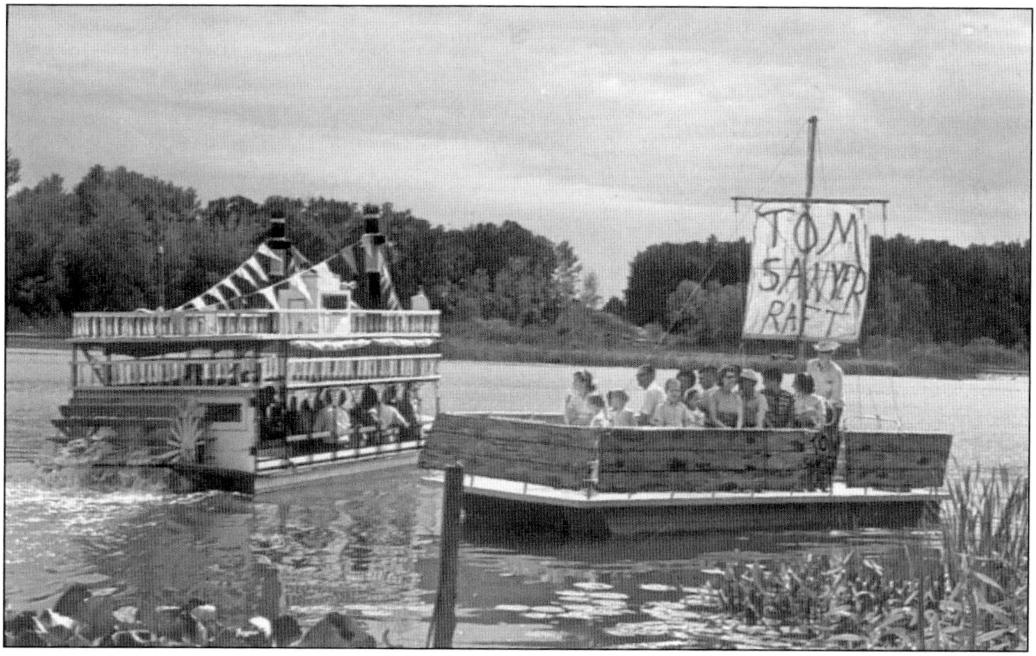

Tom Sawyer's River Raft. Tom Sawyer's River Raft takes the boys and girls for an adventuresome ride where they relive the story of Tom Sawyer and Huck Finn at Buck Lake Ranch, Angola, Indiana.

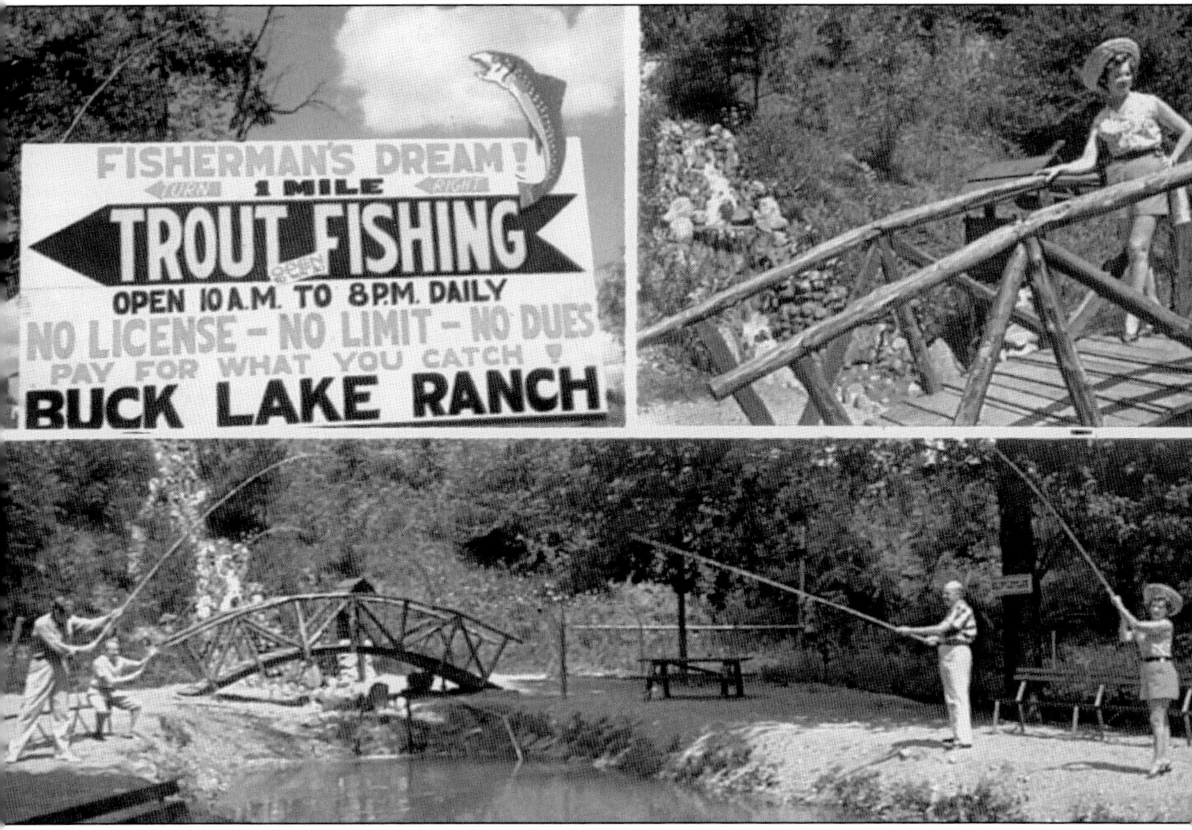

BUCK LAKE RANCH, ANGOLA, INDIANA. A fisherman's dream has come true at Buck Lake Ranch where fees for fishing are low, pay for what you catch, only 10¢ per inch, including icing and packaging. No state license is required, as these trout are privately owned with no limit attached. You'll catch rainbow trout the lazy way you've always dreamed of; they fight with the same lightning-swift charges and high leaps as in wilder elements.

(Opposite Top) **YACHT CLUB REGATTA, CLEAR LAKE.** Sail boats were a common sight on Clear Lake. This was an upscale lake area.

(Opposite Bottom) **TERRACE GARDEN, CLEAR LAKE, INDIANA.** The waterslide can be seen in the background.

CLEAR LAKE

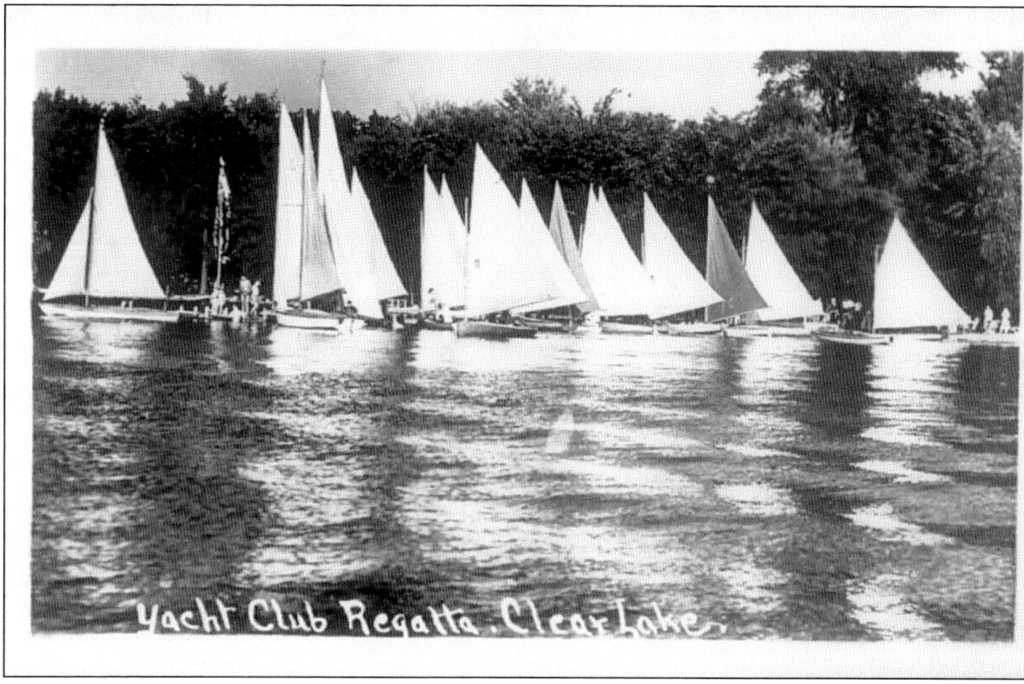
Yacht Club Regatta. Clear Lake.

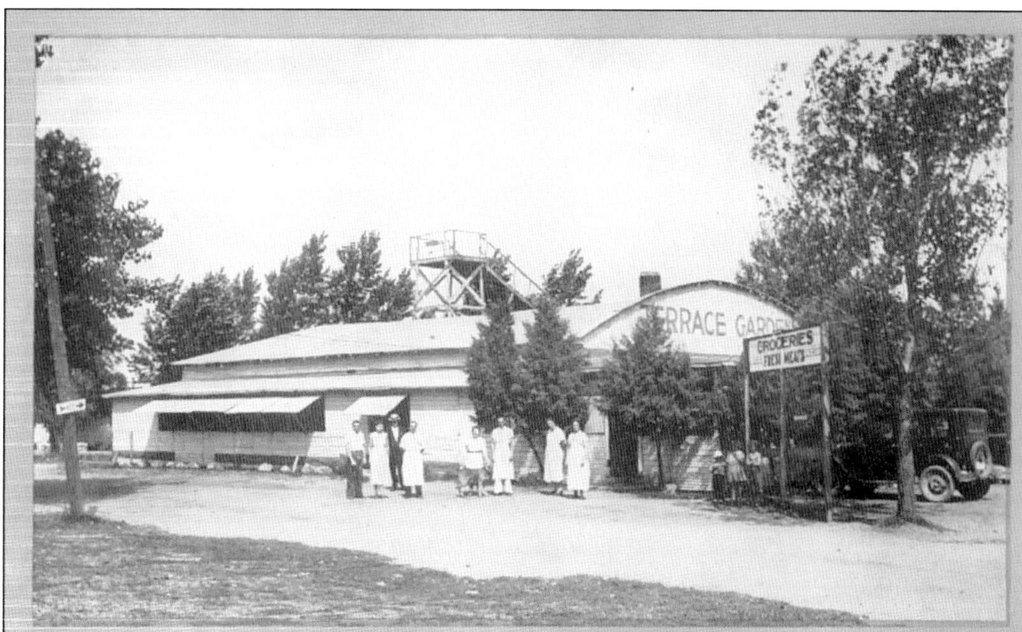
TERRACE GARDEN
GROCERIES
FRESH MEATS
TERRACE GARDEN, CLEAR LAKE, IND.
C-330

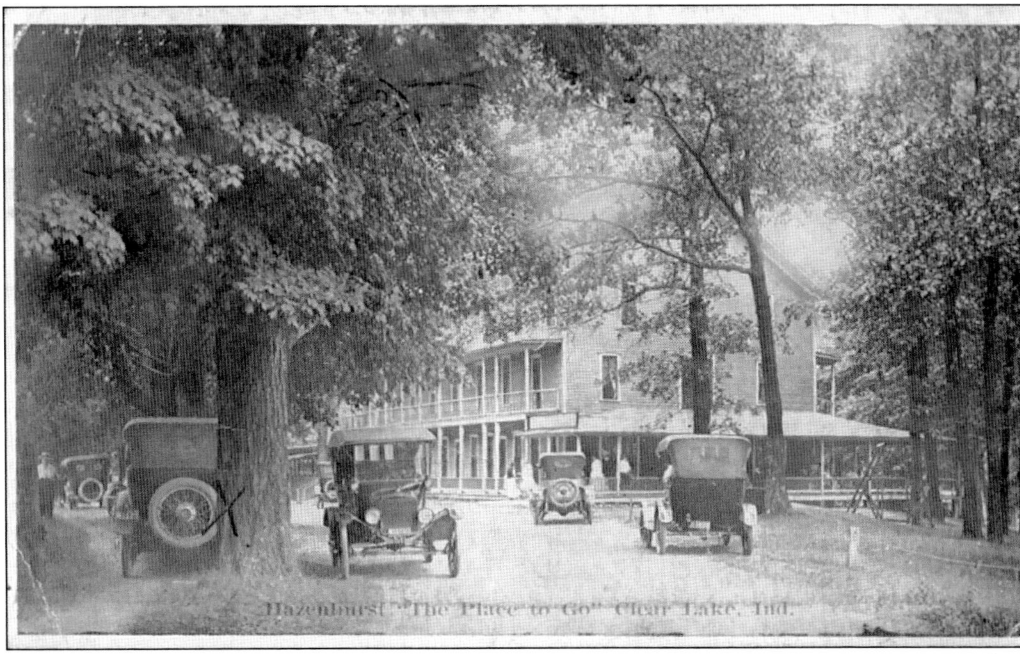

HAZENHURST "THE PLACE TO GO" CLEAR LAKE, INDIANA, *c.* 1923. Many came to spend their vacation at the Hazenhurst.

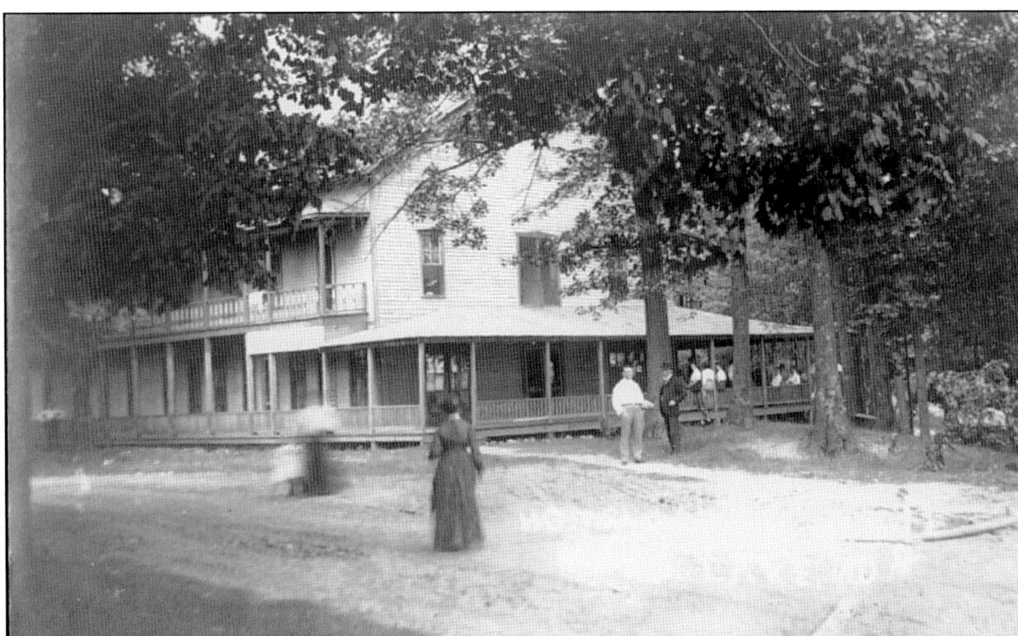

HOTEL LAKE WOOD, CLEAR LAKE, INDIANA, *c.* 1907. Guests are well dressed by today's standards.

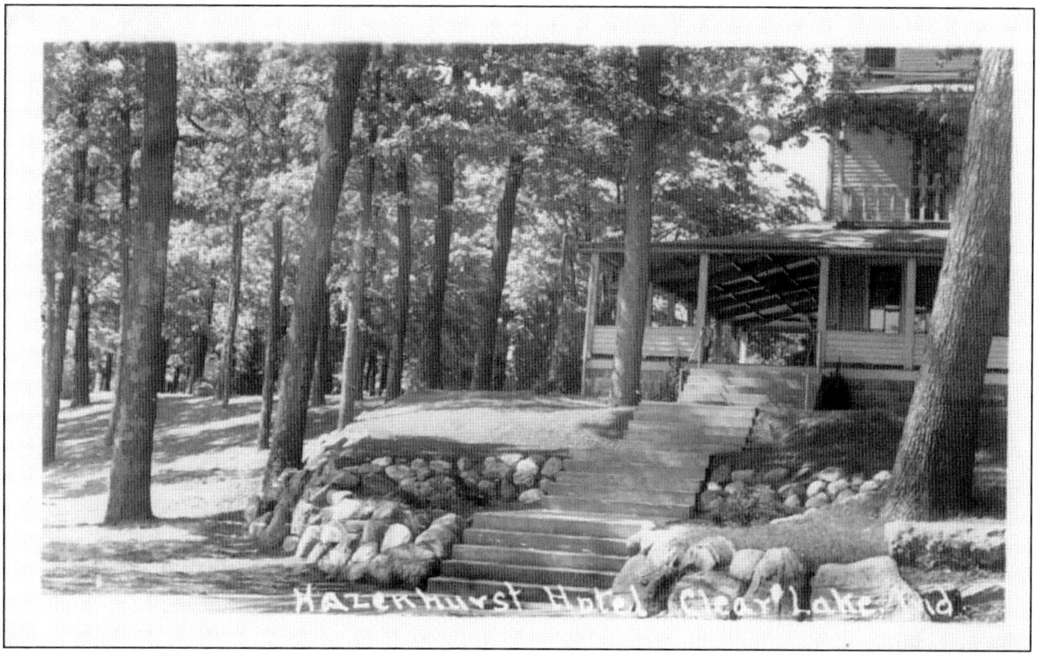

HAZENHURST HOTEL, CLEAR LAKE, INDIANA. The wrap-around porches provided a place to relax in a cool breeze.

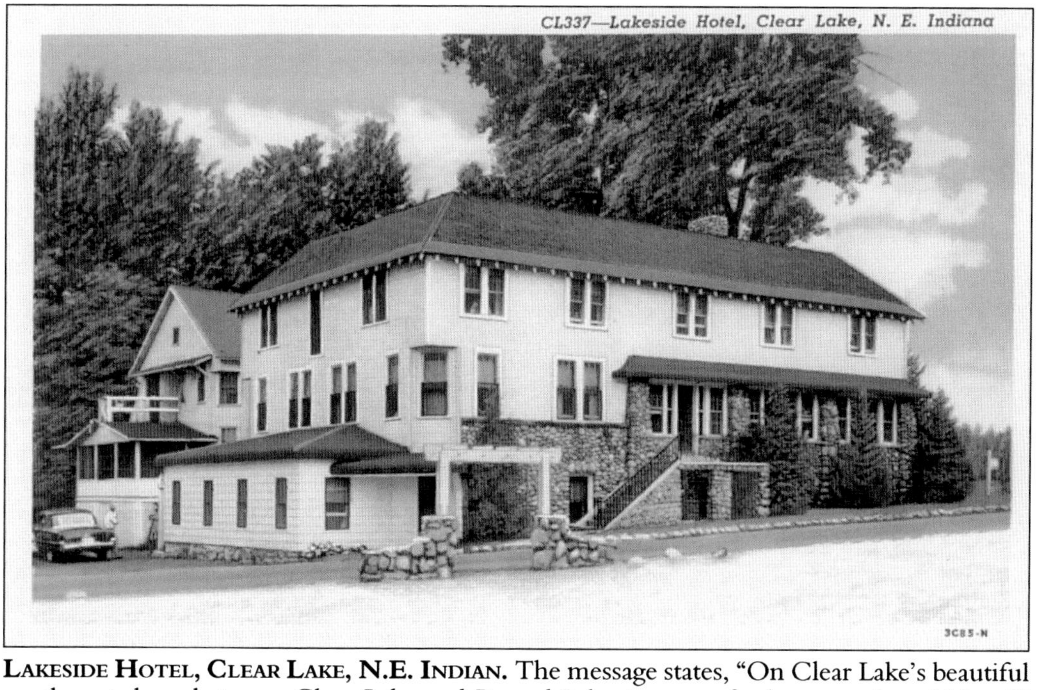

LAKESIDE HOTEL, CLEAR LAKE, N.E. INDIAN. The message states, "On Clear Lake's beautiful northwest shore between Clear Lake and Round Lake. Famous for bass, perch and bluegill fishing and fine beach."

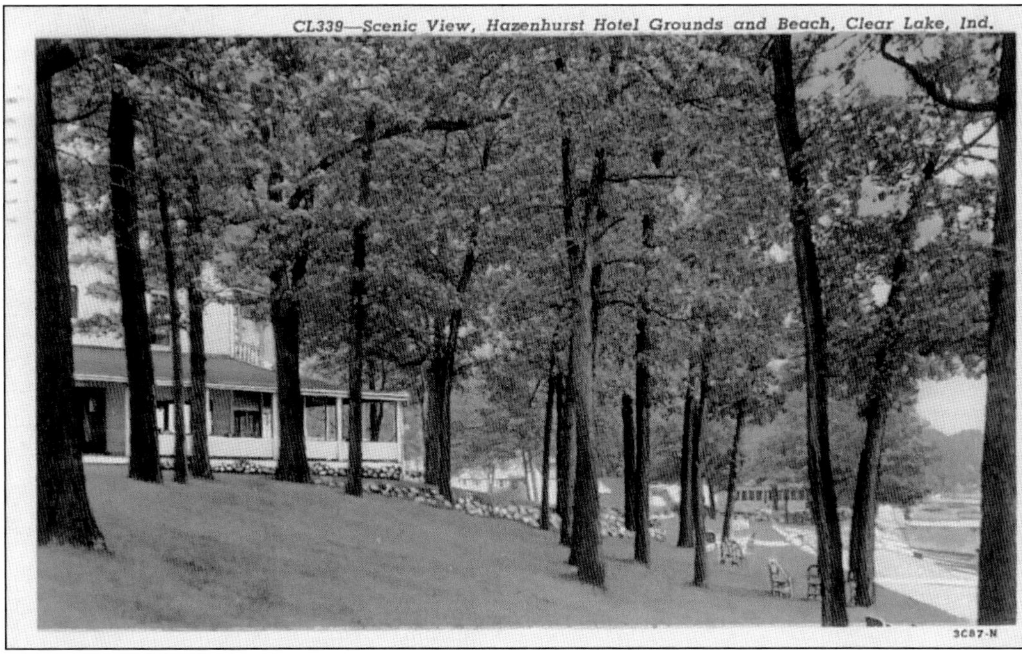

SCENIC VIEW, HAZENHURST HOTEL GROUNDS AND BEACH, CLEAR LAKE, INDIANA, *c.* 1955. This is a linen card showing the shaded lawn overlooking the beach.

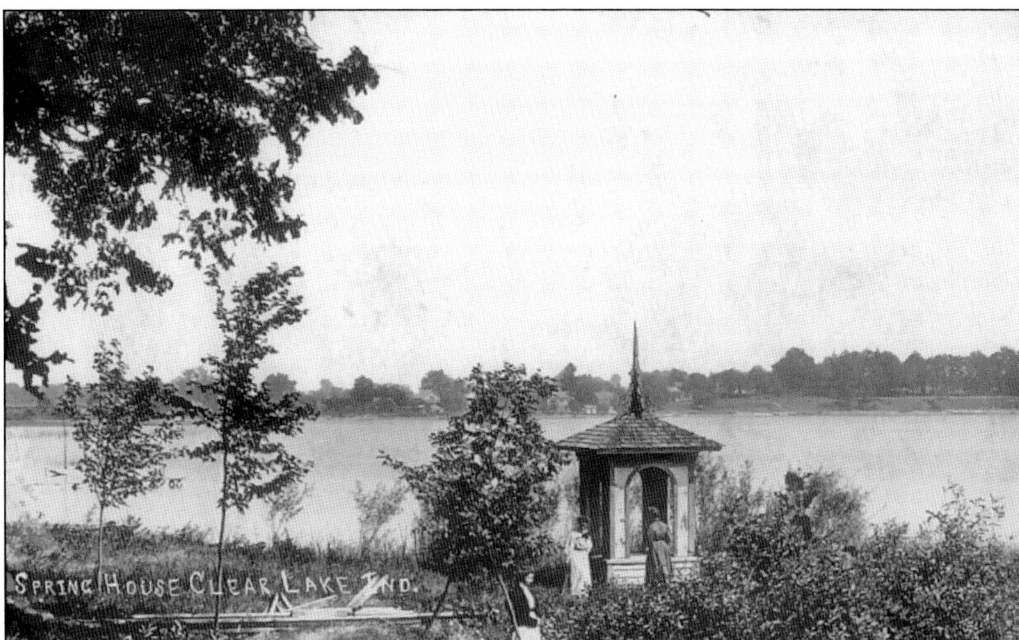

SPRING HOUSE CLEAR LAKE, INDIANA. This card is addressed to "Mr. B. Shanly, Nickle, Plate Round House, Ft. Wayne, Ind." The message states, "Hello Bill! We are catching lots of fish. We have sent on basket full of fish home and are gong to send another today. E.A. Worman."

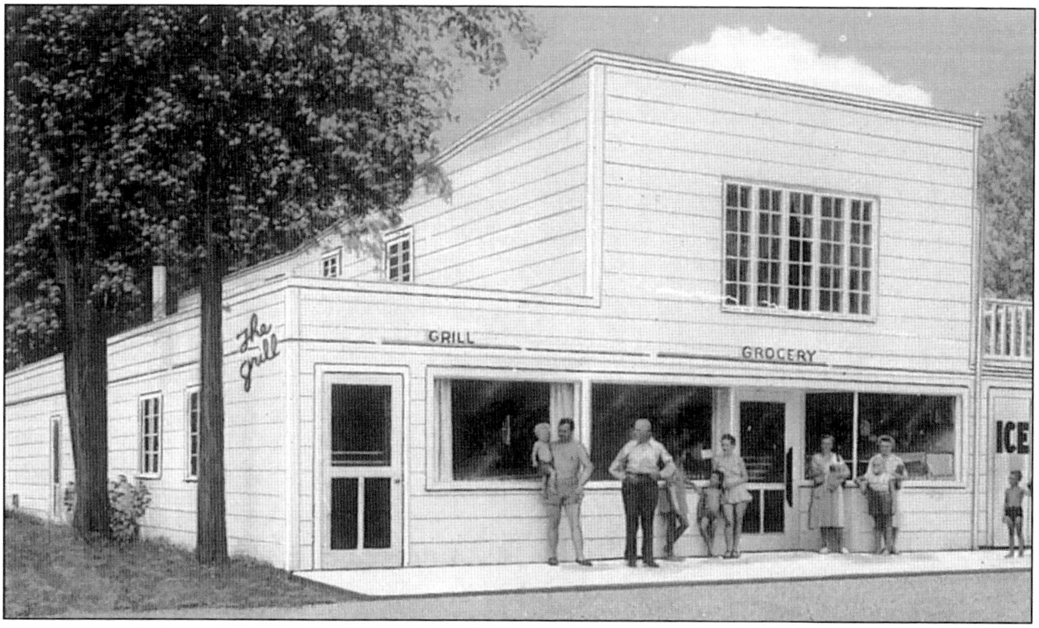

WAGGONER'S SOUTH SHORE, CLEAR LAKE, INDIANA, *c.* 1948. Located in the southeast corner on the South Shore overlooking beautiful Clear Lake, it is the social center for the entire lake, providing "Two sources of good food." Waggoner's Food Store offers the same shopping ease as their customers are accustomed to at home. "The Grill" of modern design provides a meeting place for visitors and cottagers who spend happy evenings over steaks, chops, or that famous "Burgie Basket," and exchanging friendly tales of that big fish that got away.

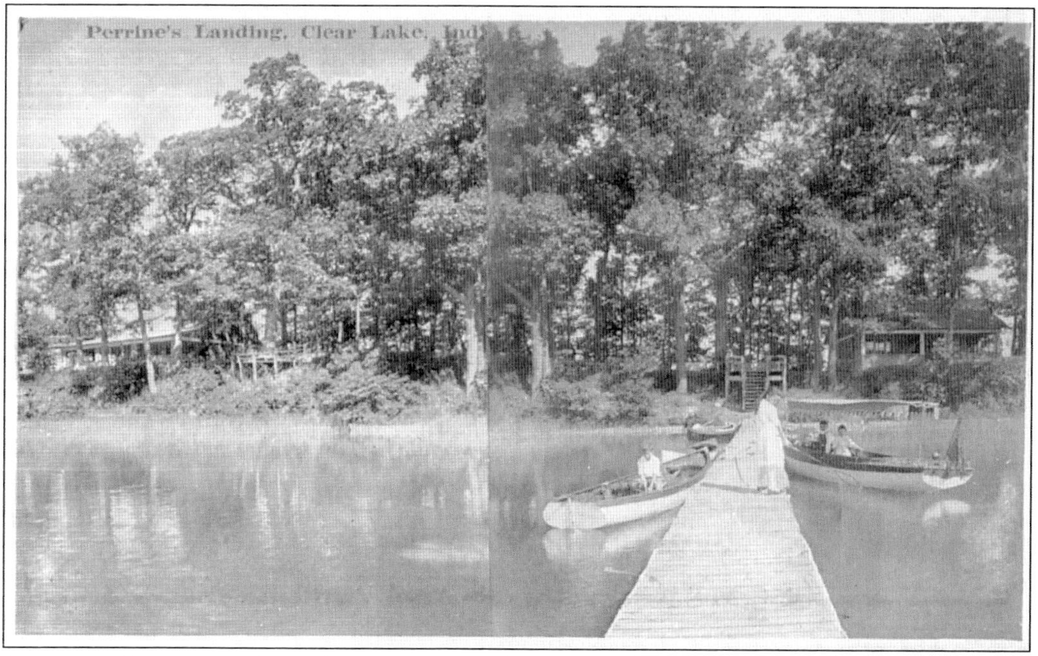

PERRINE'S LANDING, CLEAR LAKE, INDIANA. An unusually long dock is pictured above.

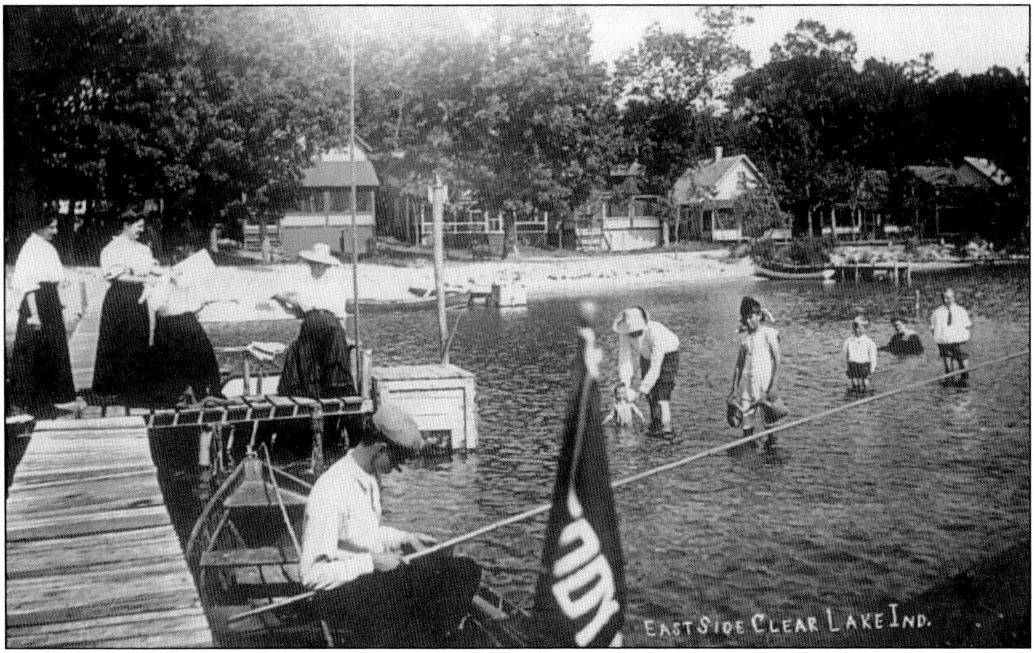

EAST SIDE CLEAR LAKE, INDIANA. Bathers appear to be fully dressed.

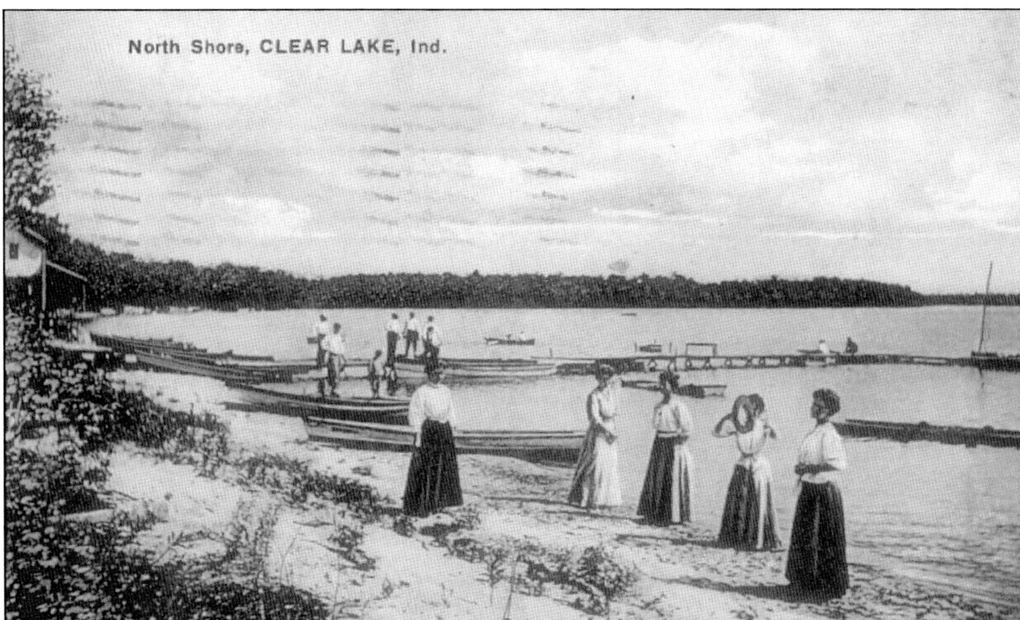

NORTH SHORE, CLEAR LAKE, INDIANA, *c.* 1909. The men in the background seem to be looking at the ladies in the foreground.

THE ARTZ COTTAGE, CLEAR LAKE, INDIANA. Some cottages were landmarks on the lake.

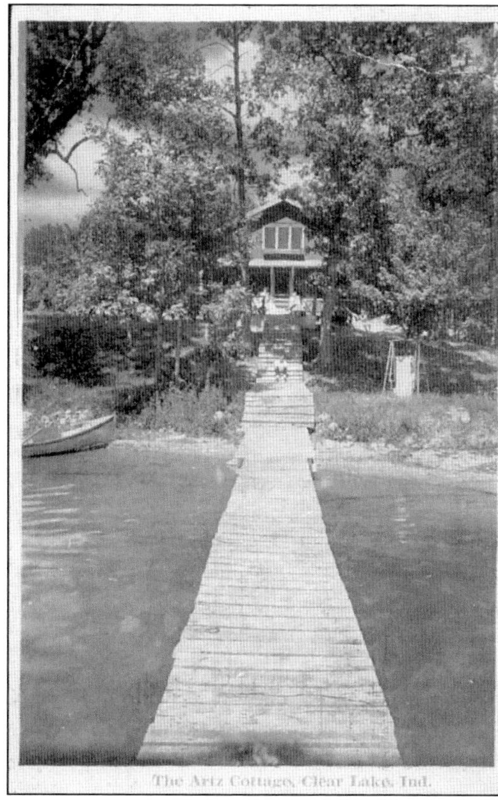

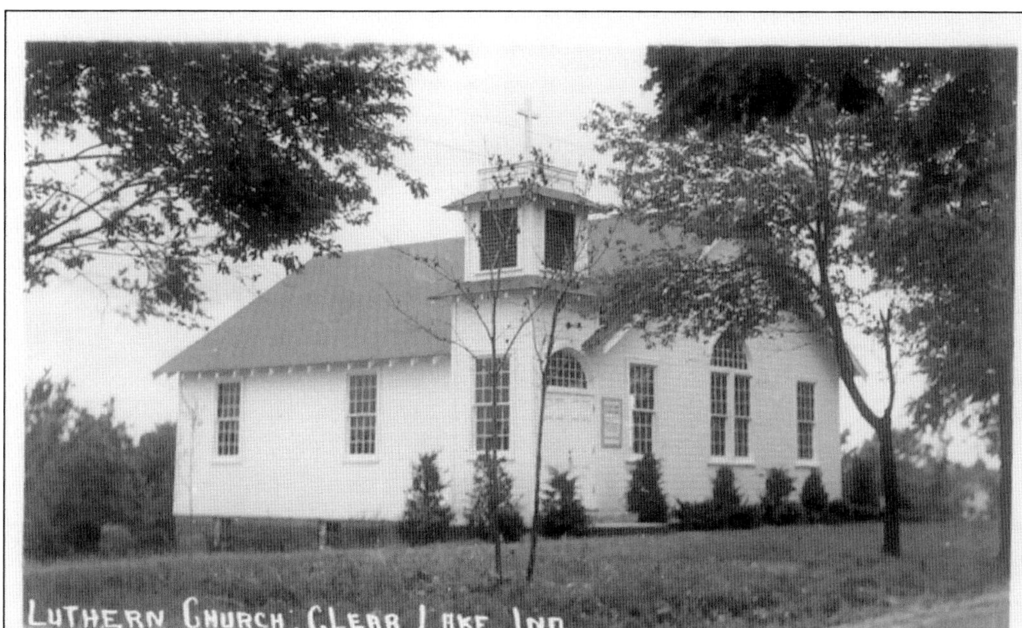

LUTHERAN CHURCH, CLEAR LAKE, INDIANA. Clear Lake was a community of both permanent and seasonal residents.

Crooked Lake

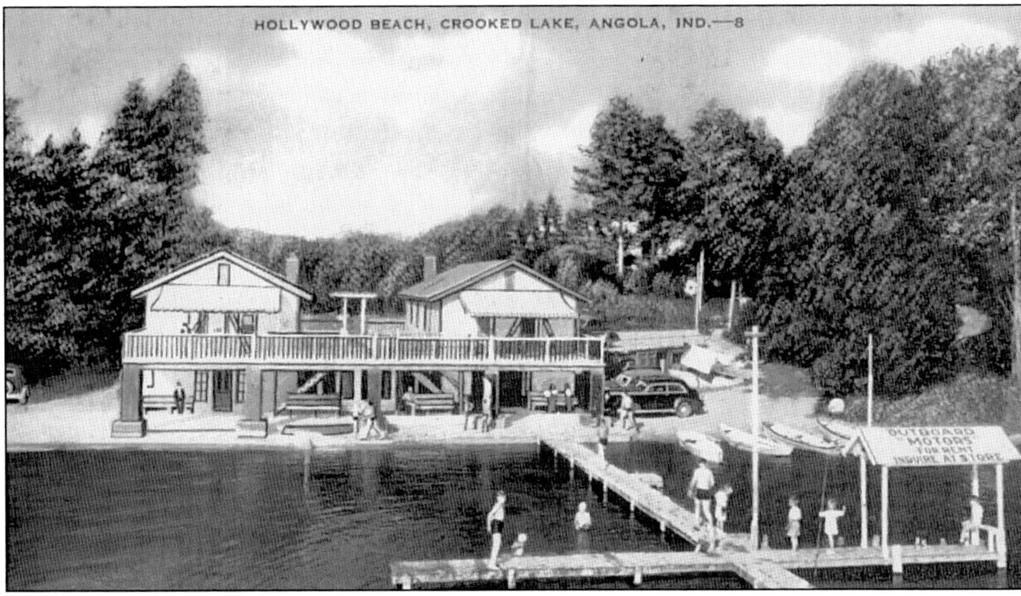

Hollywood Beach, Crooked Lake, Angola, Indiana. The sign on the canopy reads, "Outboard Motors for Rent—Inquire at Store."

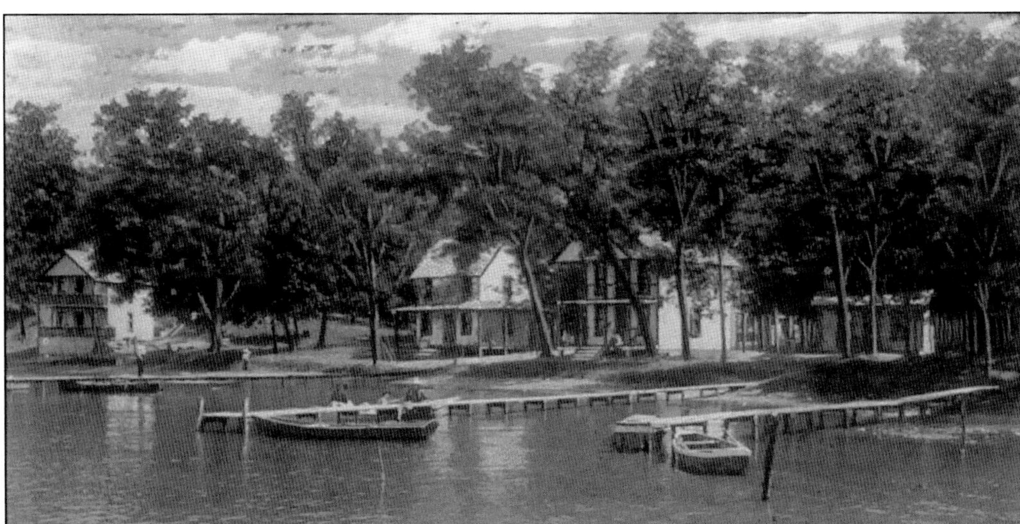

Pebble Beach, Crooked Lake, Near Angola, Indiana, c. 1931. The message states, "This lake is prettier looking in the opposite directions. Our address will be Tour 24C. Canadian Pacific 24 Boulevard des Capusines, Paris France. It takes about two weeks for mail to get to a tour and postage is 5¢. We will be so glad to hear from you. Wish you might see our roses delphiniums and likes, we'll think of you. Florence."

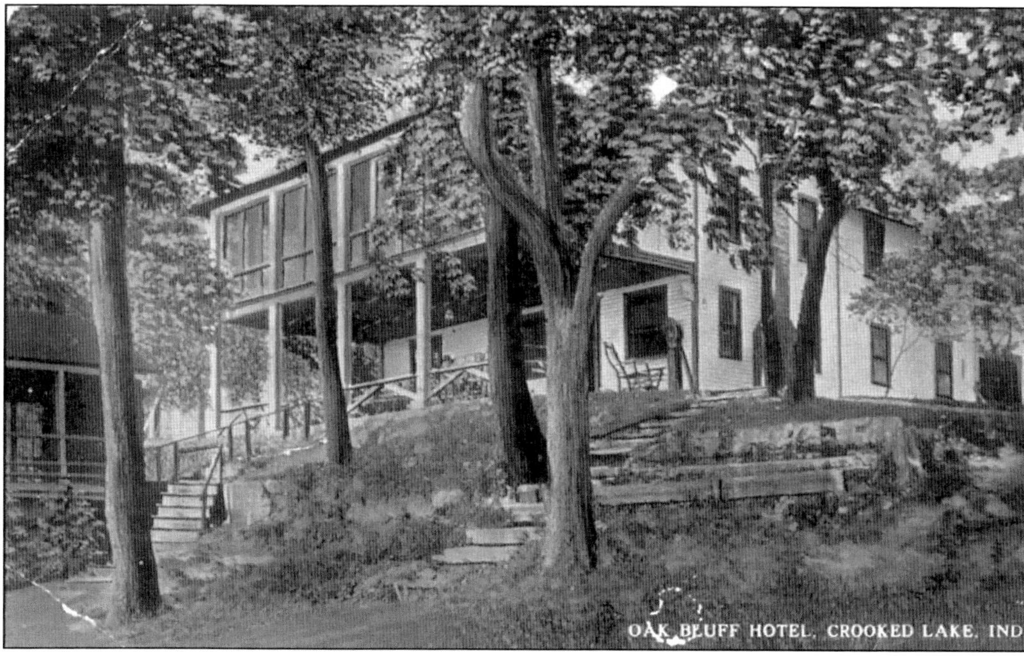

OAK BLUFF HOTEL, CROOKED LAKE, INDIANA, *C.* 1917. This small resort hotel provided vacation accommodations.

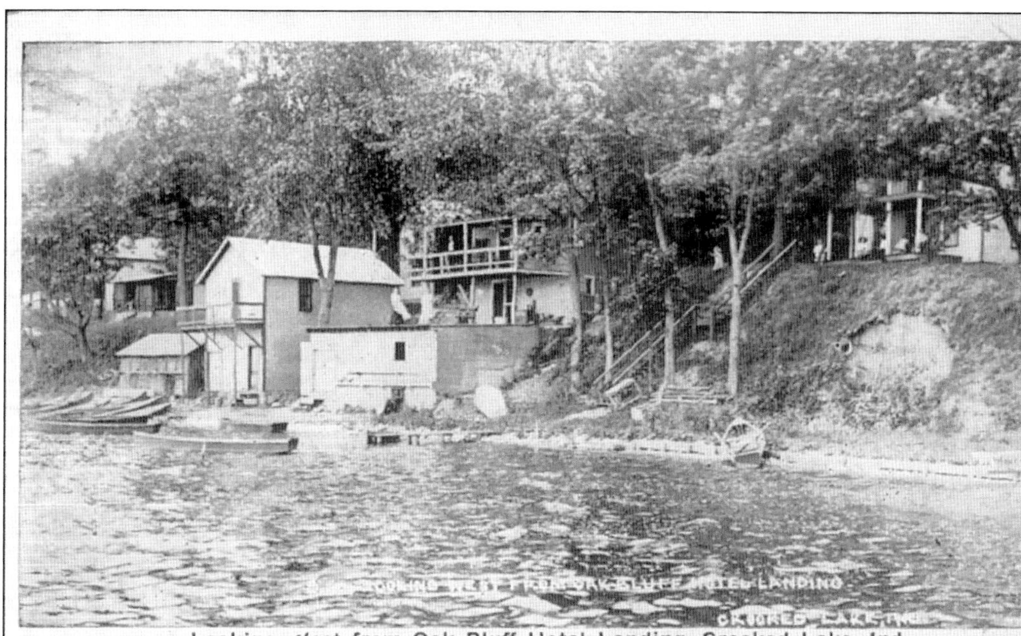

LOOKING WEST FROM OAK BLUFF HOTEL LANDING, CROOKED LAKE, INDIANA, *C.* 1922. Boat houses are built into the bluff.

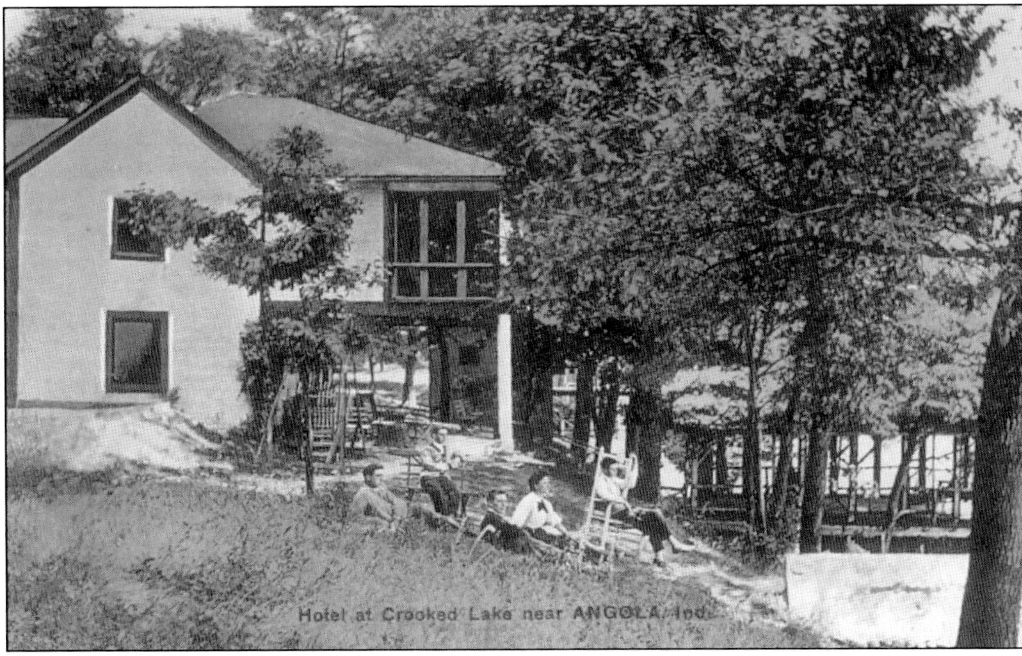

Hotel at Crooked Lake Near Angola, Indiana. Porches up and down provided cool breezes.

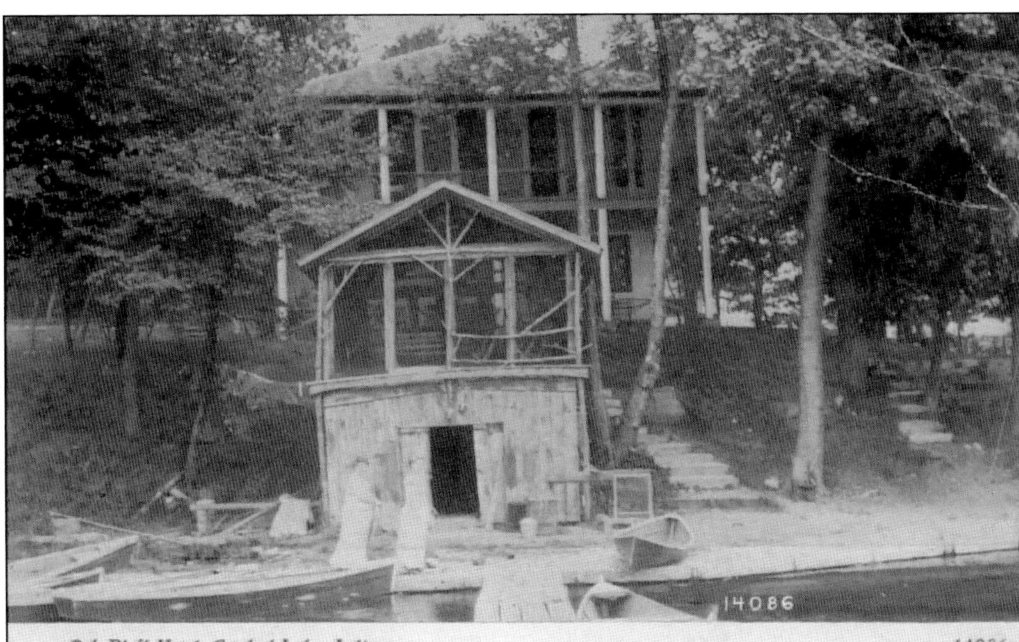

Oak Bluff Hotel, Crooked Lake, Indiana, *c.* 1913. This is another view from the front.

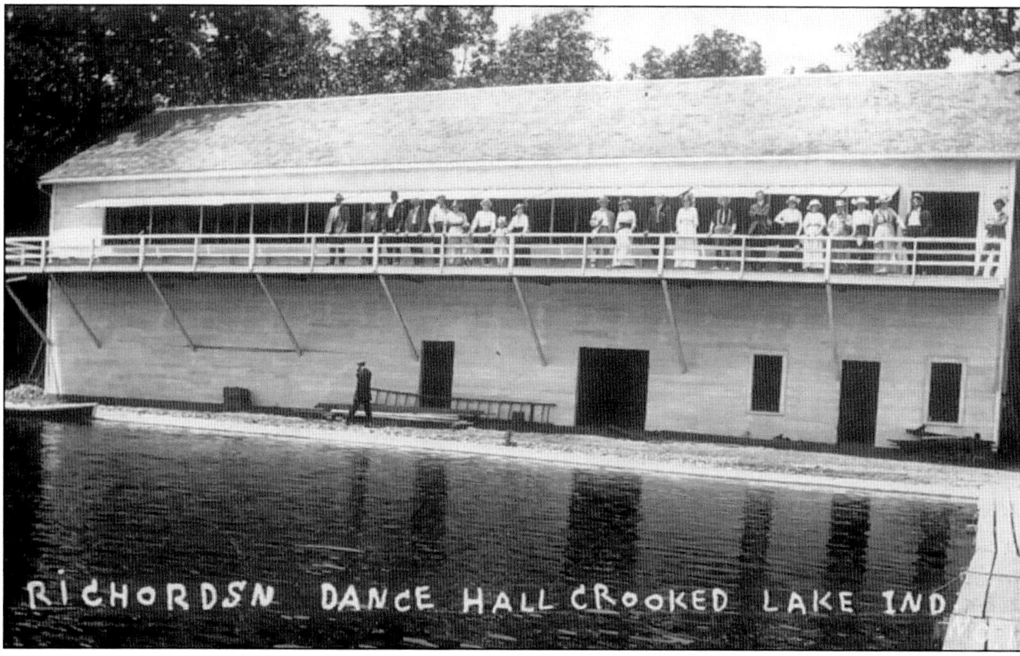

RICHARDSON DANCE HALL, CROOKED LAKE, INDIANA, *c.* 1914. Dance halls were located on many of Steuben County's lakes.

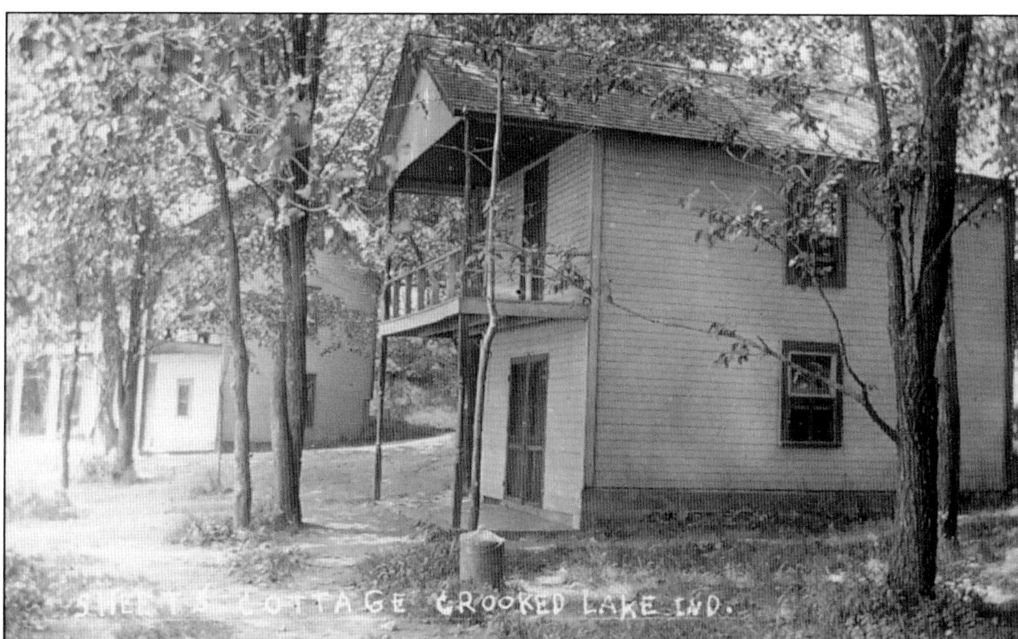

SHEETS COTTAGE, CROOKED LAKE, INDIANA. Seen here is a modest cottage.

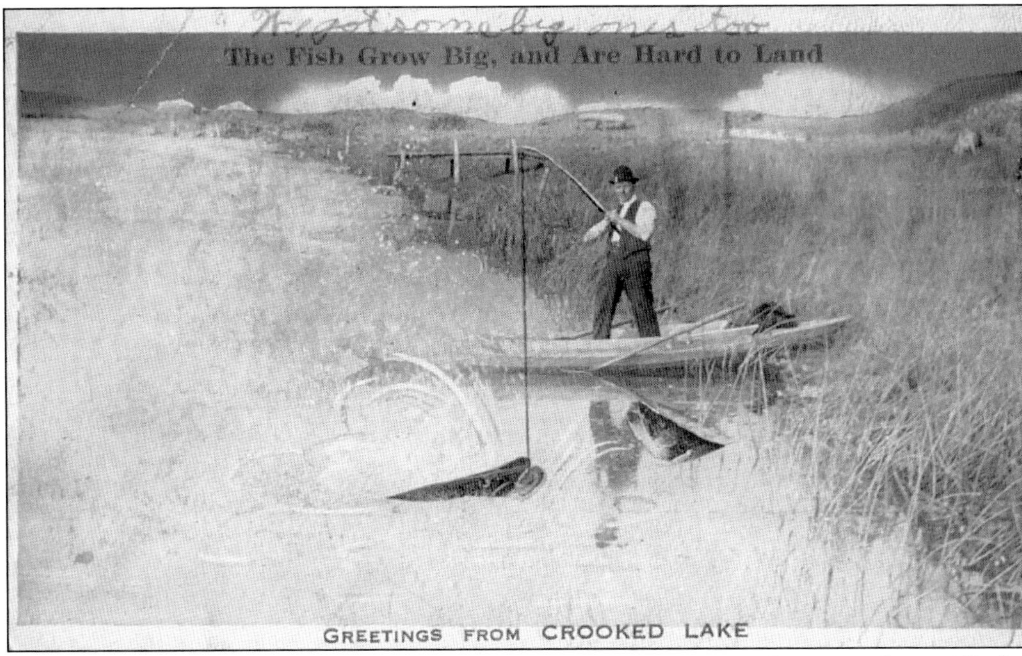

The Fish Grow Big, and are Hard to Land, Greetings from Crooked Lake. He has hooked a big one!

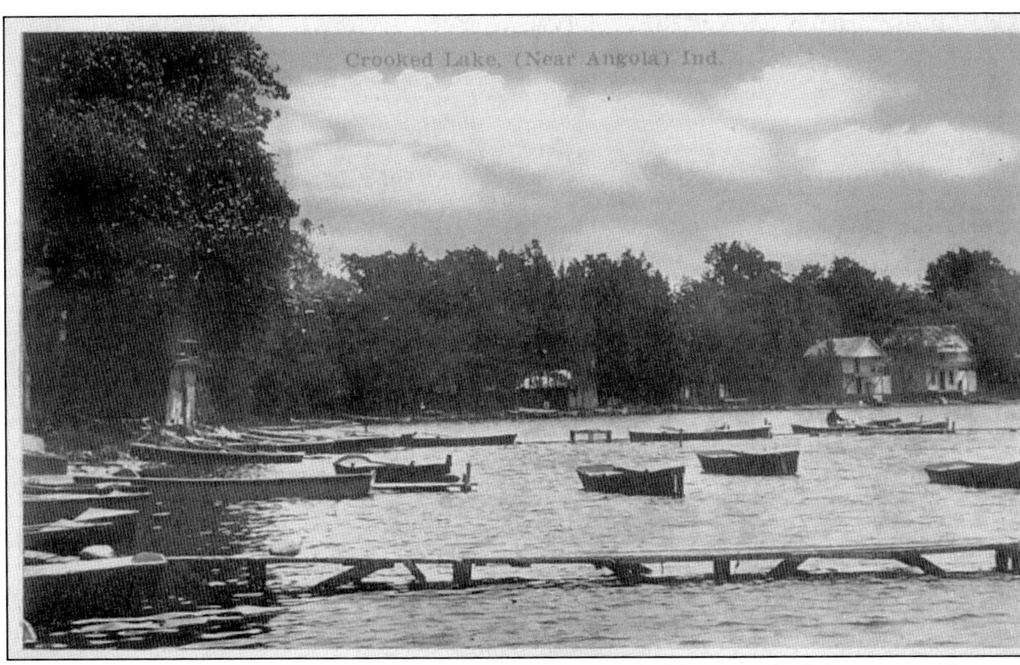

Crooked Lake, (Near Angola) Indiana. Docks extended far into the lake to provide space for boats.

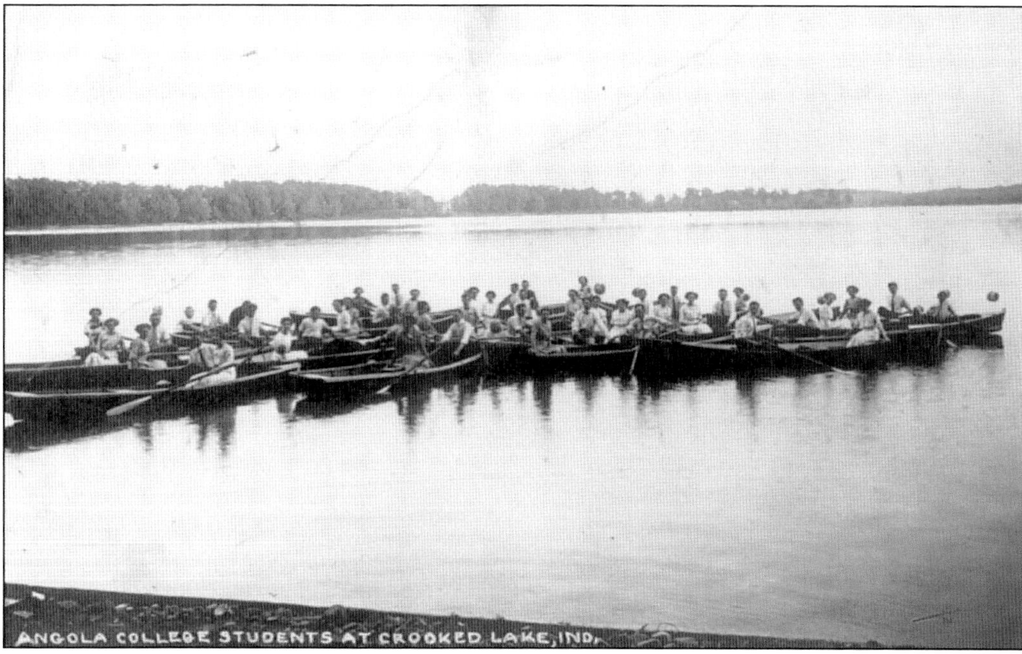

ANGOLA COLLEGE STUDENTS AT CROOKED LAKE, INDIANA, *c.* 1913. An activity on the lake is shown here.

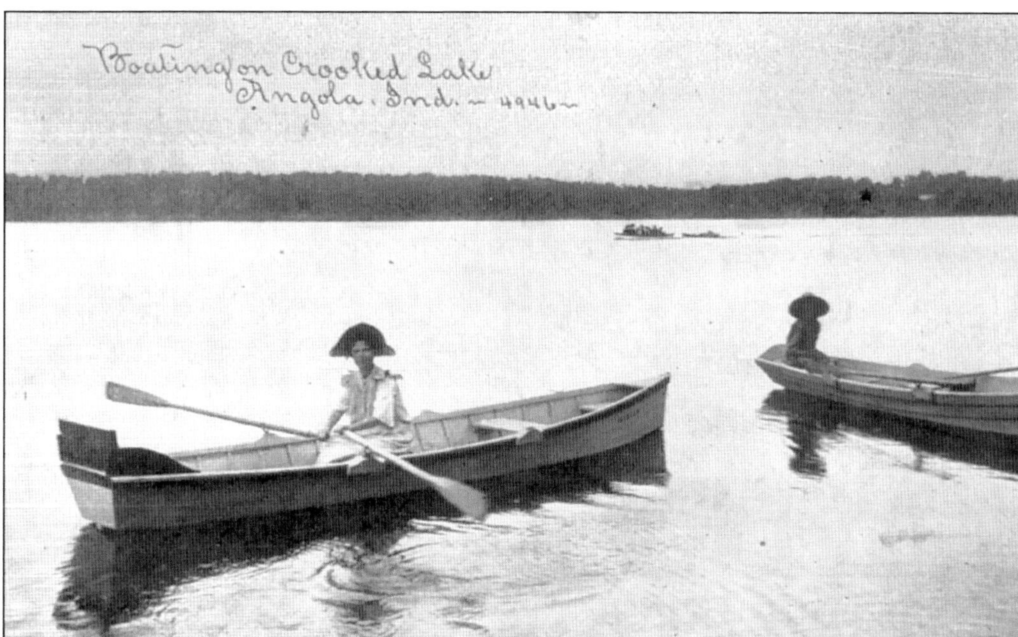

BOATING ON CROOKED LAKE, ANGOLA, INDIANA, *c.* 1914. The message states, "I am at Crooked Lake for the week, am having a nice time eating fish. Uncle Bill and Auntie Lib."

Fox Lake

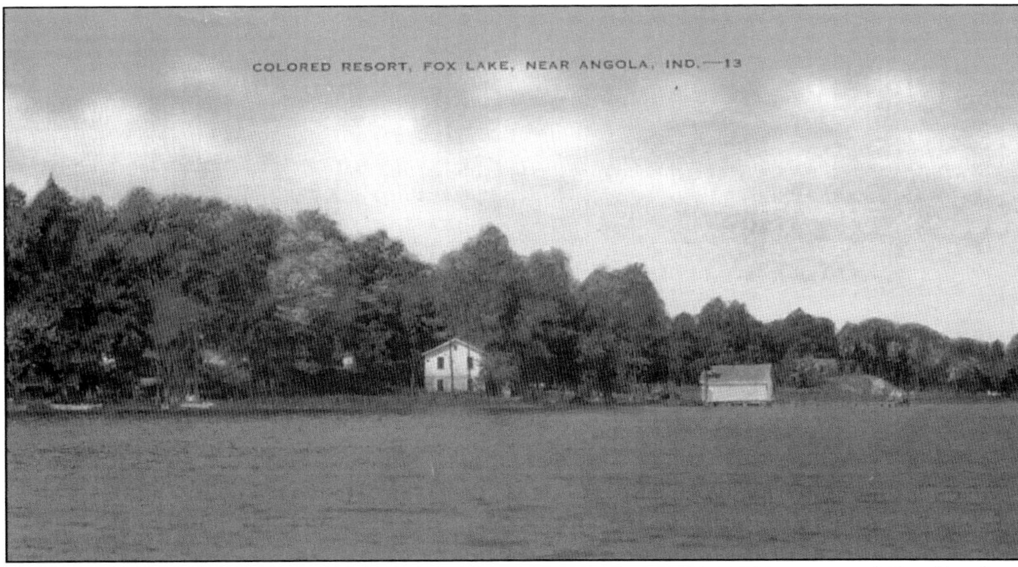

Colored Resort, Fox Lake, Near Angola, Indiana, *c.* 1946. This resort, 1.5 miles from Angola, located on Fox Lake, offers swimming, boating, fishing, horseback riding, etc. This was an ideal spot for the vacation minded.

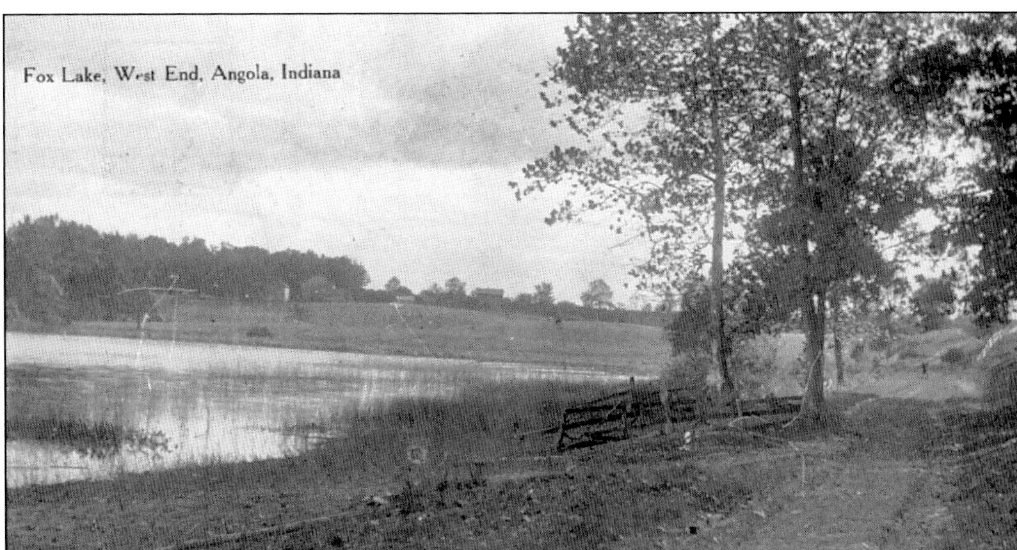

Fox Lake, West End, Angola, Indiana, *c.* 1912. Fox Lake was developed by a group of African Americans mainly from Fort Wayne and Indianapolis. In the days of segregation, even northern states, particularly Indiana, allowed segregation. It was especially prevalent in resort areas.

HAMILTON LAKE

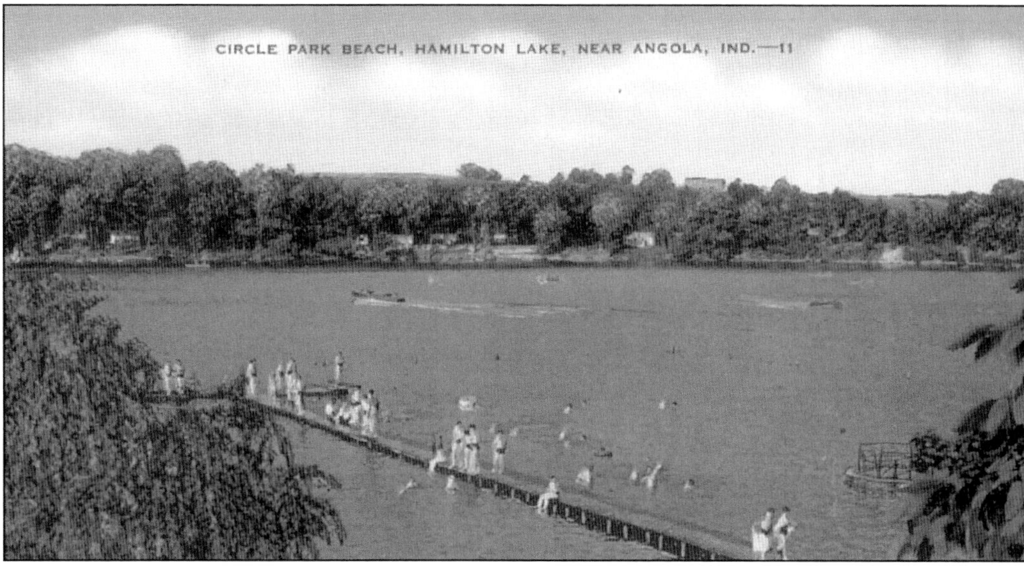

CIRCLE PARK BEACH, HAMILTON LAKE, NEAR ANGOLA, INDIANA. Circle Park Beach is located on the shore of beautiful Hamilton Lake about 14 miles from Angola. This park is an ideal recreational spot for old and young alike.

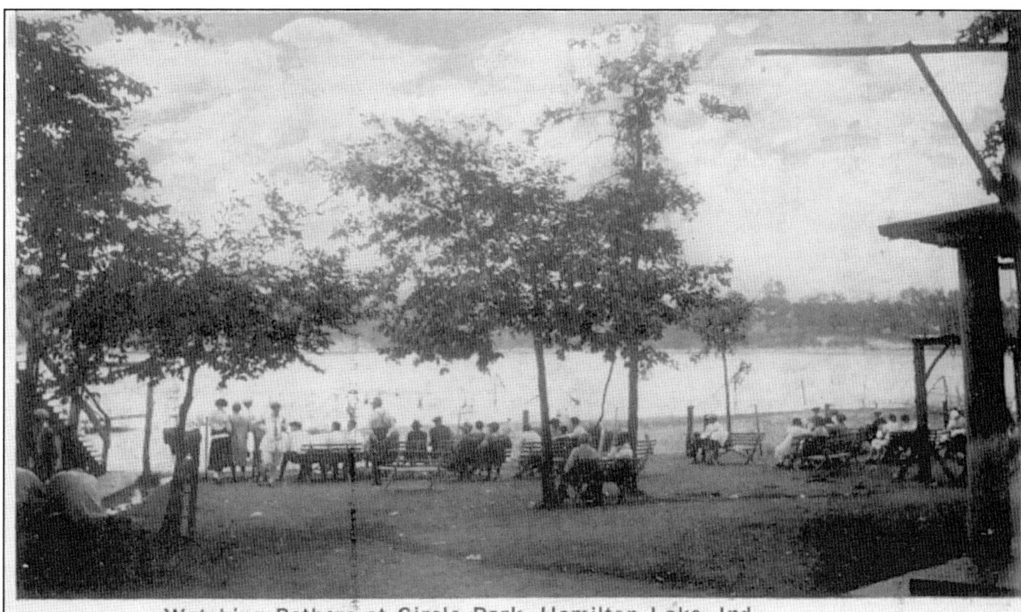

WATCHING BATHERS AT CIRCLE PARK, HAMILTON LAKE, INDIANA. Circle Park offered a host of activities.

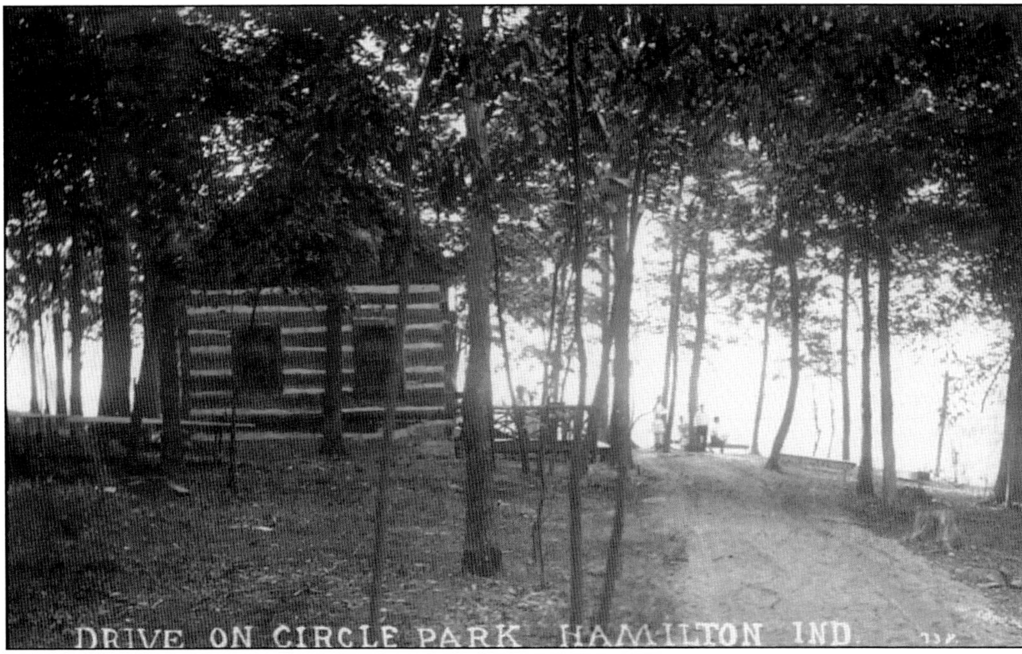

Drive on Circle Park, Hamilton, Indiana. The log cabin store sold groceries to campers and picnickers. It was located in a log house moved from near Terry Lake.

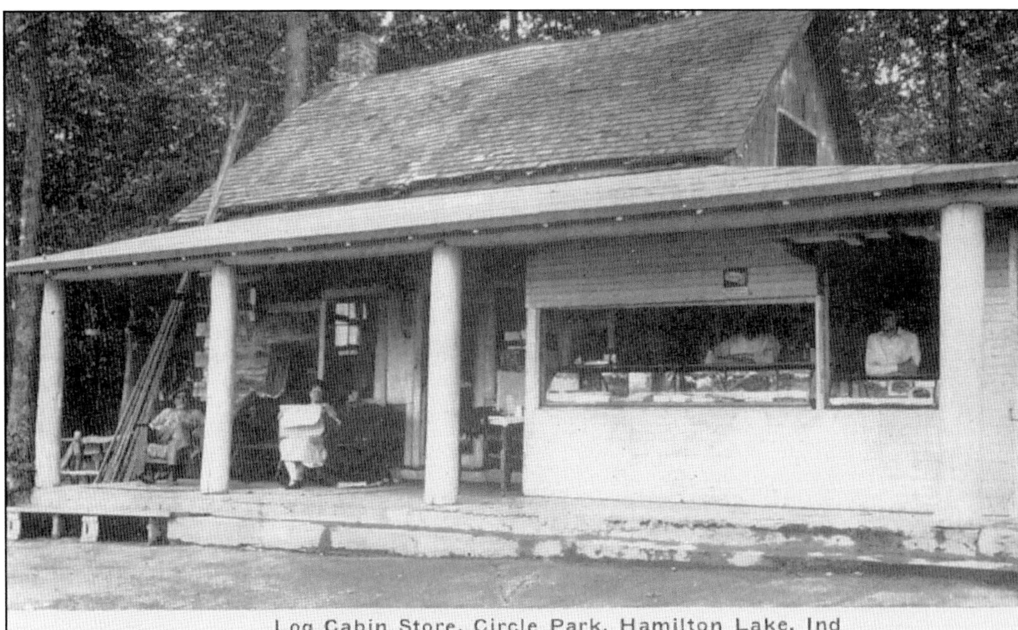

Log Cabin Store, Circle Park, Hamilton Lake, Indiana. The log house was the birthplace of the author's grandfather, Carl R. Smith.

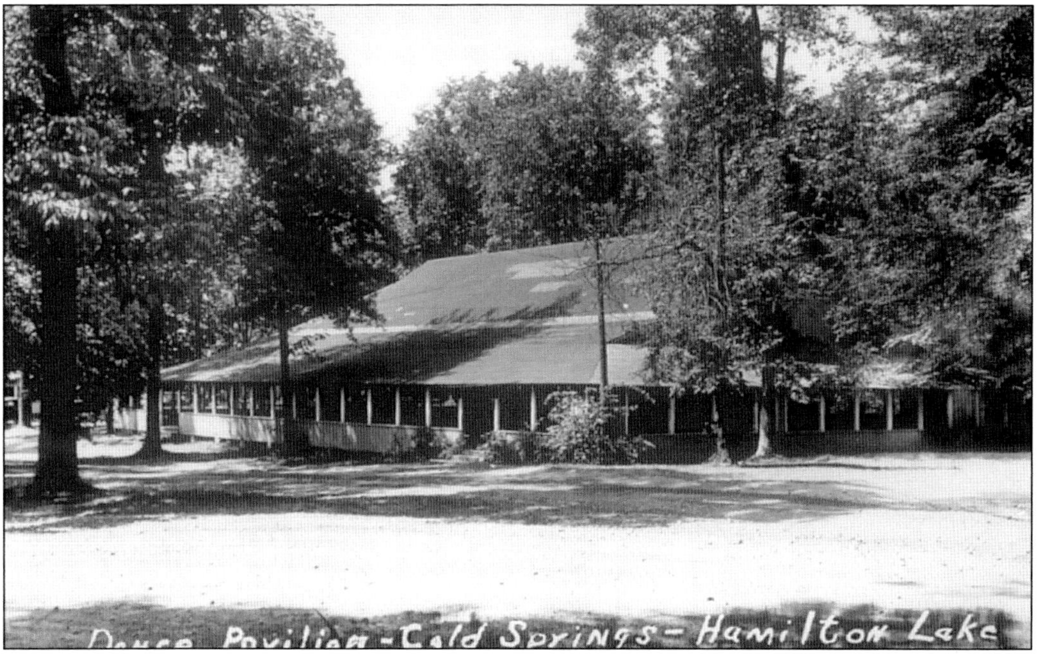

DANCE PAVILION, COLD SPRINGS, HAMILTON LAKE, INDIANA. The pavilion hosted many of the big bands of the 1930s and 1940s. Record hops hosted by W.O.W.O. Radio's Disc Jockeys Bob Chase, Don Chevilet, Bob Seivers, and Jack Underwood were extremely popular among the area's teenagers in the 1950s and 1960s.

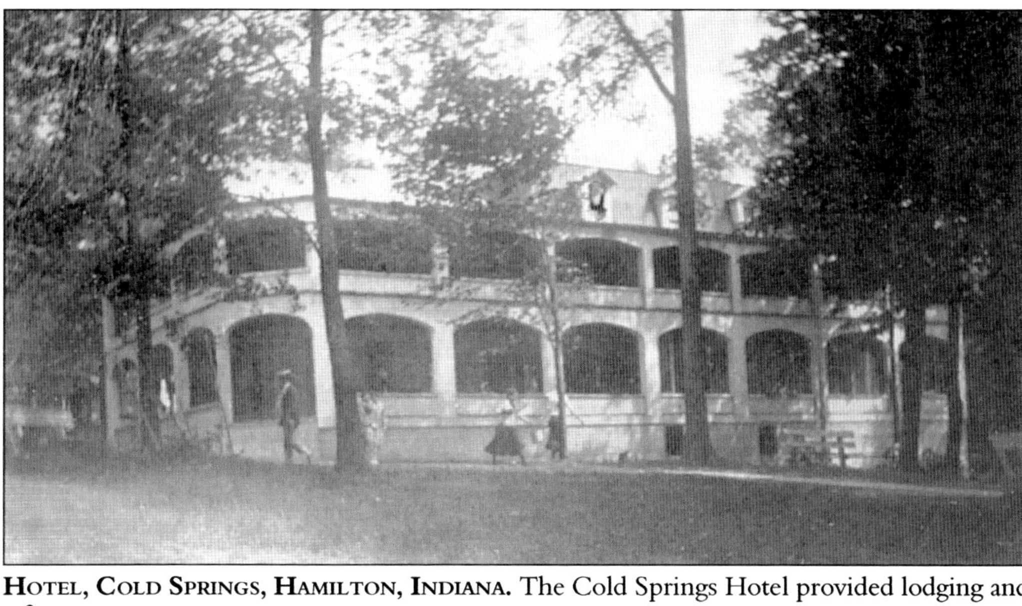

HOTEL, COLD SPRINGS, HAMILTON, INDIANA. The Cold Springs Hotel provided lodging and a fine restaurant.

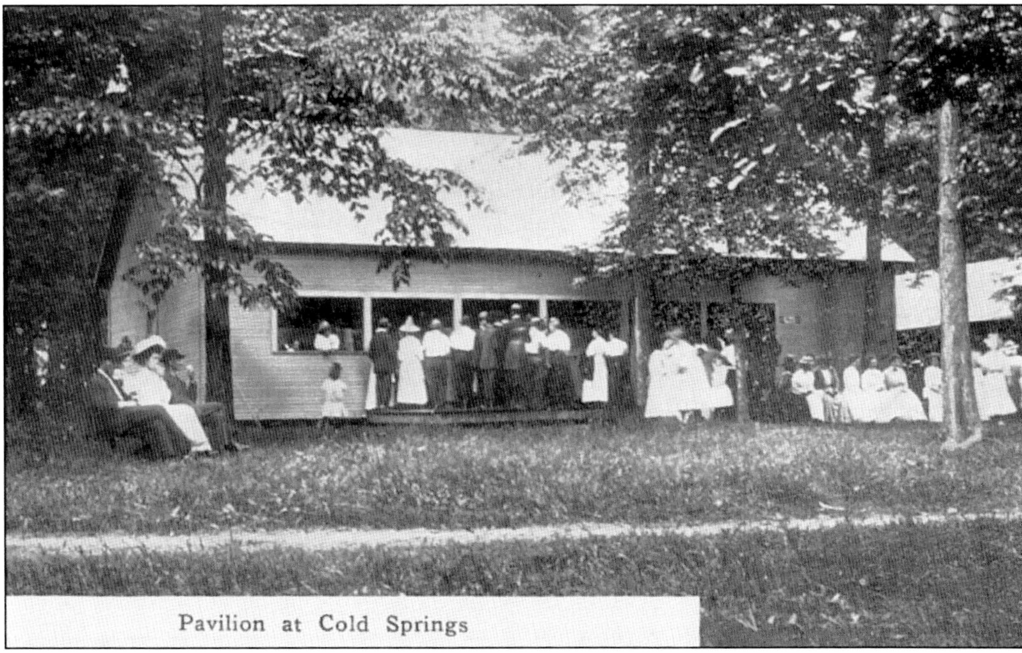

PAVILION AT COLD SPRINGS, HAMILTON, INDIANA, *c.* 1912. The pavilion dates from the early part of the century.

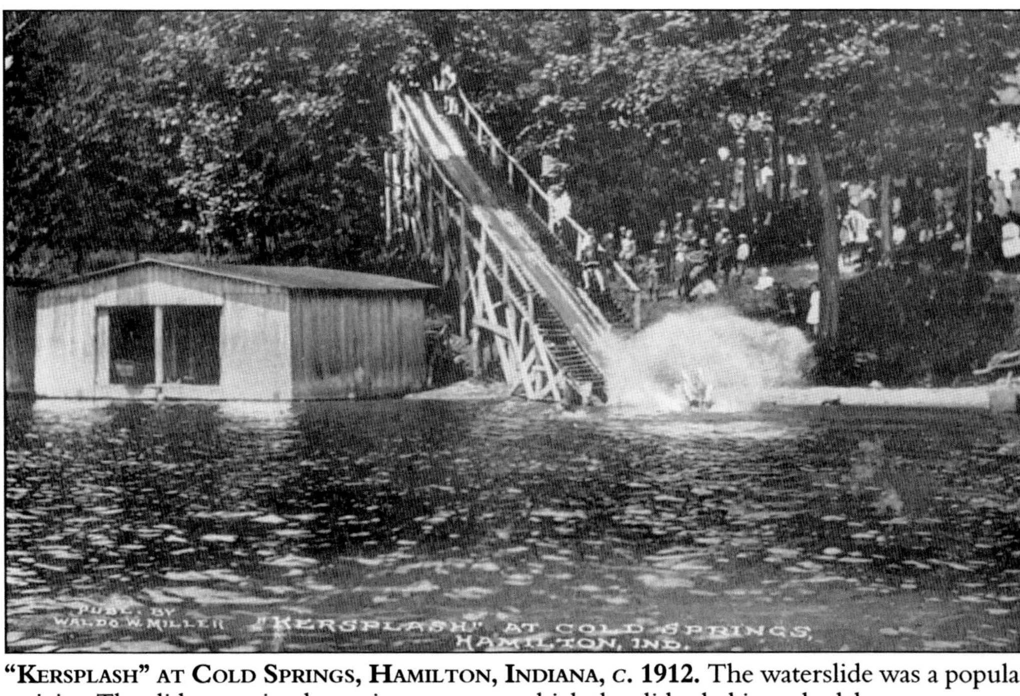

"KERSPLASH" AT COLD SPRINGS, HAMILTON, INDIANA, *c.* 1912. The waterslide was a popular activity. The slide contained running water on which the slide sled into the lake.

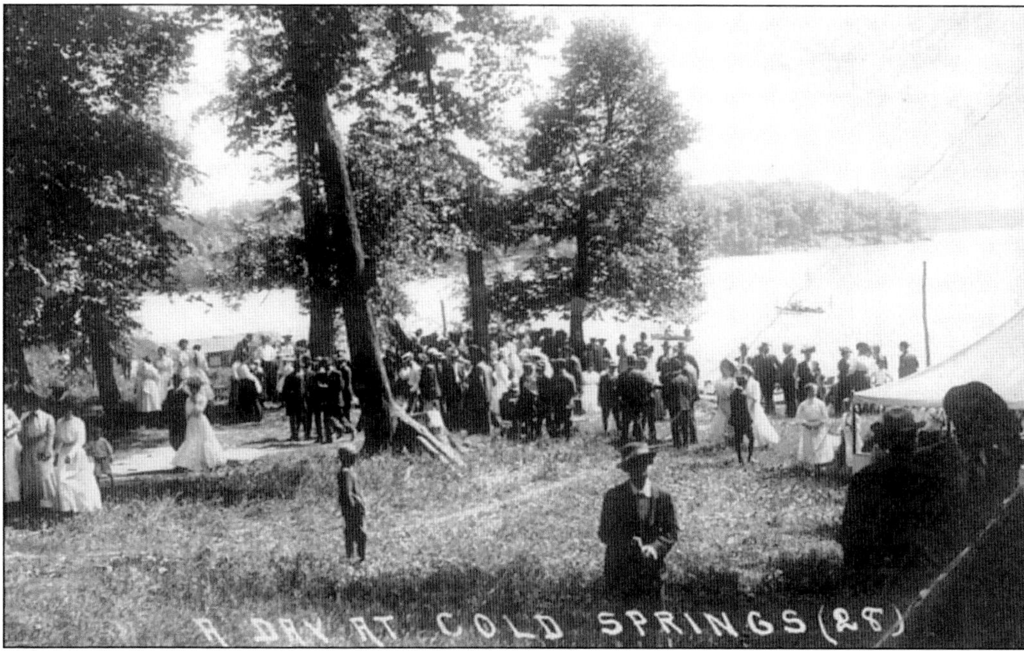

A Day at Cold Springs, Hamilton, Indiana. This was a popular place for company picnics and family reunions.

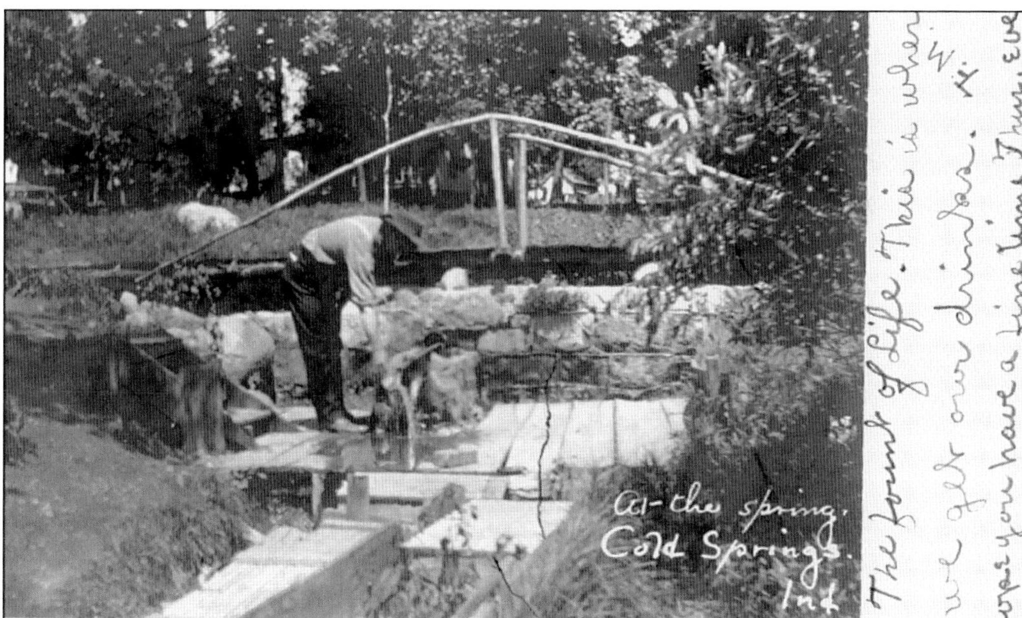

At the Spring, Cold Springs, Hamilton, Indiana. There was a "cold spring" at Cold Springs. Fresh cold water bubbled from an iron pipe.

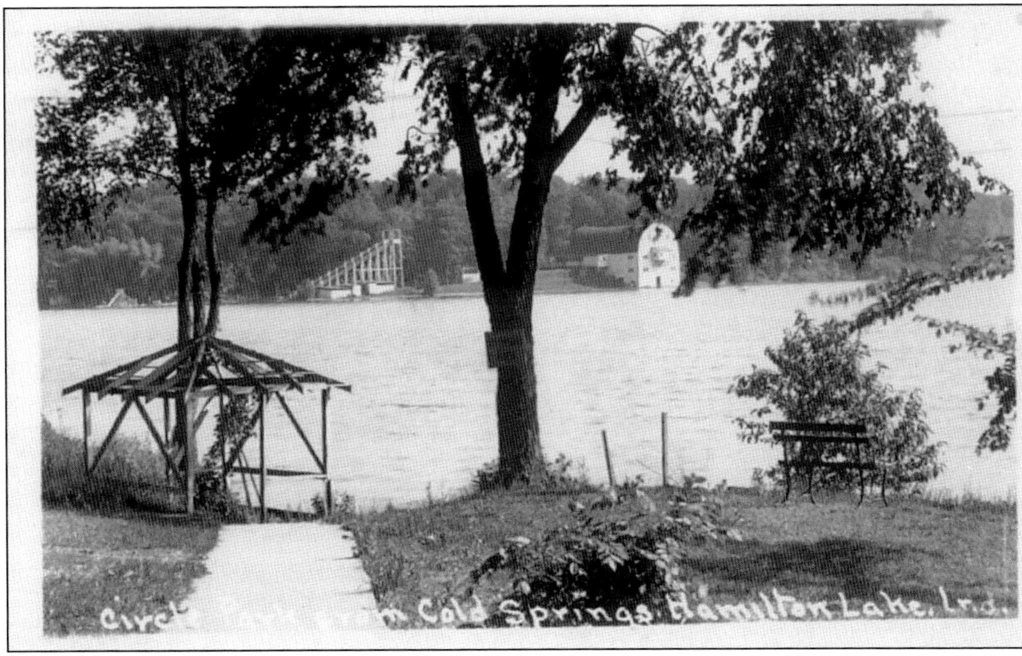

CIRCLE PARK FROM COLD SPRINGS, HAMILTON LAKE, INDIANA, *c.* 1940. The Circle Park Waterslide is between the trees. The dining hall and skating rink building is on the right.

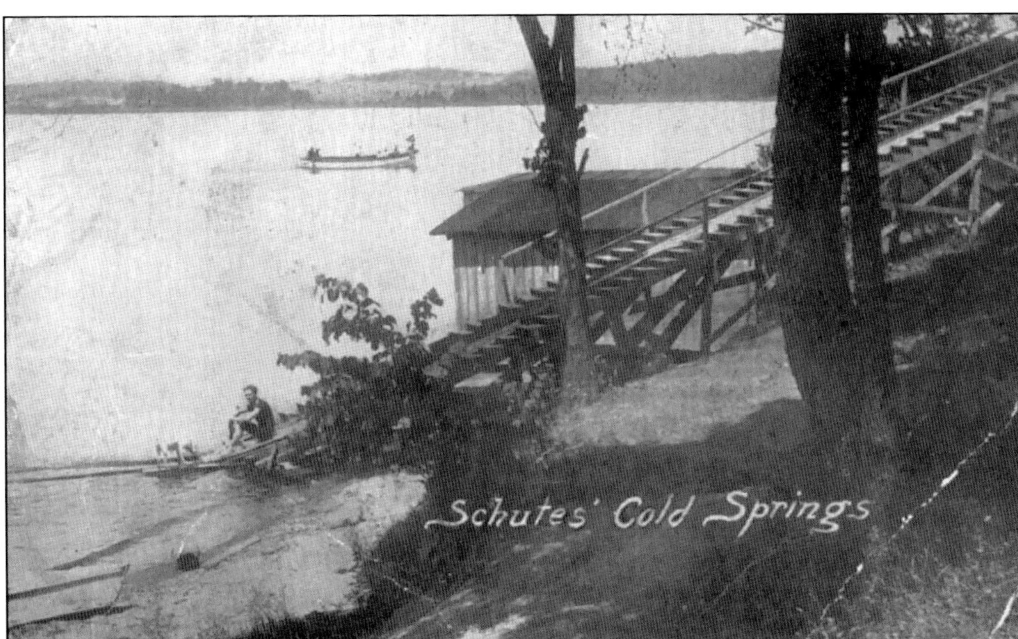

SCHUTE'S COLD SPRINGS, HAMILTON, INDIANA, *c.* 1910.

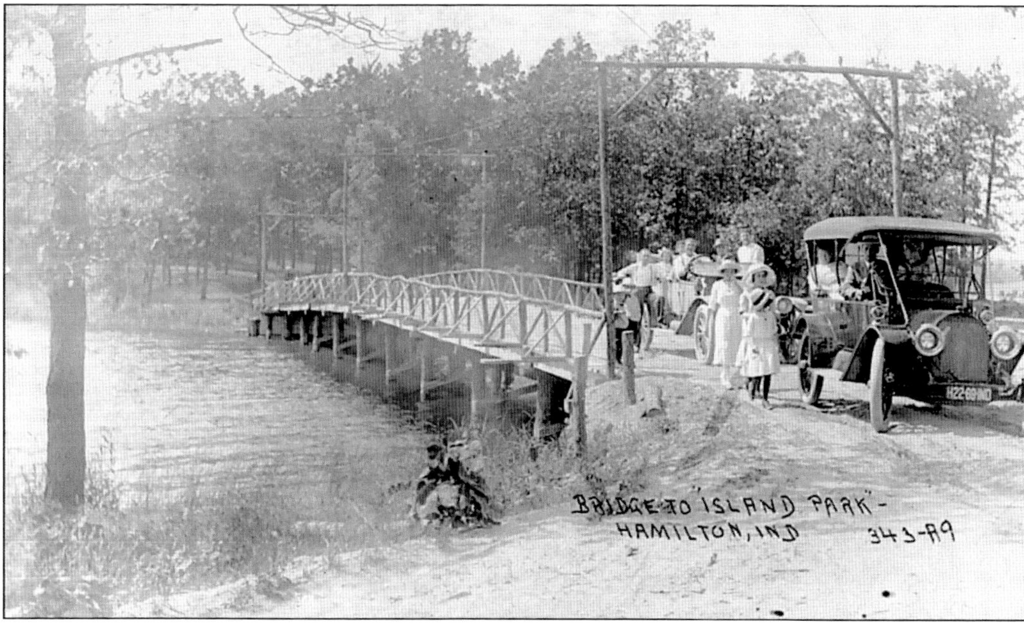

Bridge to Island Park, Hamilton, Indiana. The wooden bridge was the only access to Island Park.

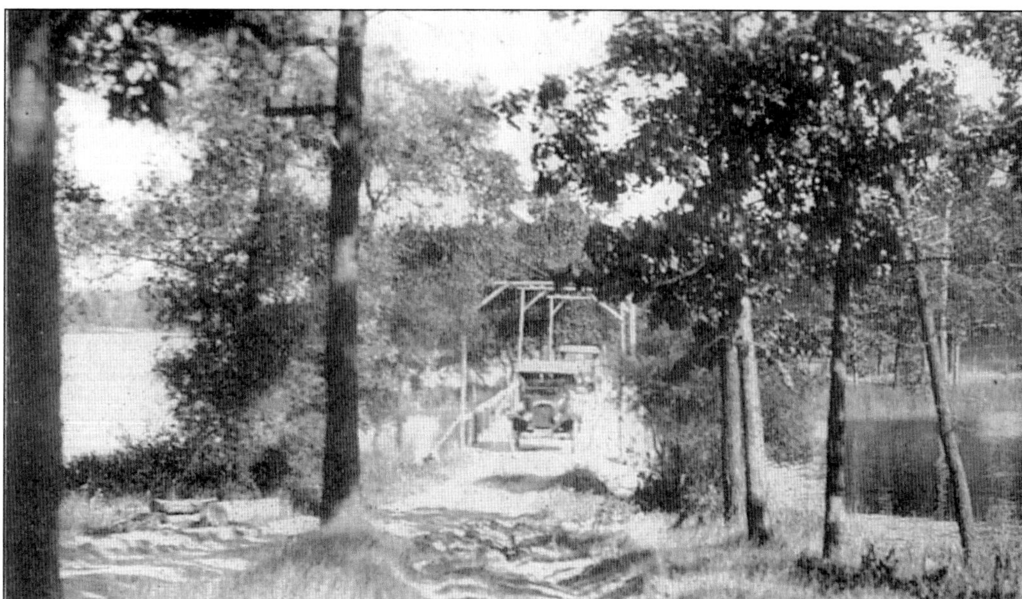

Bridge from Island Park

Bridge from Island Park. Seen here is another view from Island Park.

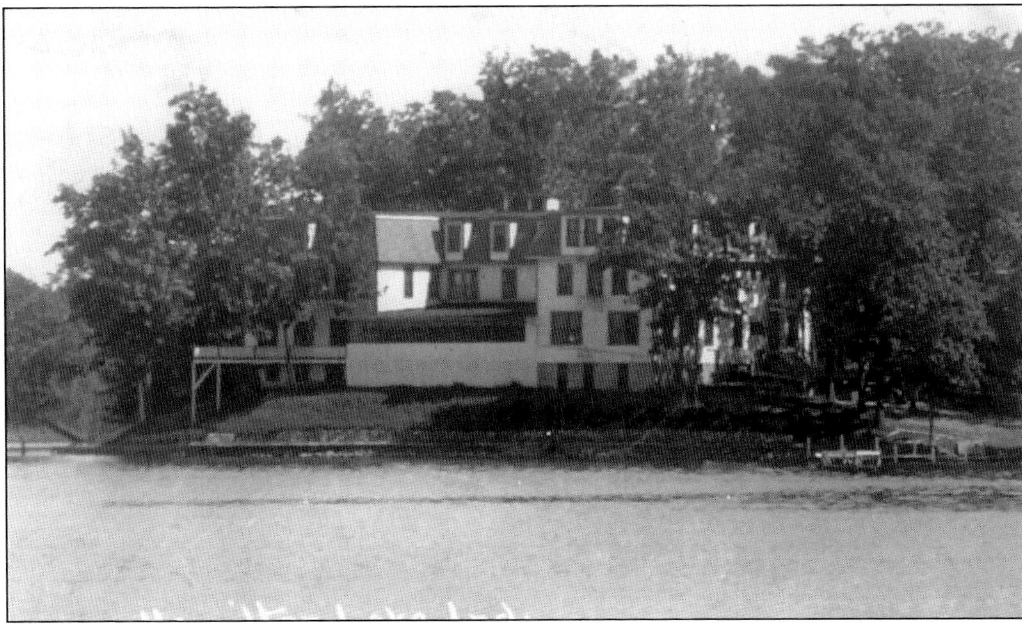

Hamilton Lake, Indiana, c. 1943. The Island Park Hotel is shown from the lake side.

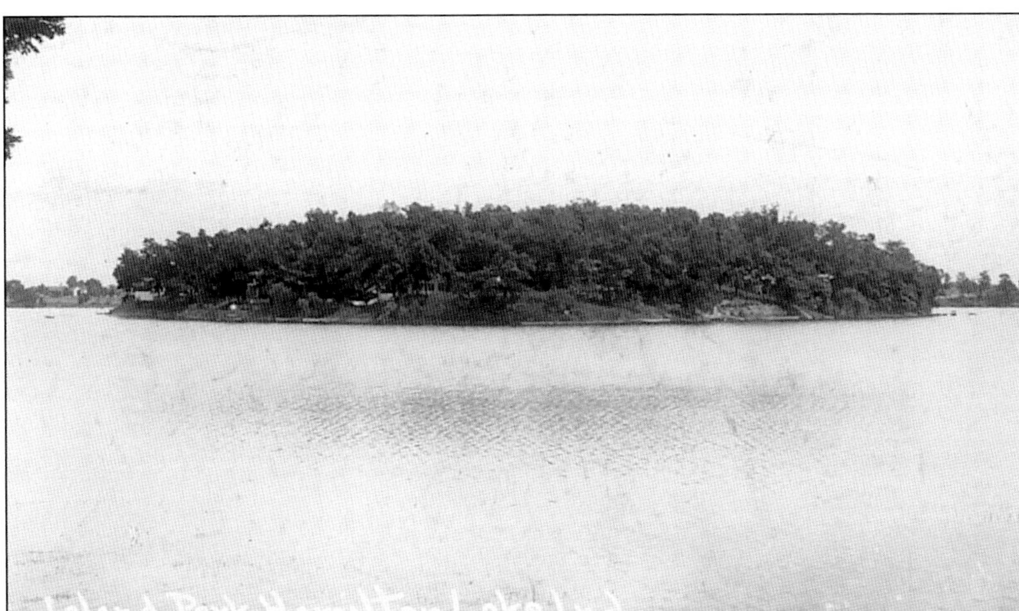

Island Park, Hamilton Lake, Indiana, 1943. The Island Park provided an ideal secluded place for cottages and a resort hotel.

PENN PARK, HAMILTON LAKE, INDIANA. Seen here is another area of the lake.

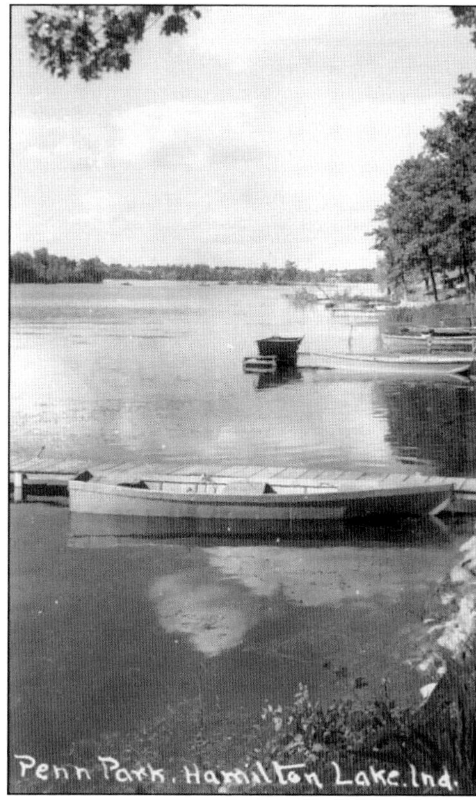

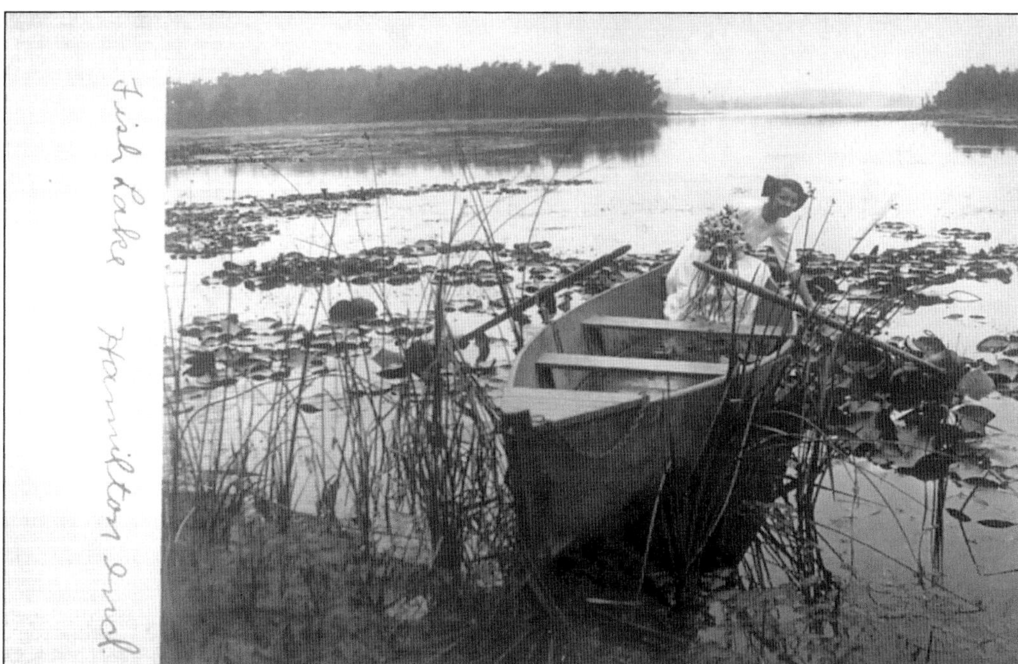

FISH LAKE, HAMILTON INDIANA, *c.* 1945. Hamilton Lake was originally known as Fish Lake.

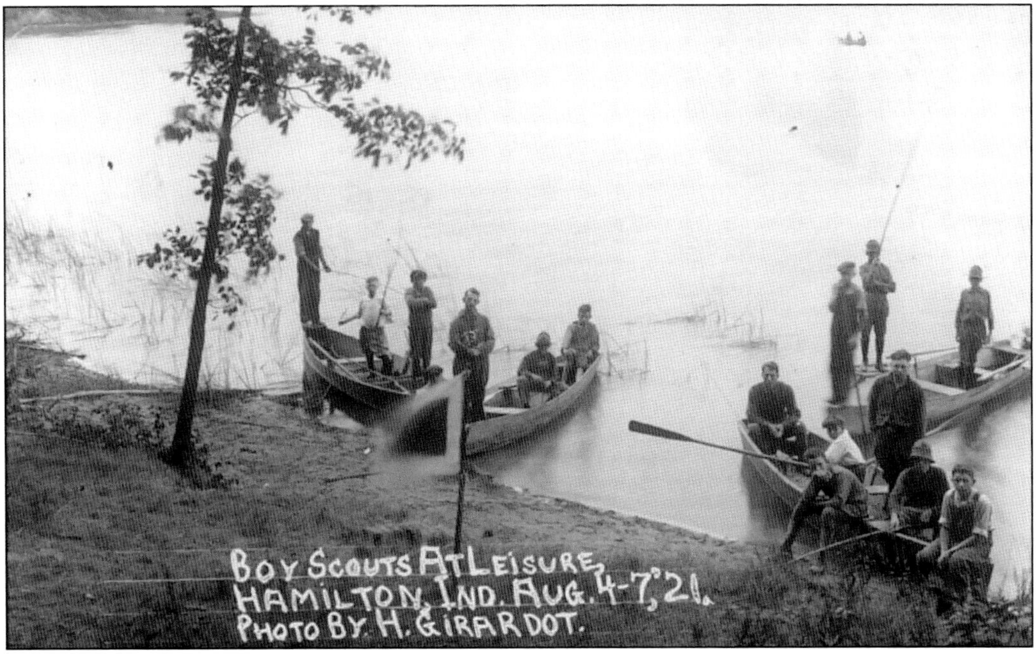

Boy Scouts At Leisure, Hamilton, Indiana, August 4–7, 1921. This was a great place for an outing.

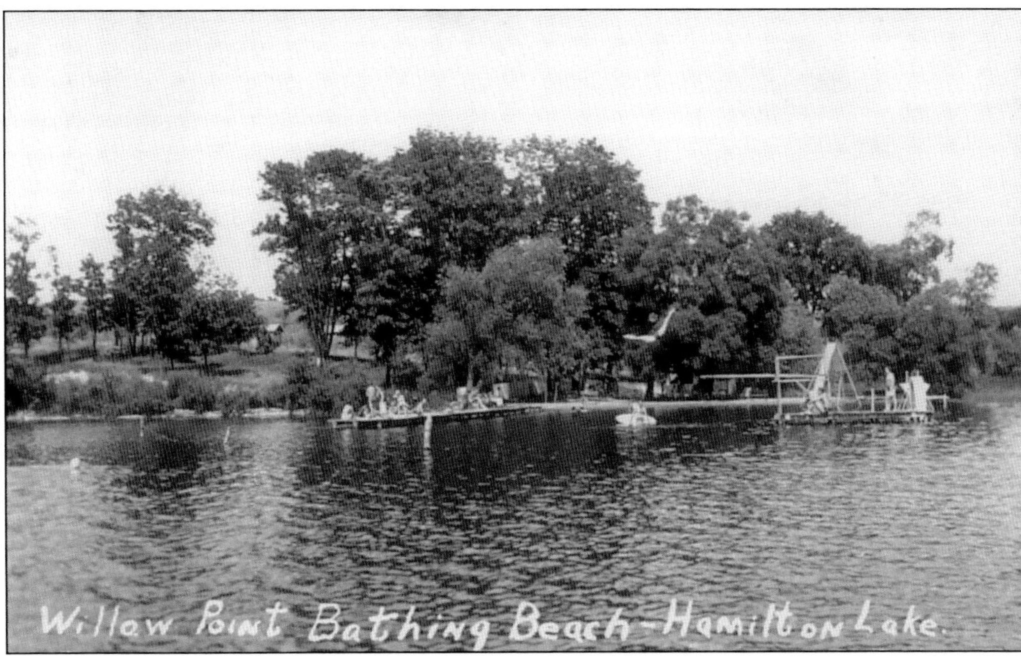

Willow Point Bathing Beach, Hamilton Lake, Indiana. The sandy bottom of the lake provided many great beaches.

Lake Gage

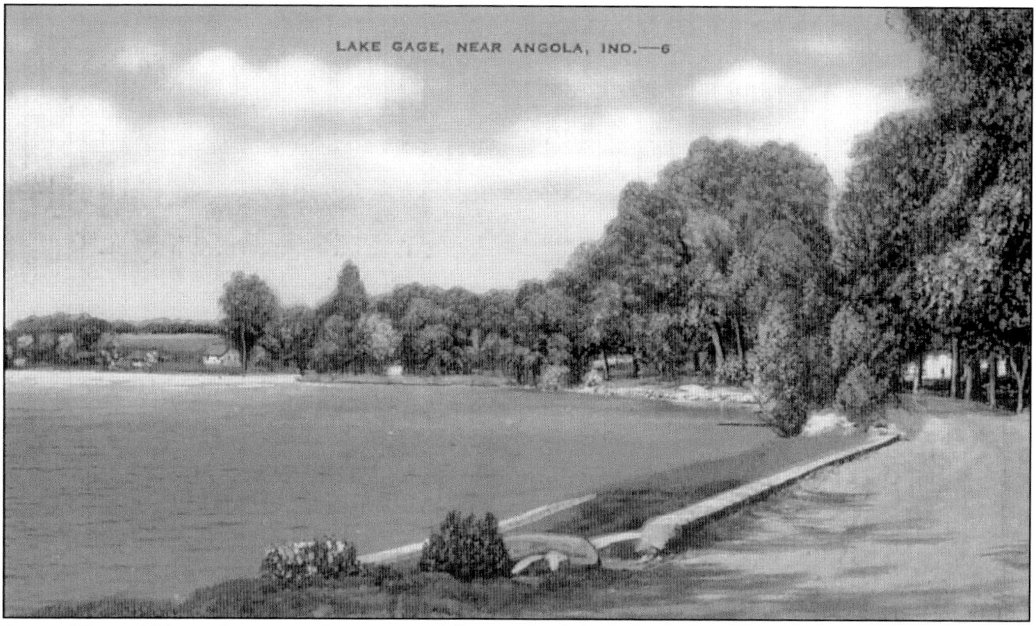

Lake Gage, Near Angola, Indiana. A linen card shows an ideal shore line.

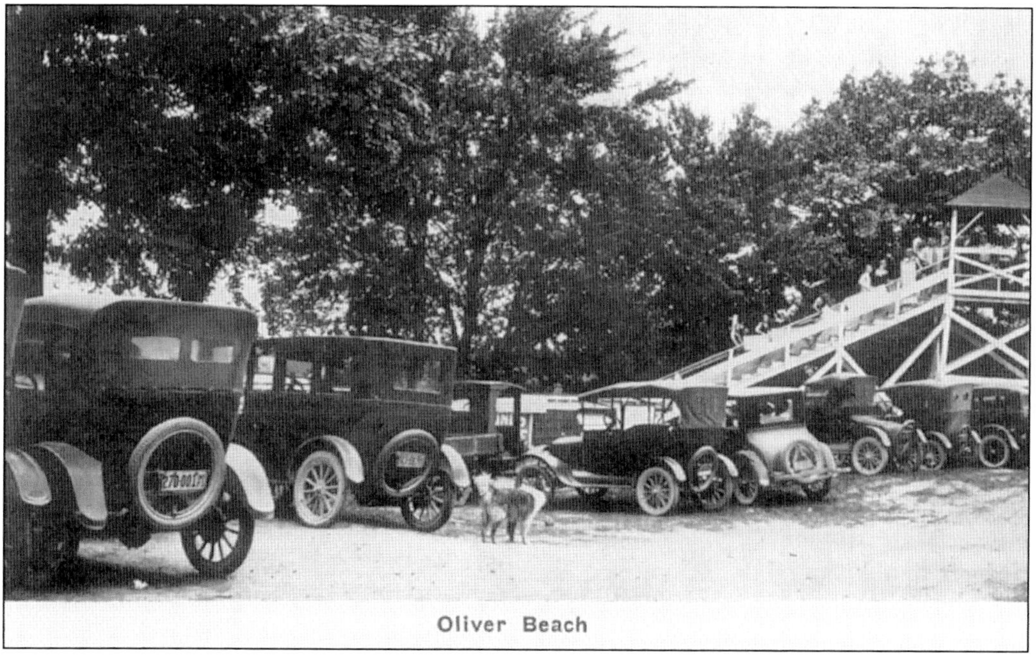

Oliver Beach. Many cars and a dog line the beach parking area.

LAKE GEORGE

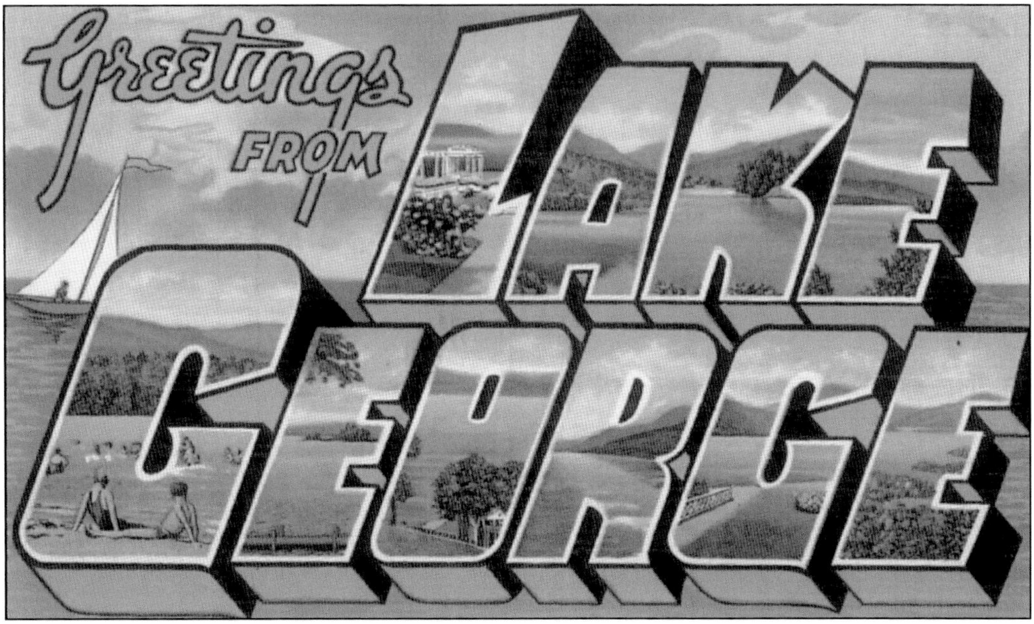

GREETINGS FROM LAKE GEORGE. Large letter linen cards were popular among collectors.

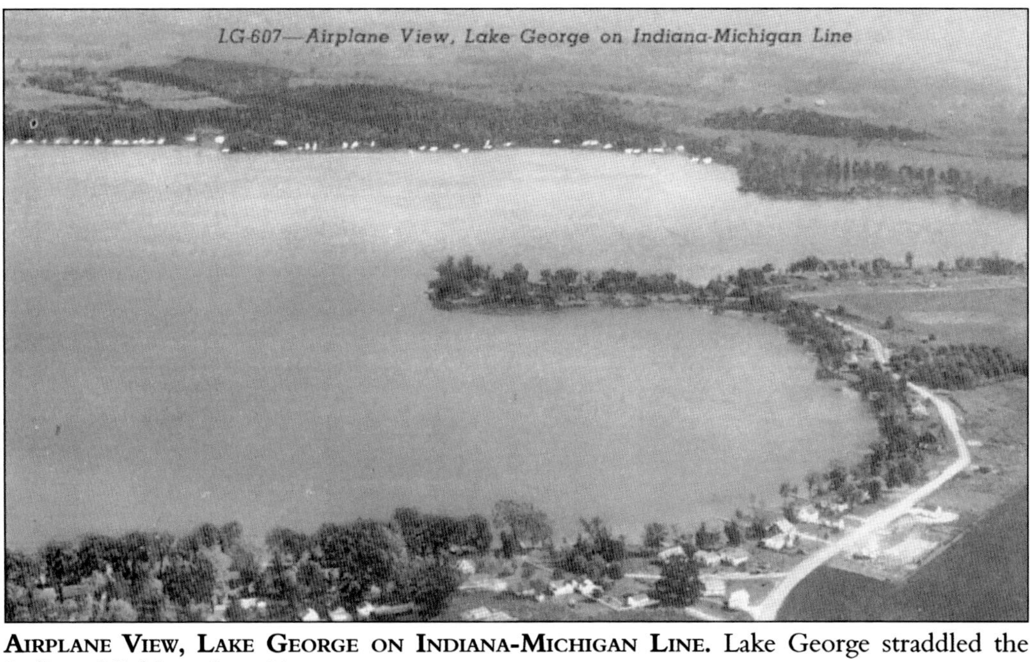

AIRPLANE VIEW, LAKE GEORGE ON INDIANA-MICHIGAN LINE. Lake George straddled the Indiana-Michigan State Line.

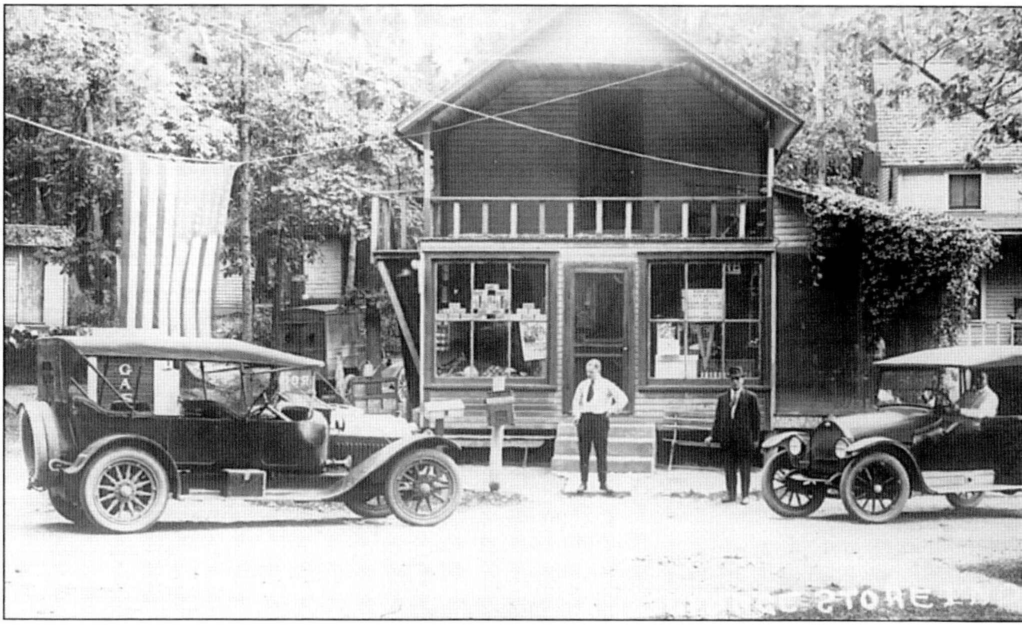

Lake George Store, Indiana. An Auburn Beauty-Six on the left is admired by the man in the center.

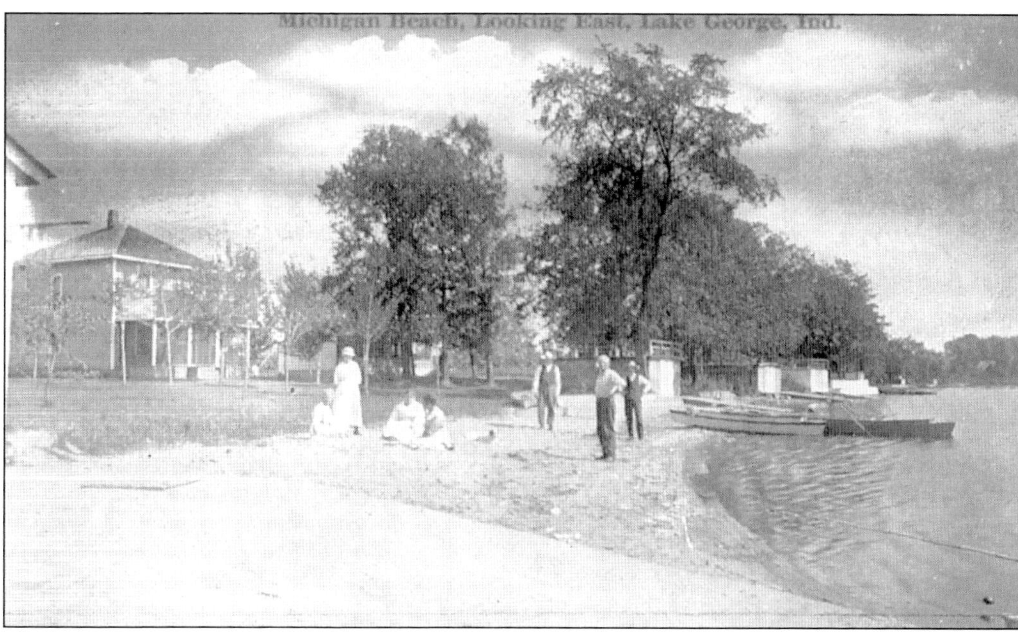

Michigan Beach, Looking East, Lake George, Indiana. The Michigan Beach was particularly fine.

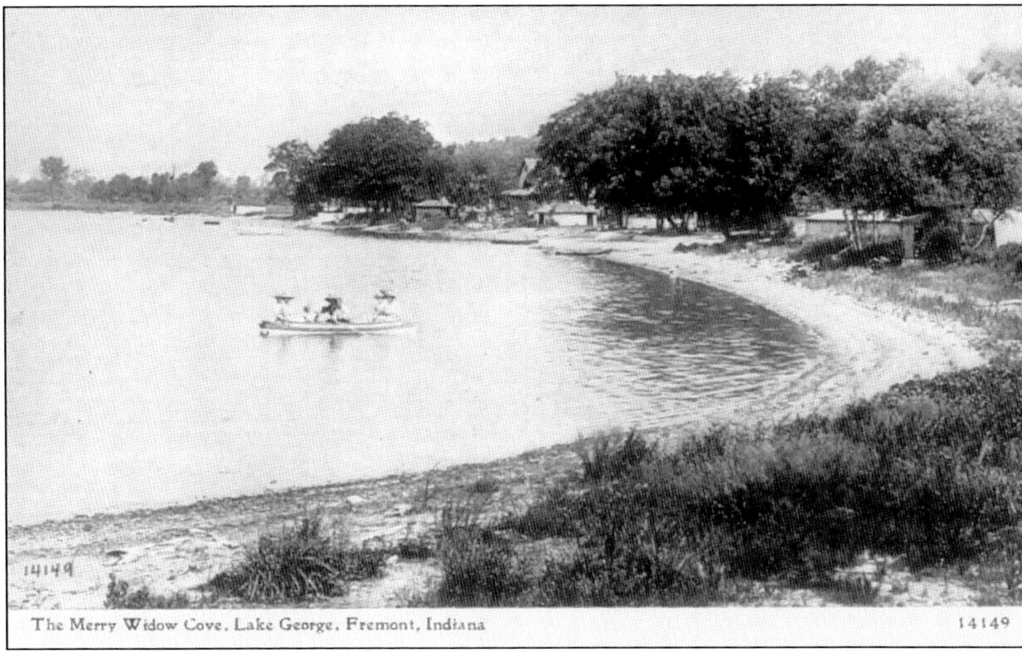

The Merry Widow Cove, Lake George, Fremont, Indiana. This is an unusual name that probably had some basis in fact.

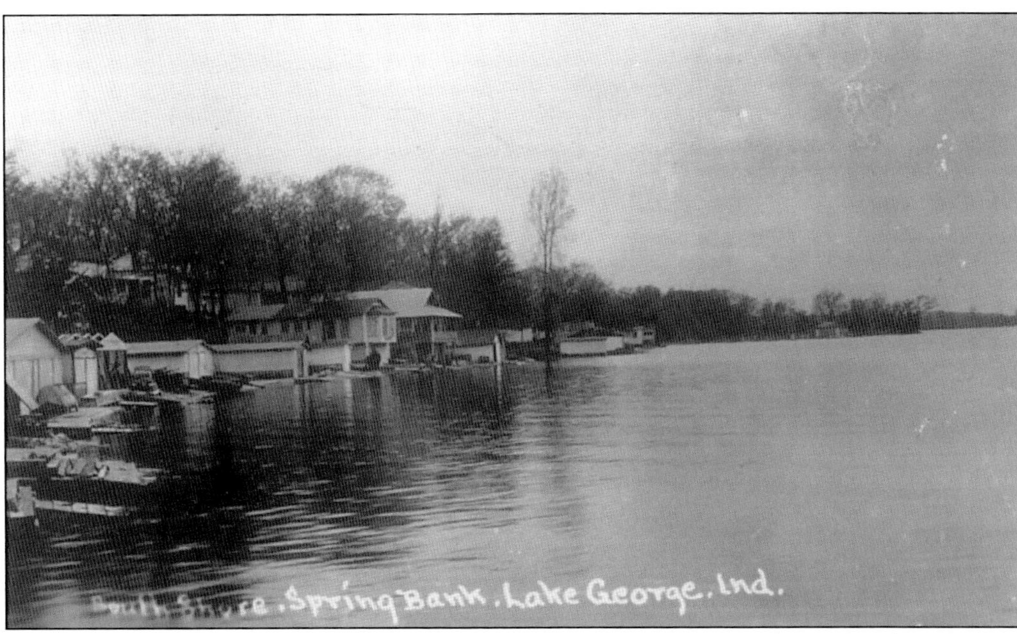

South Shore, Spring Bank. Lake George, Indiana. Boat houses clutter the shore line.

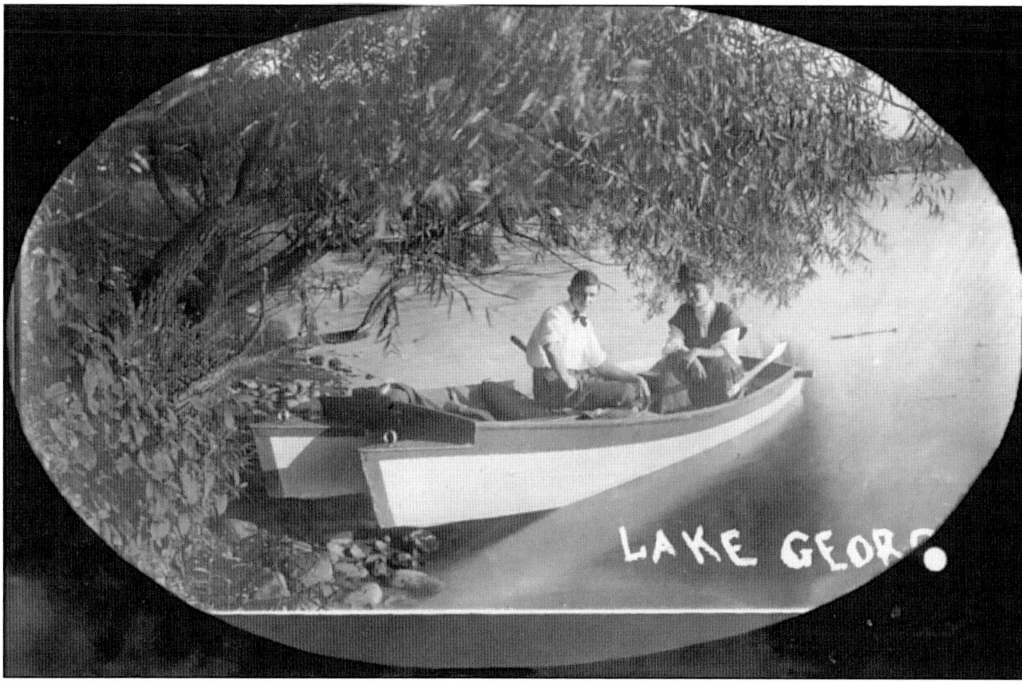

LAKE GEORGE, INDIANA. A double boat was very stable.

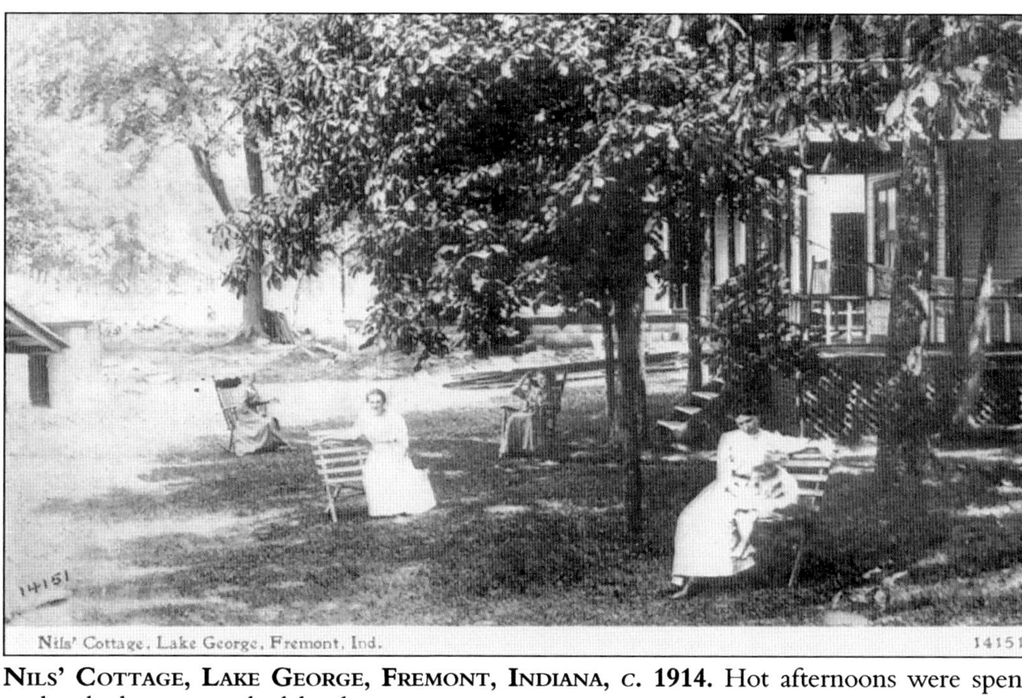

NILS' COTTAGE, LAKE GEORGE, FREMONT, INDIANA, *c.* 1914. Hot afternoons were spent under shade trees on the lake shore.

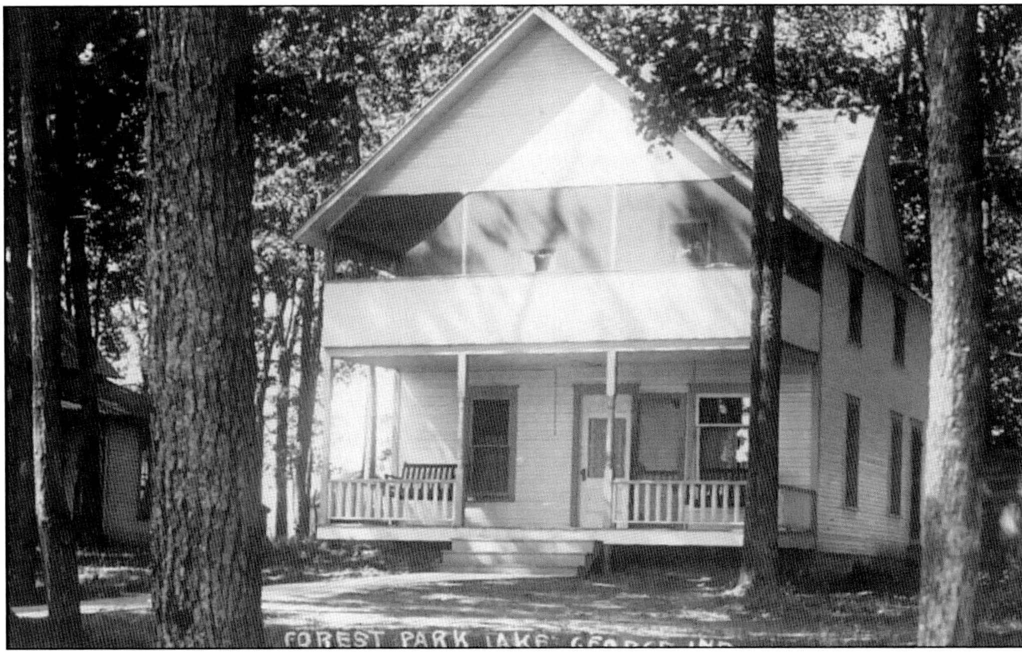

Forest Park Lake George, Indiana. Many cottages could house extended families for summer vacations.

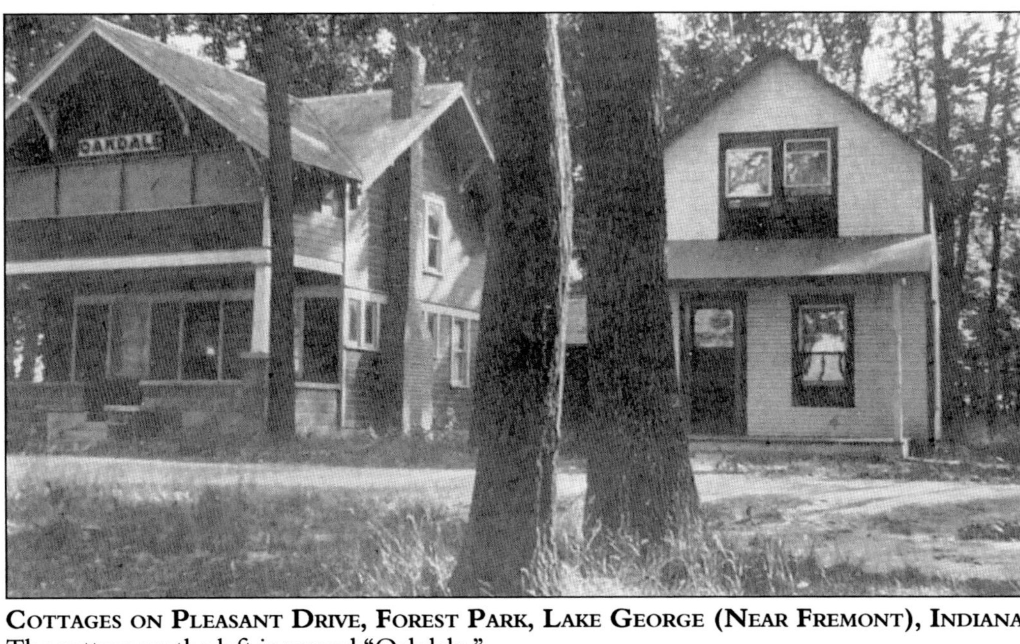

Cottages on Pleasant Drive, Forest Park, Lake George (Near Fremont), Indiana. The cottage on the left is named "Oakdale."

LAKE JAMES

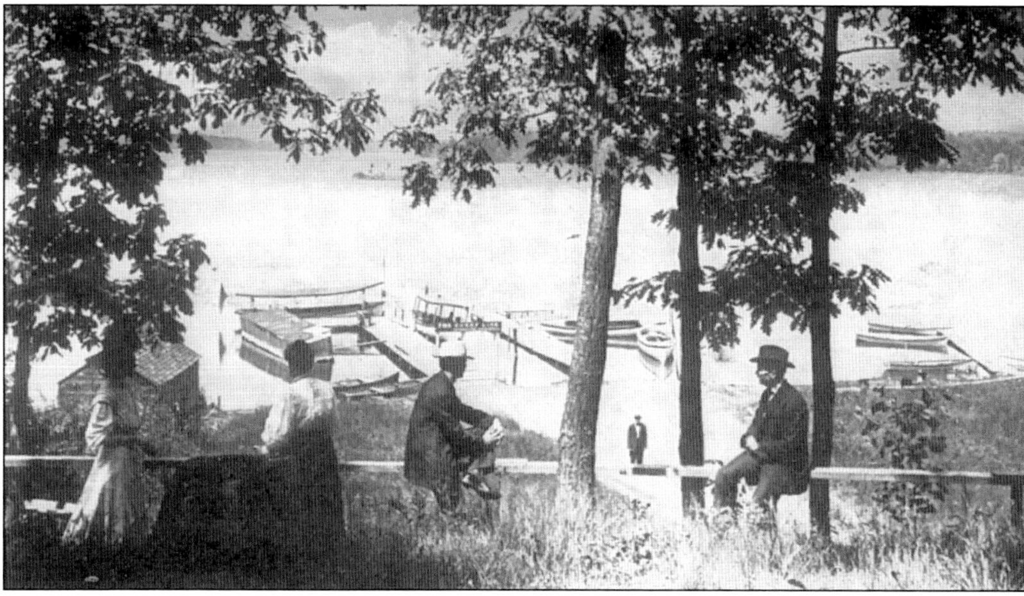

FIRST BASIN, LAKE JAMES, (NEAR ANGOLA) INDIANA. The term "basin" denotes deep areas of the lake.

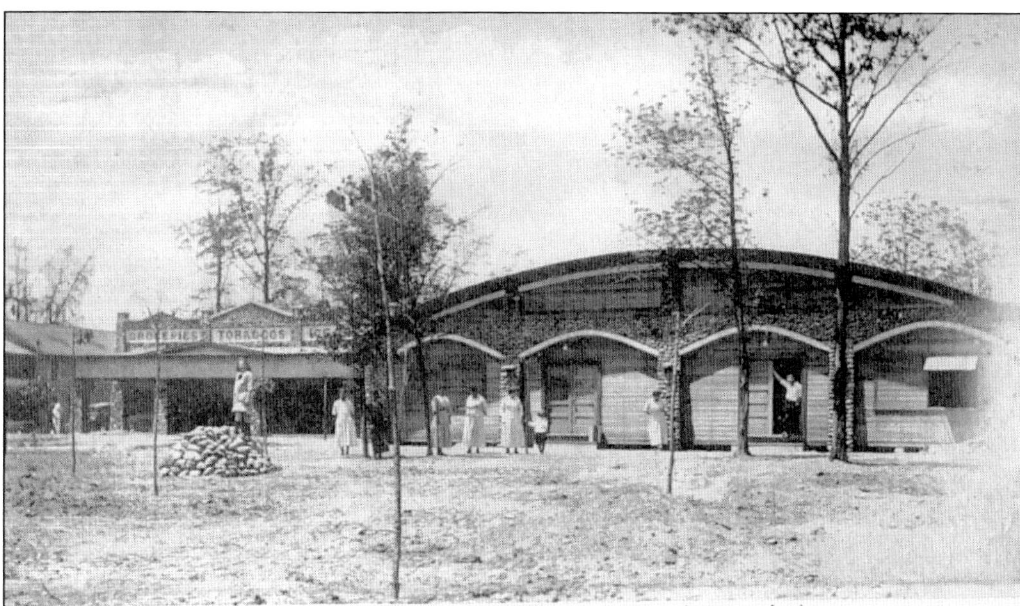

"OAKDALE," SECOND BASIN, LAKE JAMES, INDIANA. This was a popular place in its day.

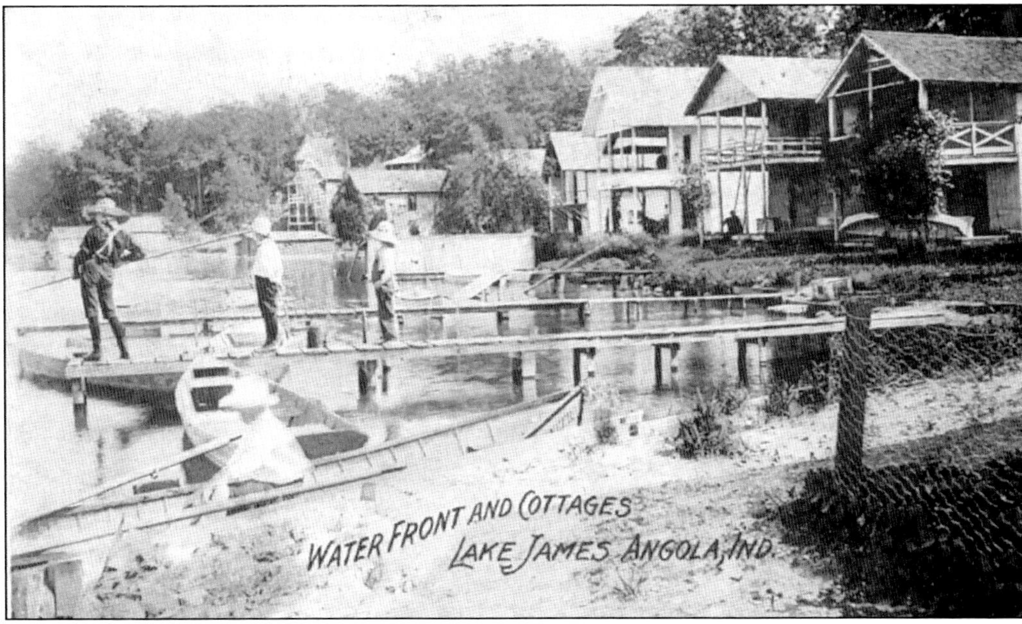

WATER FRONT AND COTTAGES, LAKE JAMES, ANGOLA, INDIANA. Cottages were built close together and had open porches on both levels where many slept on hot summer nights.

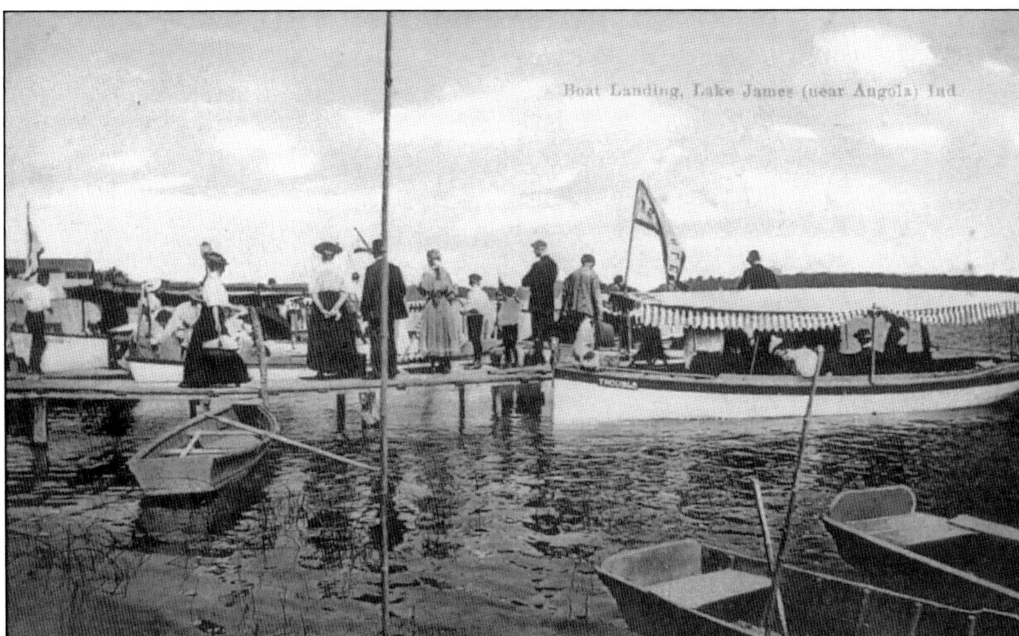

BOAT LANDING, LAKE JAMES, NEAR ANGOLA, INDIANA. The large boat was steam powered and took paying passengers for rides around the lake.

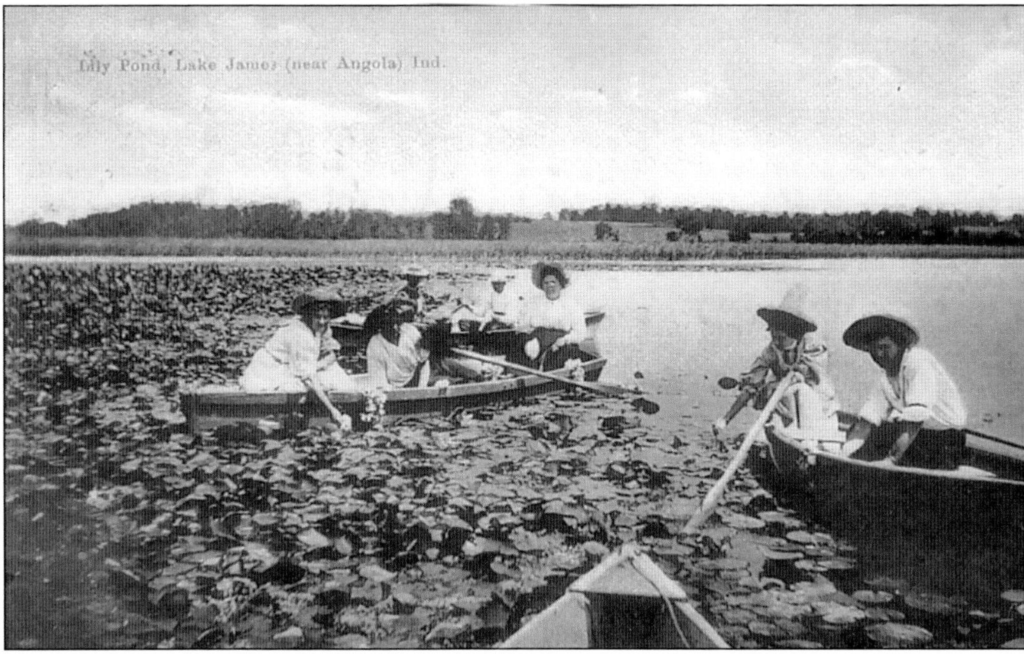

Lily Pond, Lake James, Near Angola, Indiana, *c.* 1909. Water lilies were admired by many.

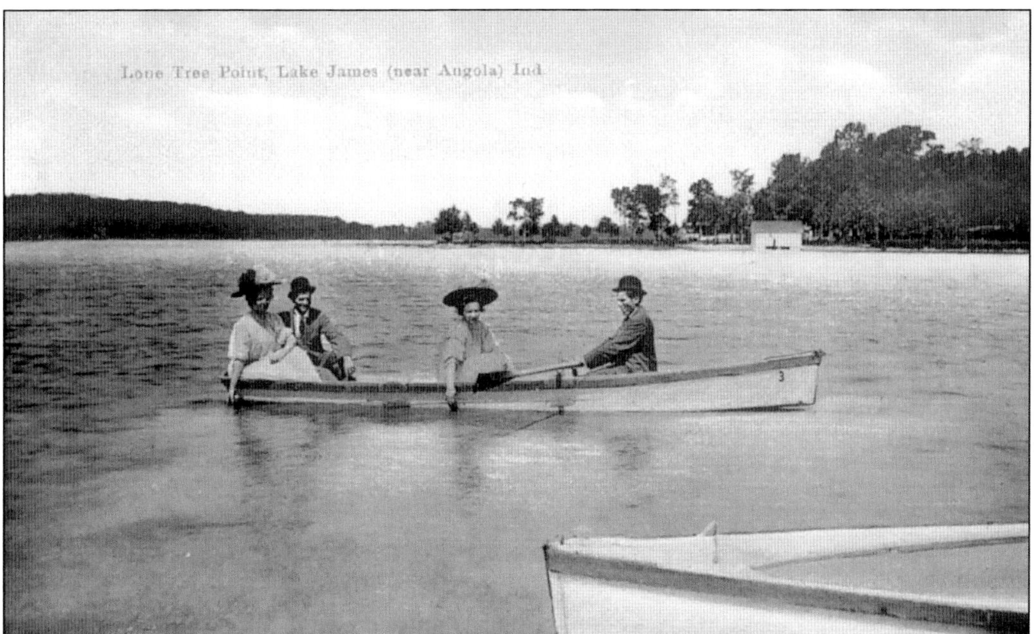

Lone Tree Point, Lake James (Near Angola) Indiana. Most areas of the lake had descriptive names.

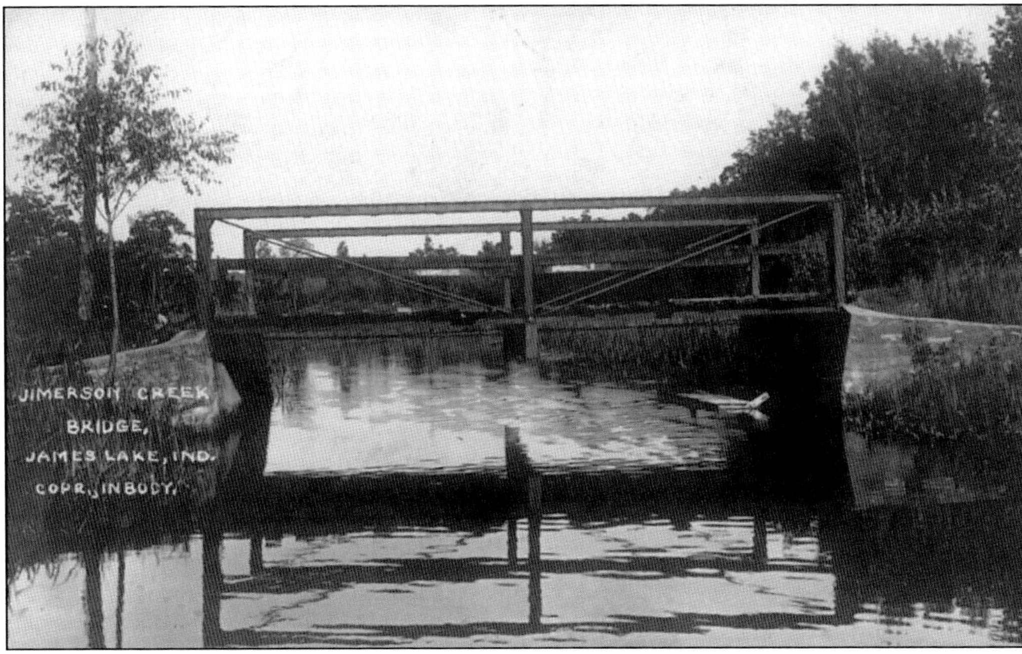

Jimerson Creek Bridge, James Lake, Indiana, *c.* 1914. The creek was a good place to fish.

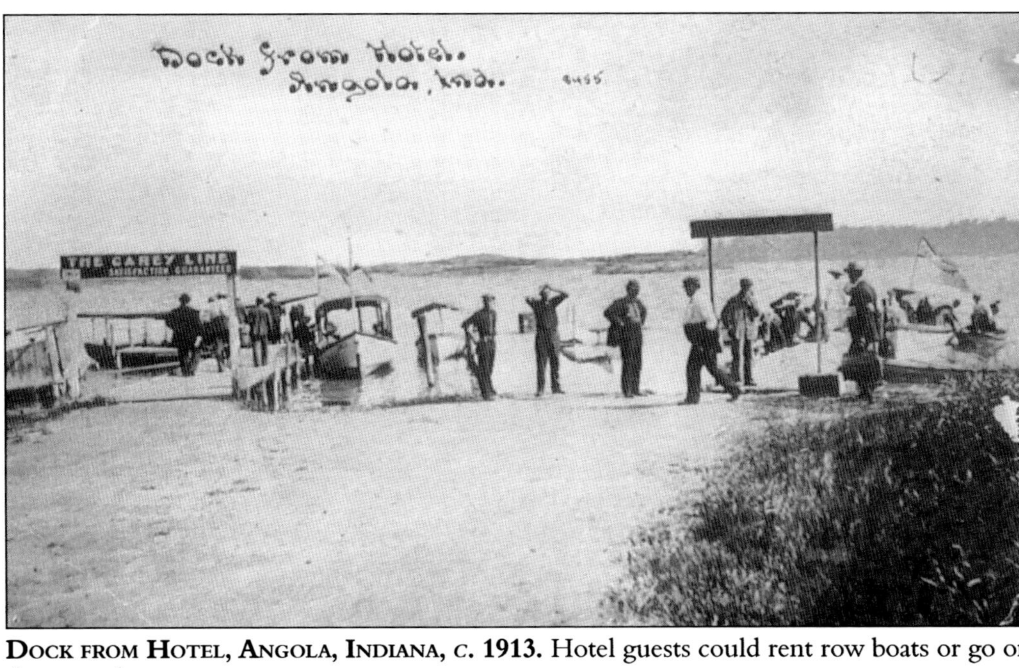

Dock from Hotel, Angola, Indiana, *c.* 1913. Hotel guests could rent row boats or go on the steam boat.

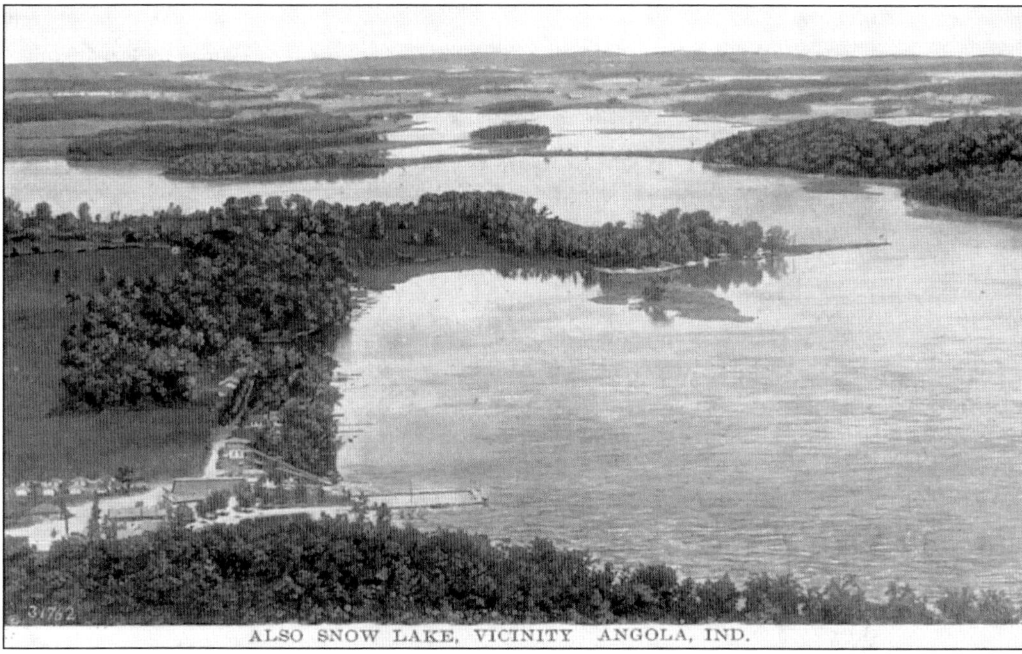

AERIAL VIEW OF WELDON'S LANDING, LAKE JAMES, WITH SECOND AND THIRD BASIN; ALSO SNOW LAKE, VICINITY, ANGOLA, INDIANA. The aerial photograph shows the meandering shore lines.

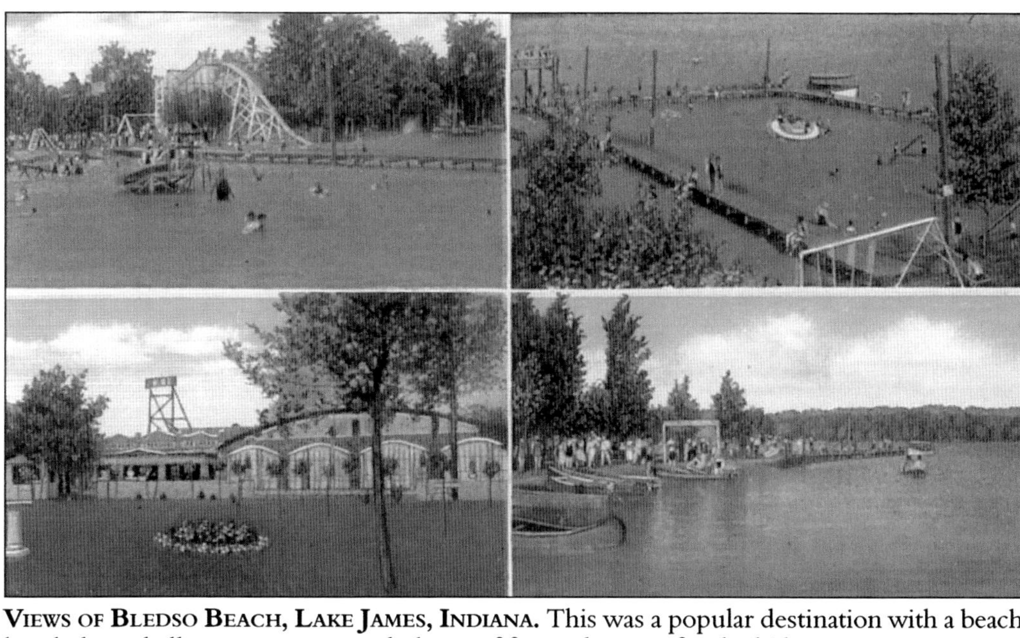

VIEWS OF BLEDSO BEACH, LAKE JAMES, INDIANA. This was a popular destination with a beach, hotel, dance hall, grocery store, and plenty of fun and games for the kids.

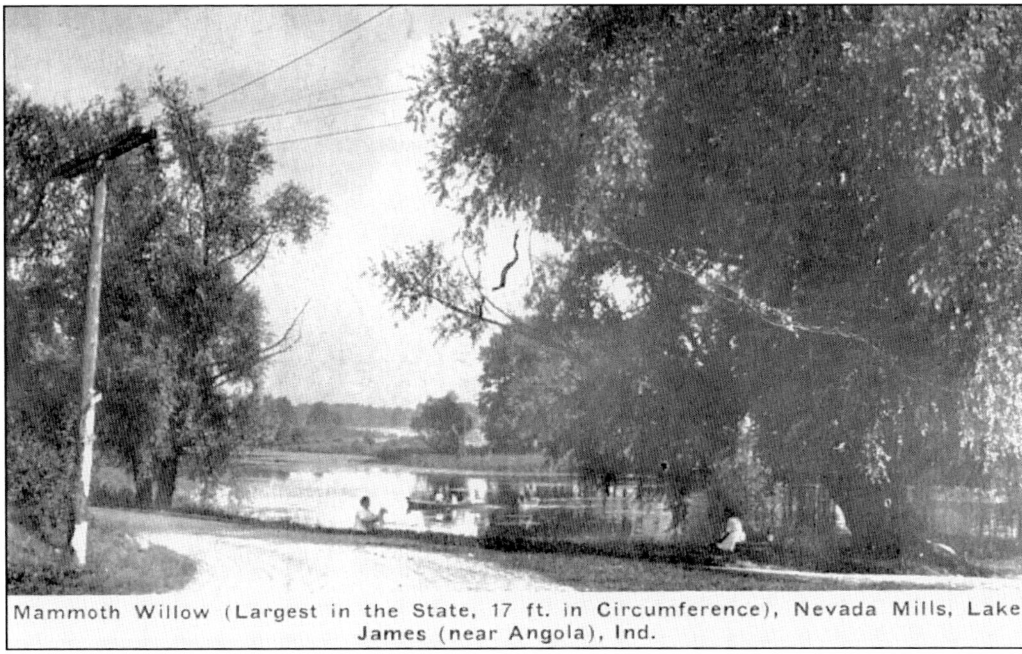

MAMMOTH WILLOW (LARGEST IN THE STATE, 17 FEET IN CIRCUMFERENCE), NEVADA MILLS, LAKE JAMES (NEAR ANGOLA), INDIANA.

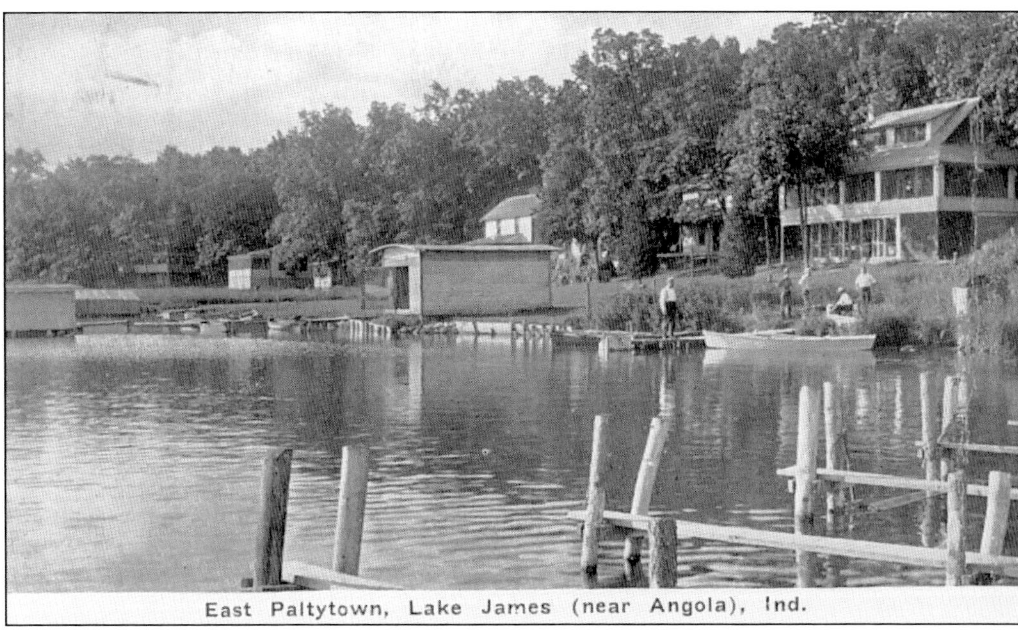

EAST PALTYTOWN, LAKE JAMES (NEAR ANGOLA), INDIANA, *C.* 1922. Paltytown was a well known area of the lake.

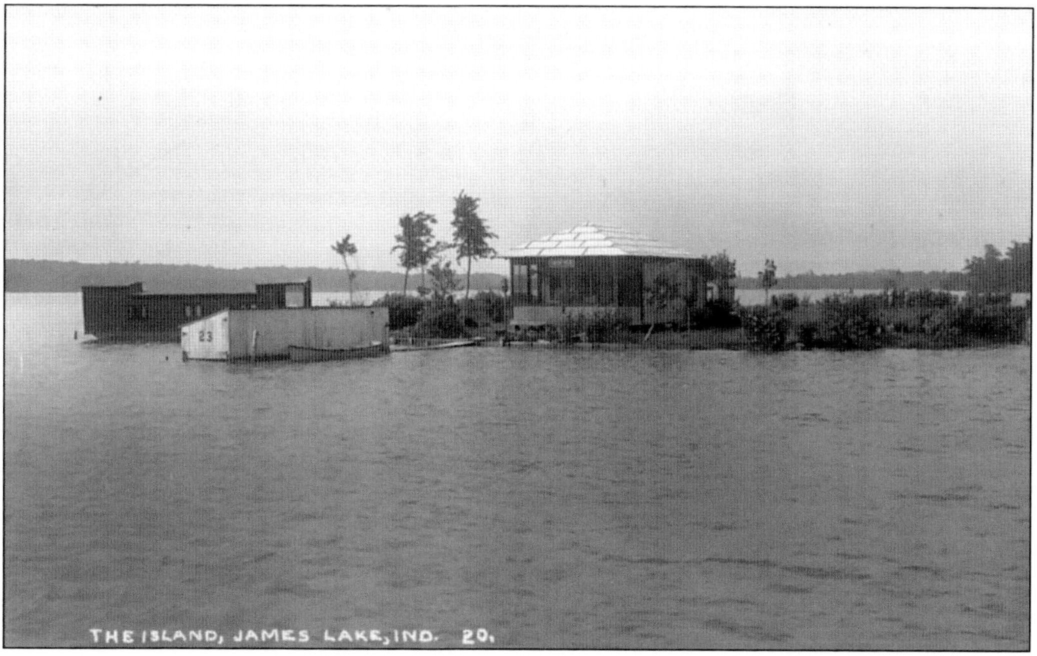

THE ISLAND, JAMES LAKE, INDIANA. An interesting house was built on the island, which was accessible by boat.

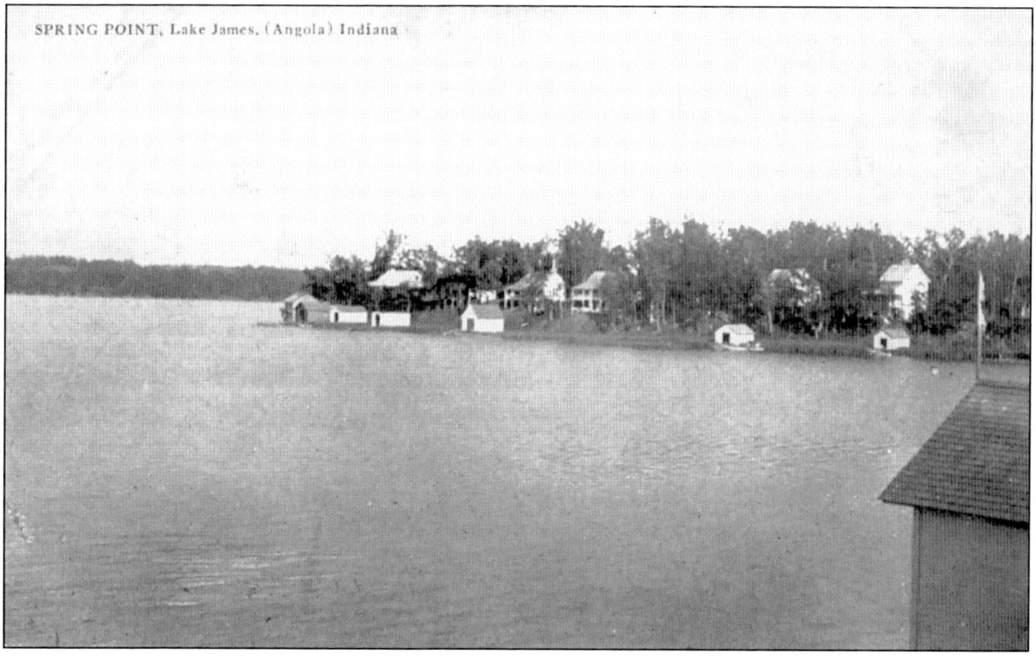

SPRING POINT, LAKE JAMES, (ANGOLA) INDIANA.

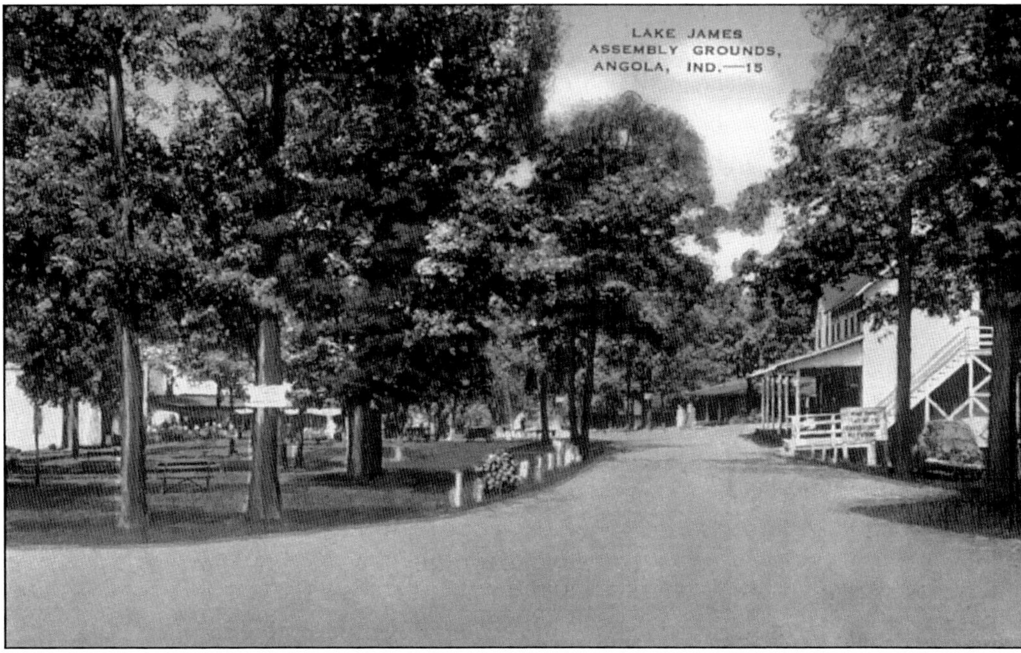

LAKE JAMES ASSEMBLY GROUNDS, ANGOLA, INDIANA. The Lake James Christian Assembly is a non-profit corporation maintained to provide a spiritual renewal, instruction, inspiration, and fellowship. Its natural beauty, accessibility, and seclusion provide an ideal location for such a center.

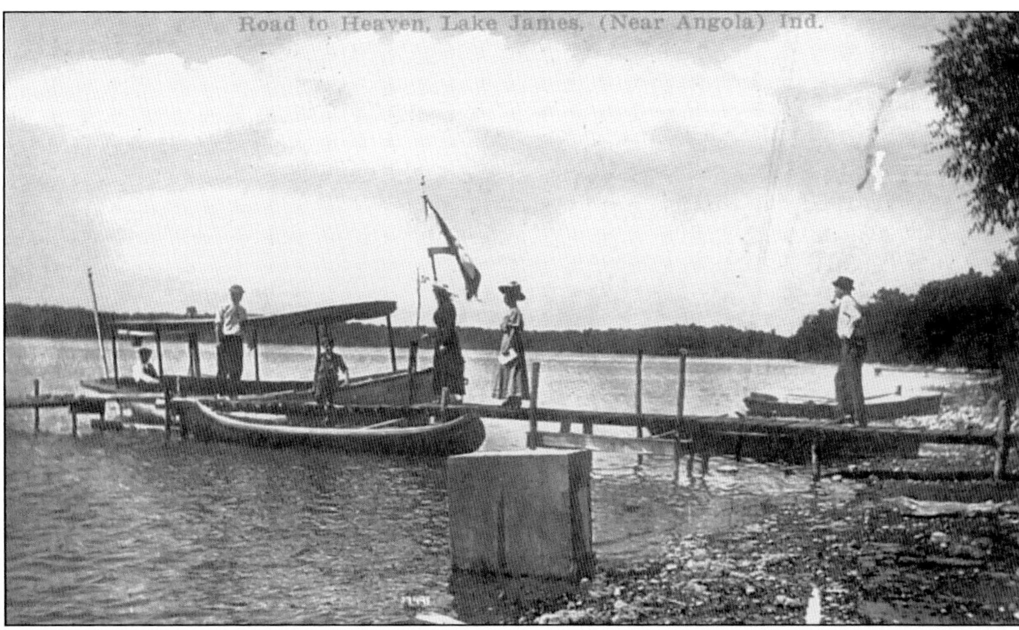

ROAD TO HEAVEN, LAKE JAMES, (NEAR ANGOLA) INDIANA. Many considered a week at the lake as a week in heaven.

Pokagon State Park

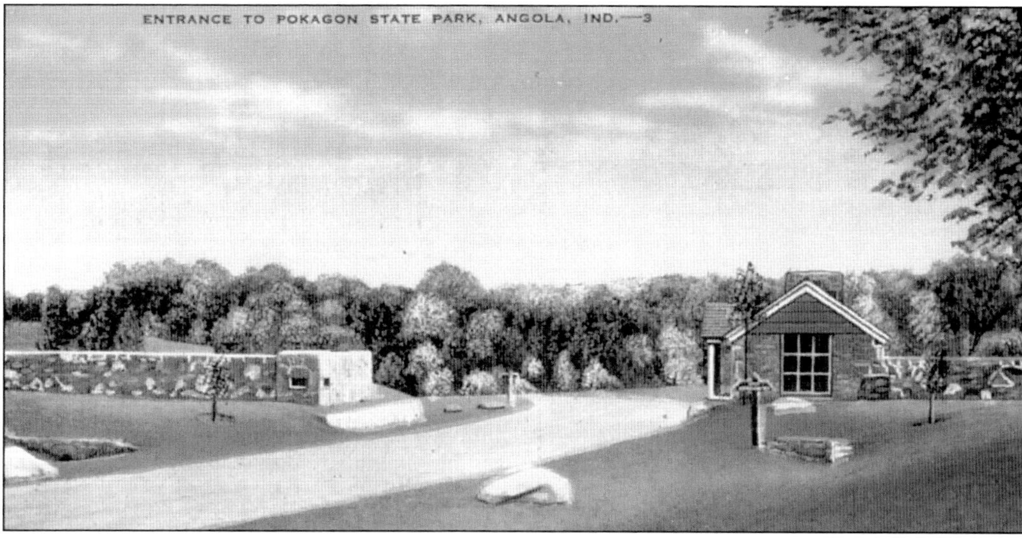

Entrance to Pokagon State Park, Angola, Indiana. Pokagon is one of the premier state parks in Indiana. It offers both summer and winter activities.

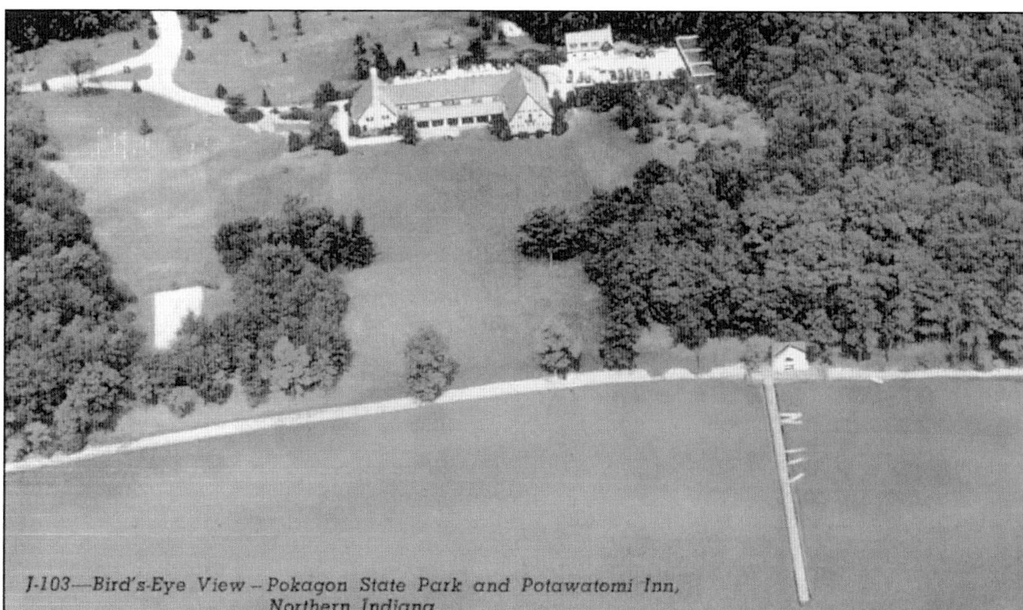

Bird's-Eye View, Pokagon State Park and Potawatomi Inn, Northern Indiana, c. 1947. This Northern Indiana playground is on beautiful Lake James, where nature's ever-changing beauty is always its best. It's located in Steuben County, 2 miles north of Angola on Route 27.

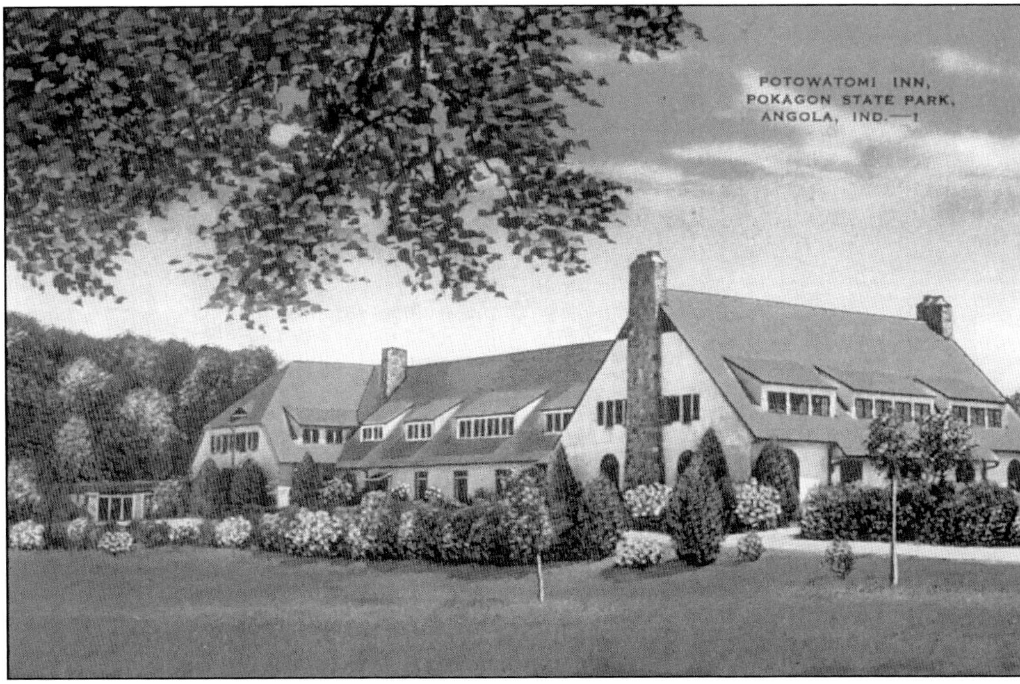

POTOWATOMI INN, POKAGON STATE PARK, ANGOLA, INDIANA. This has been a popular place for many generations. It offers hotel and dining facilities.

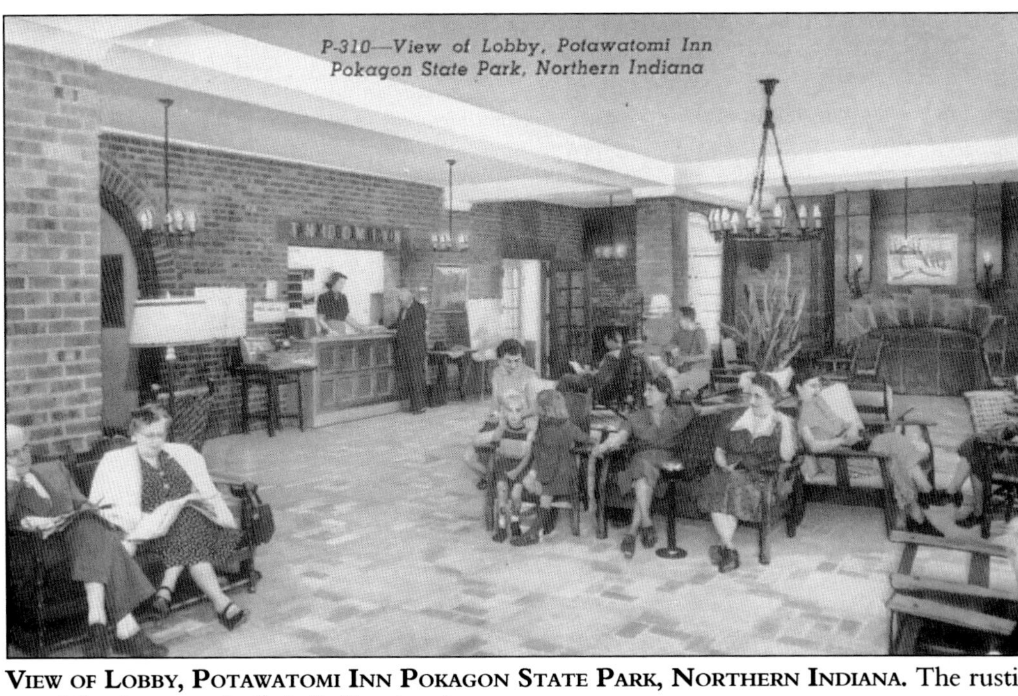

VIEW OF LOBBY, POTAWATOMI INN POKAGON STATE PARK, NORTHERN INDIANA. The rustic wood furniture was built in Indiana's prisons.

POKAGON STATE PARK. "THE HUT" TOBOGGAN SLIDE. The ride starts in the tower where the toboggan is placed on the track, the riders get on, and then the track is tipped for a fast ride on the ice.

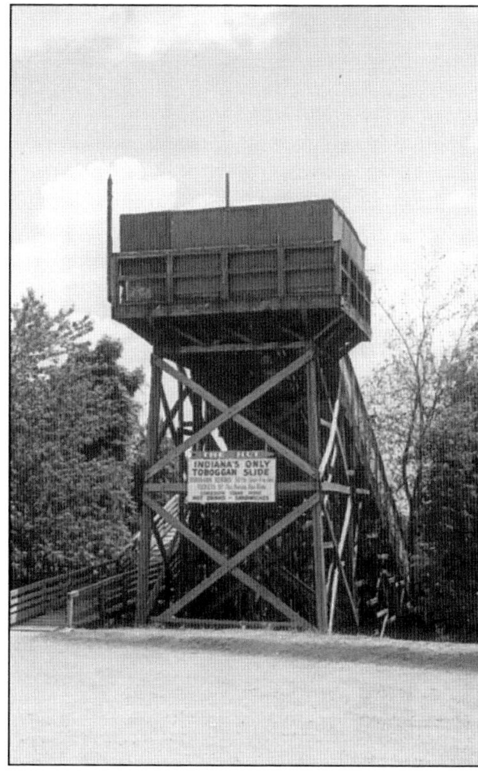

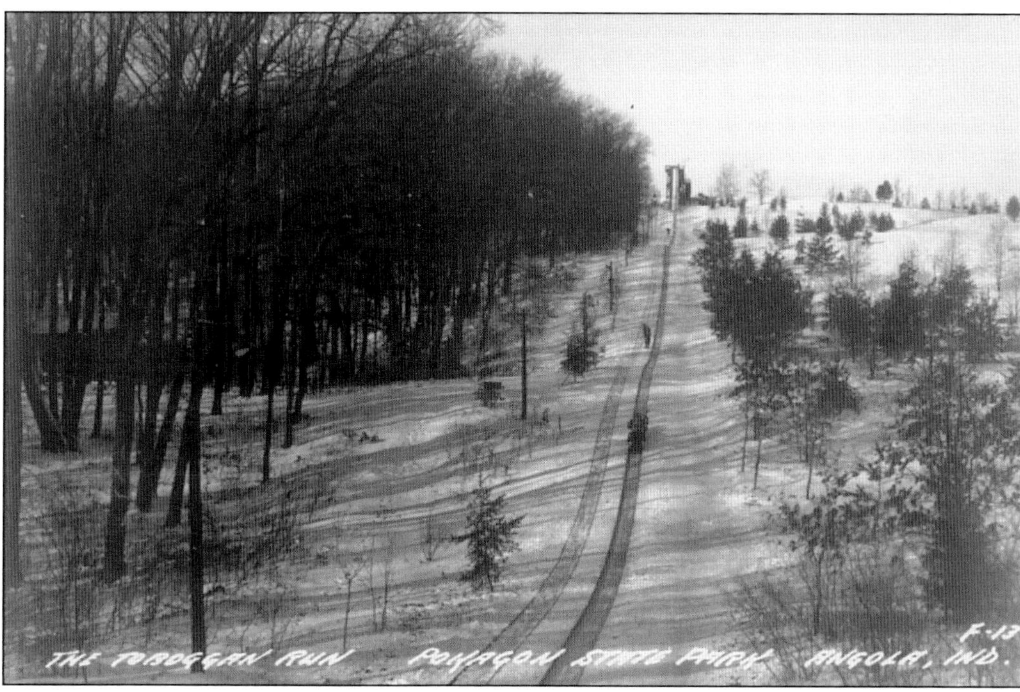

THE TOBOGGAN RUN, POKAGON STATE PARK, ANGOLA, INDIANA. Two tracks are used for a fast ride down, followed by a slow walk back up the hill!

Silver Lake

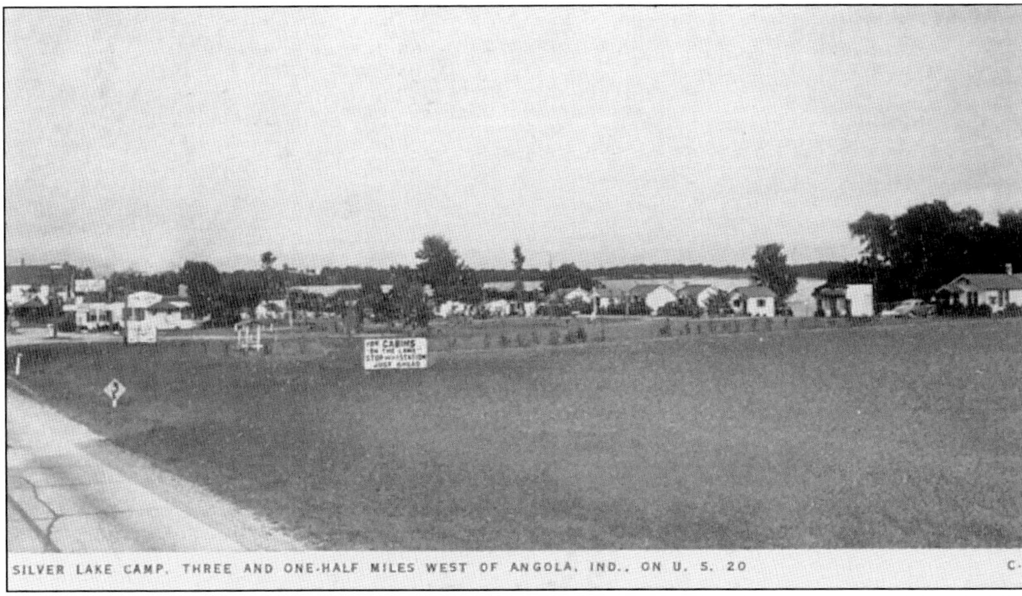

Silver Lake Camp, 3.5 Miles of Angola, Indiana, on U.S. 20. The sign states: "For Cabins on the Lake Stop at the Station Just Ahead."

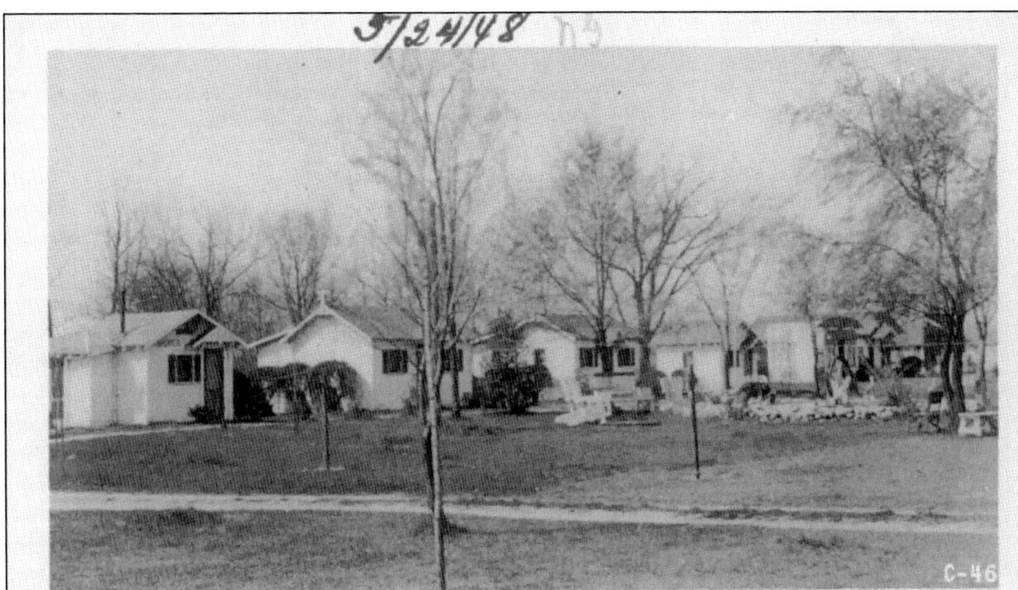

Wells Silver Lake Court, 3.5 Miles West of Angola, Indiana. on U.S. 20. Tourist cabins were a popular choice for automobile travelers. They were later connected into a motel.

Snow Lake

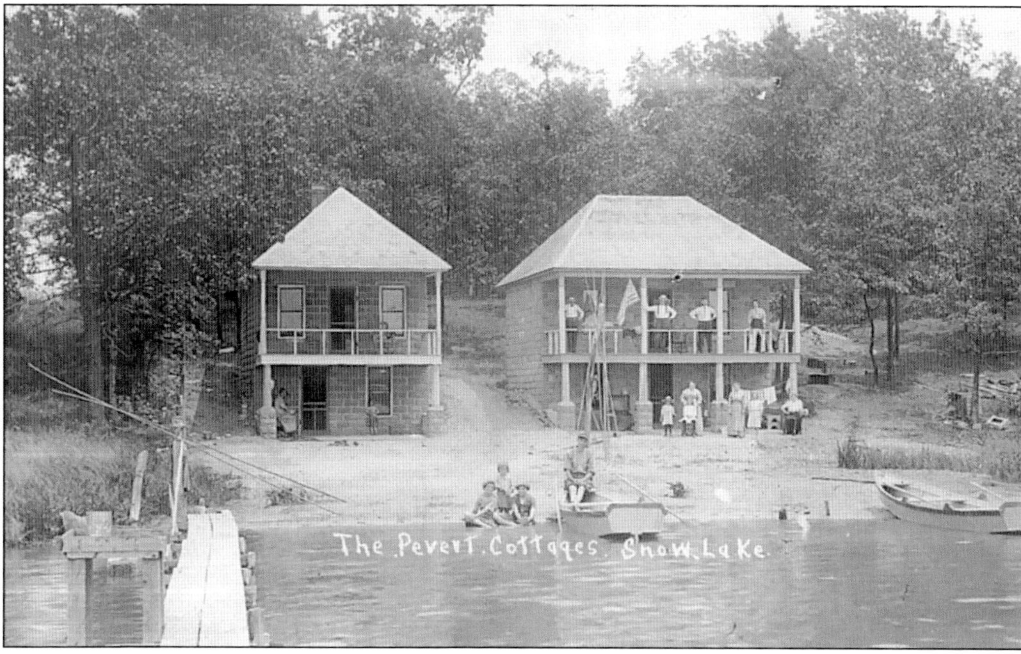

The Pevevt Cottage, Snow Lake. The whole family poses for a photograph.

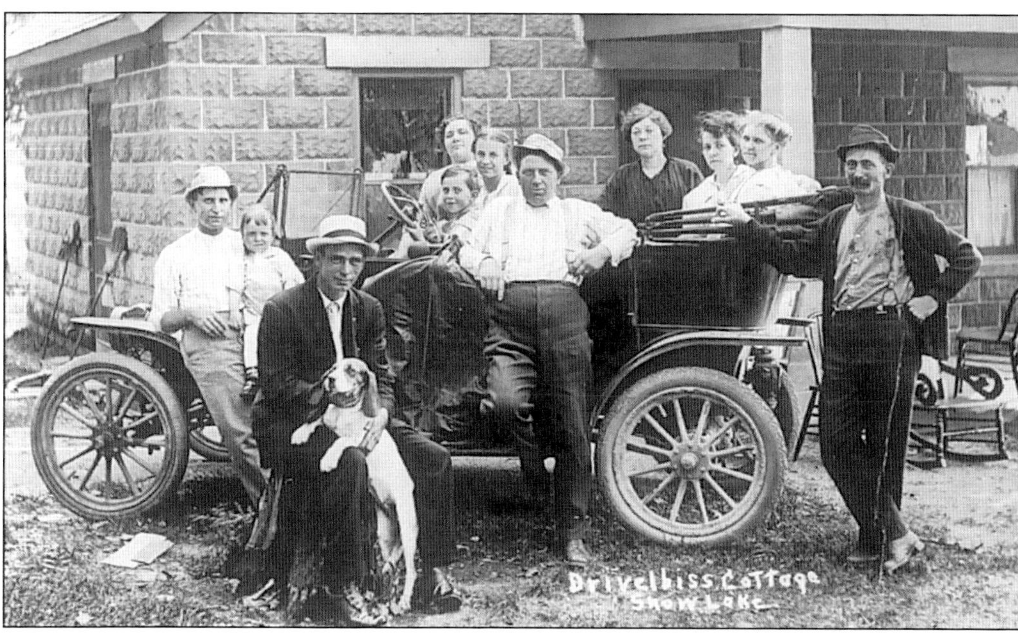

Drivelbiss Cottage, Snow Lake. Seen here is the cottage and the touring car.

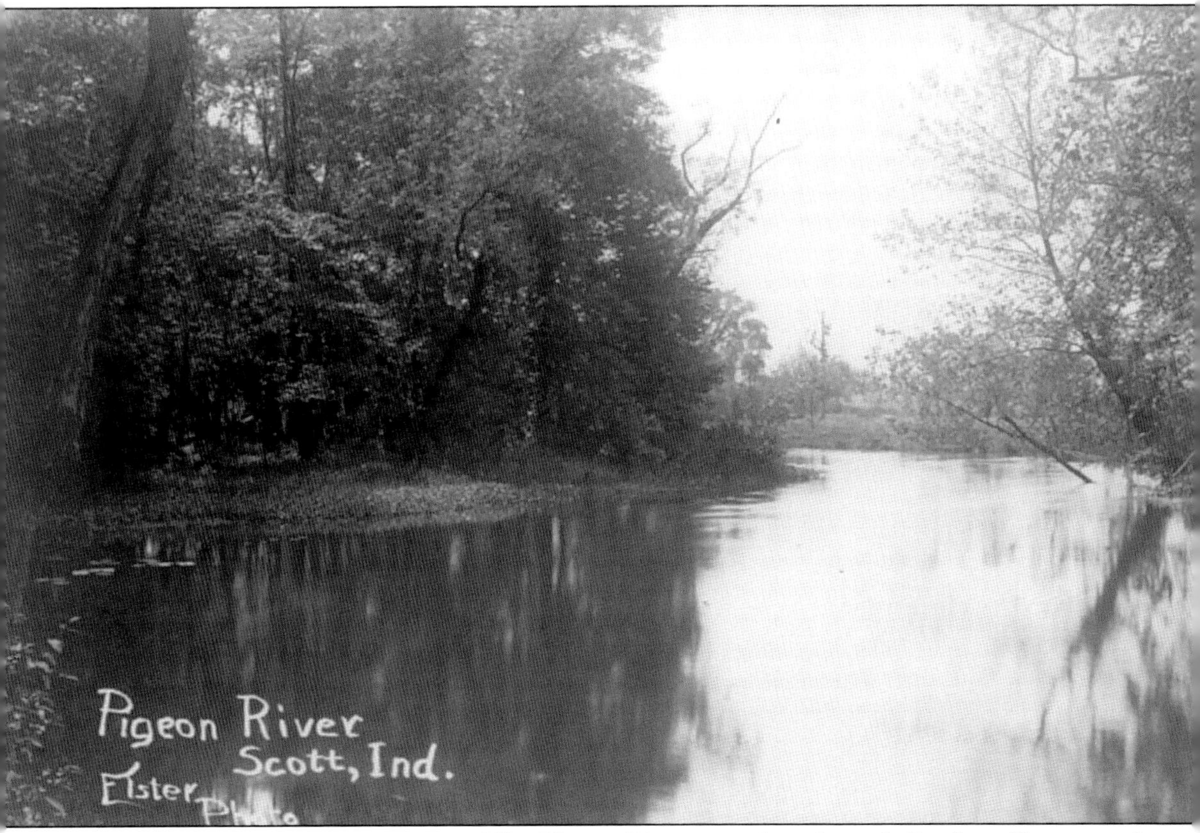

PIGEON RIVER, SCOTT, INDIANA. The Pigeon River meanders through Steuben County and provides a scenic venue for a canoe ride.

Seven

METZ

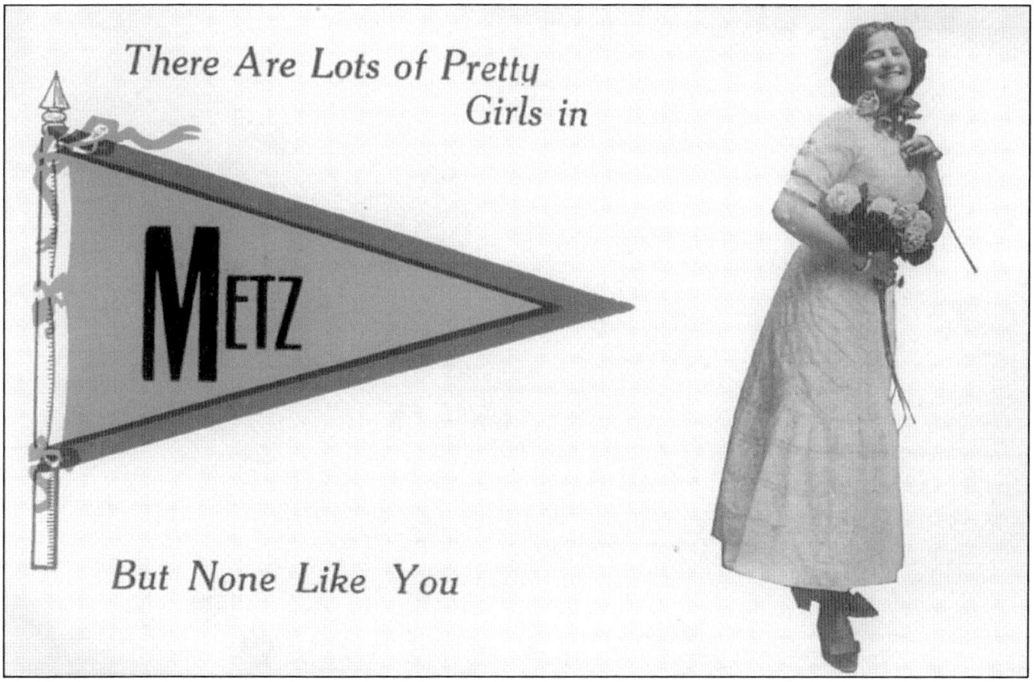

THERE ARE LOTS OF PRETTY GIRLS IN METZ BUT NONE LIKE YOU. No other cards were found for the Village of Metz.

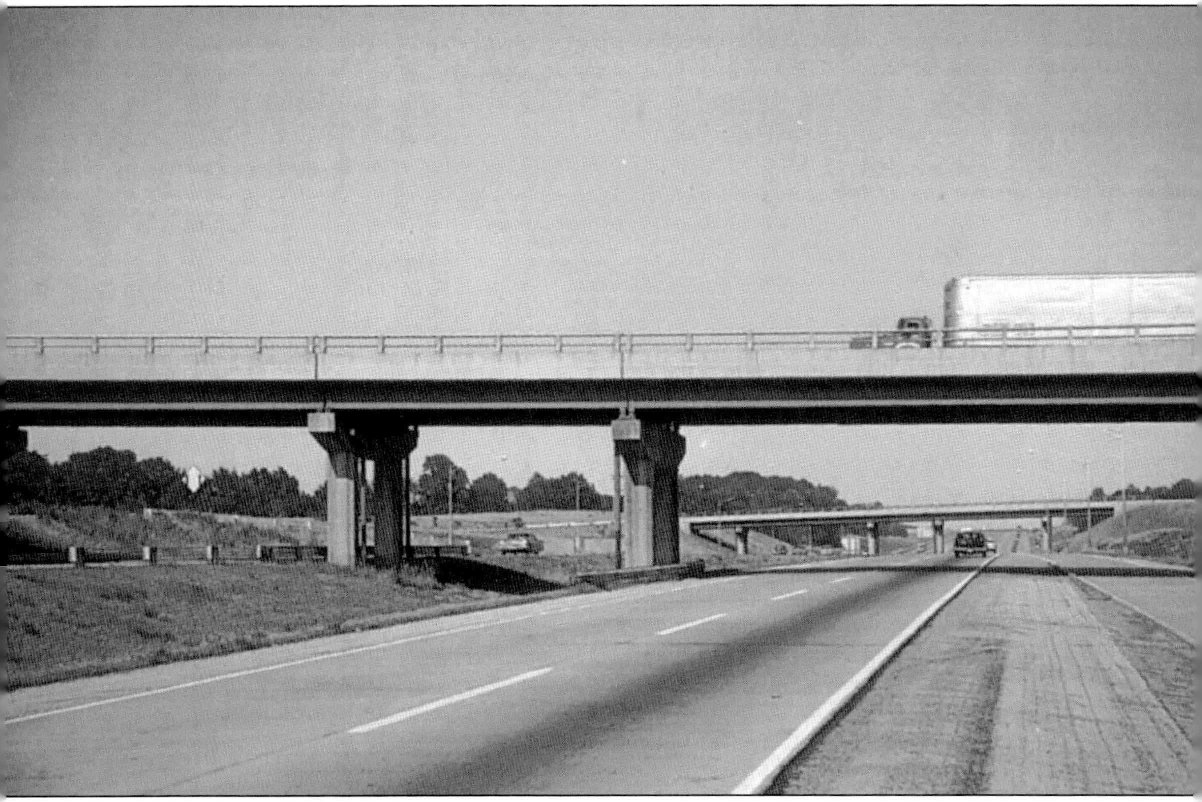

Northern Indiana Toll Road. In its 156-mile sweep across Northern Indiana, the road affords a panoramic view of some of the world's largest industries, some of the Midwest's finest resort and farm lands. There are 249 underpasses and overpasses that eliminate all grade crossings.

Eight

Orland

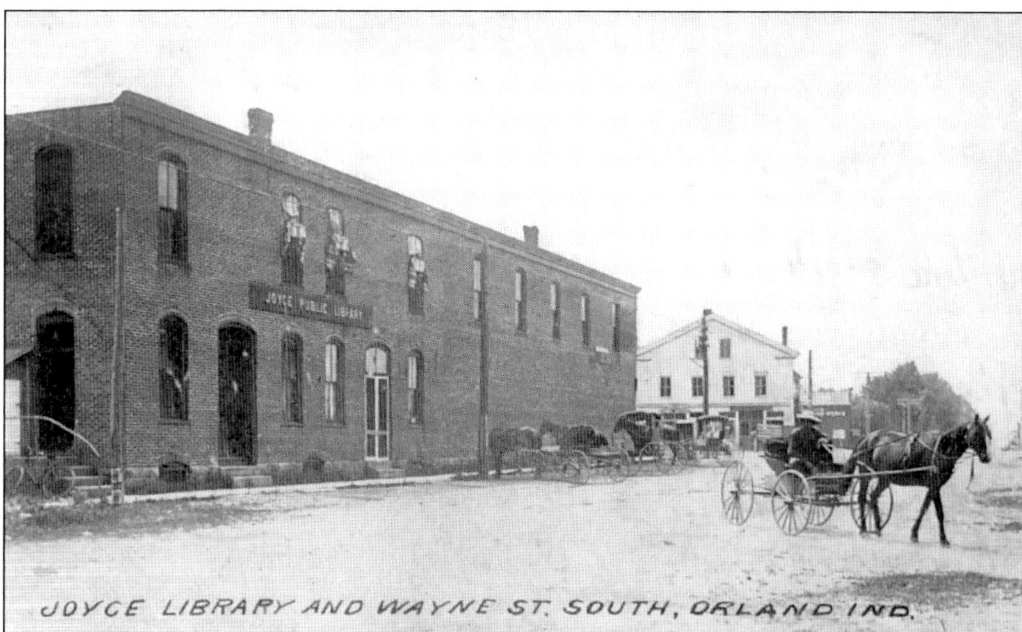

Joyce Library and Wayne Street South, Orland, Indiana, *c.* 1917. The library was a popular place as evidenced by the many rigs tied to the hitching rack.

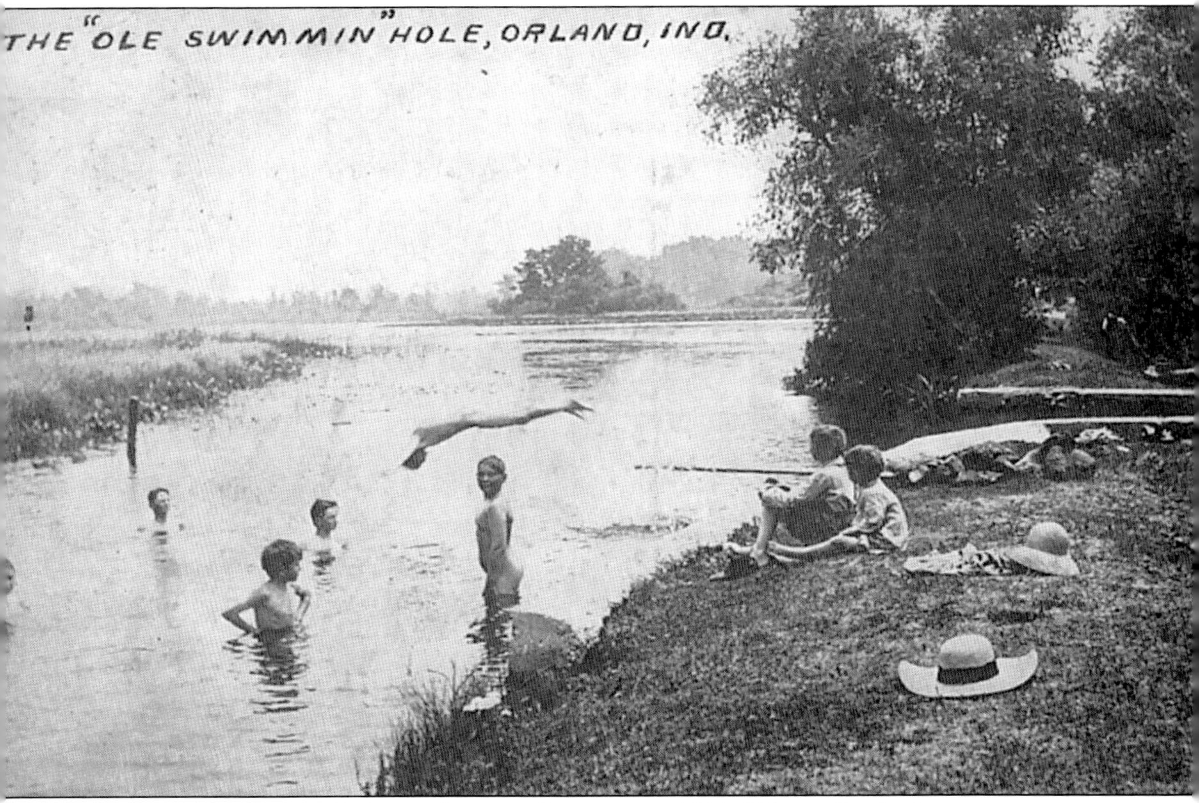

The "Ole Swimmin" Hole, Orland, Indiana, *c.* 1914. Skinny dipping!

Nine

PLEASANT LAKE

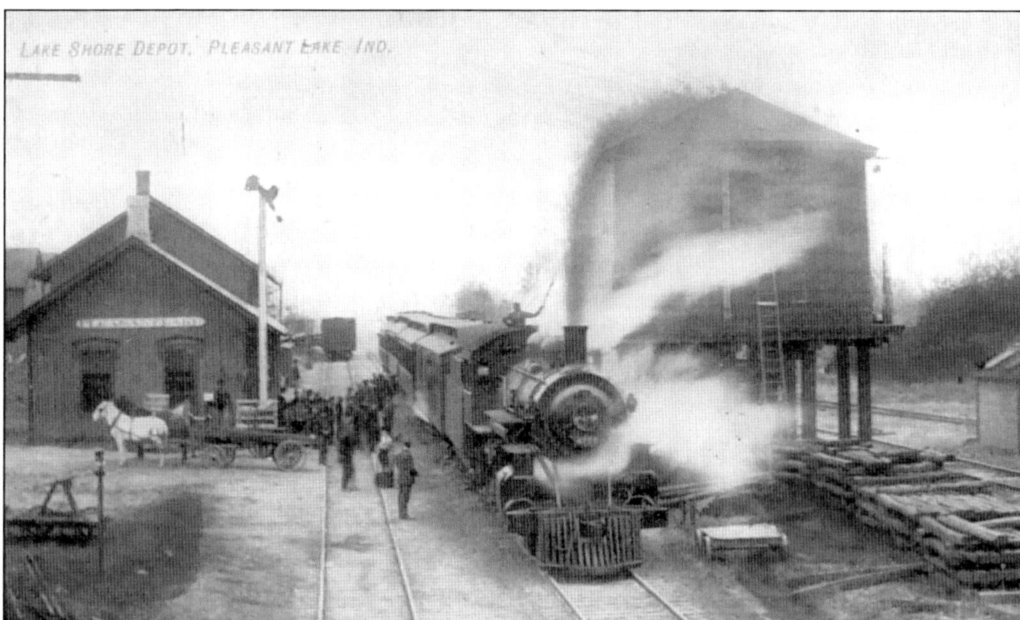

LAKE SHORE DEPOT, PLEASANT LAKE, INDIANA. The passenger train has just arrived and is "letting off steam."

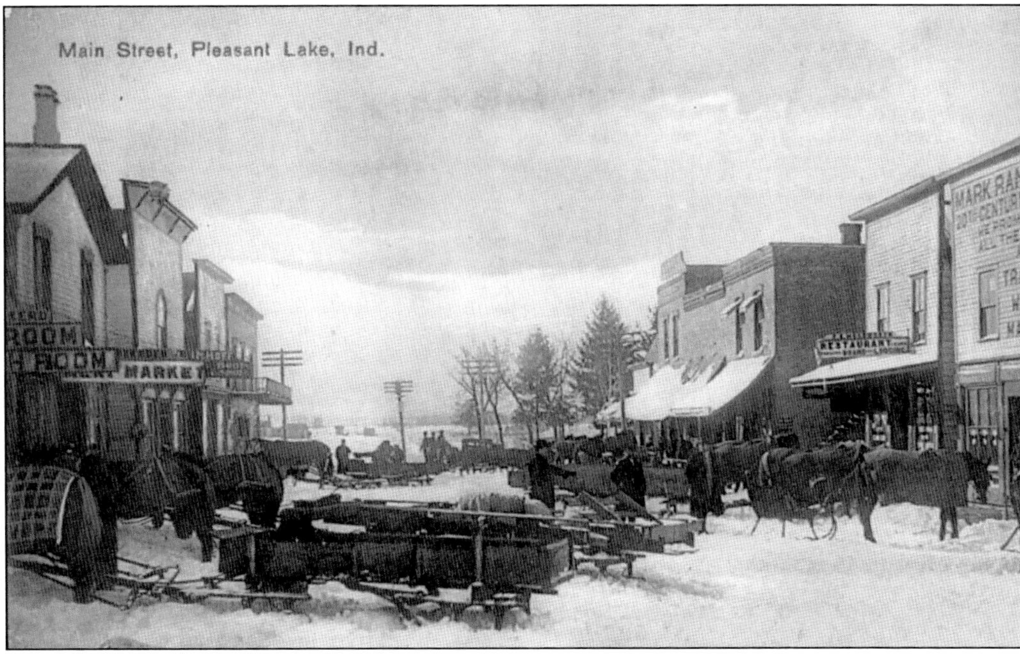

Main Street, Pleasant Lake, Indiana. This is an unusual winter scene with many sleds and sleighs. The signs on the left include, "Rooms, Meat Markets" and "Imhoff Shoes & Boots." The signs on the right include "Mark Ransberg—Twentieth Century Drugs and Restaurant."

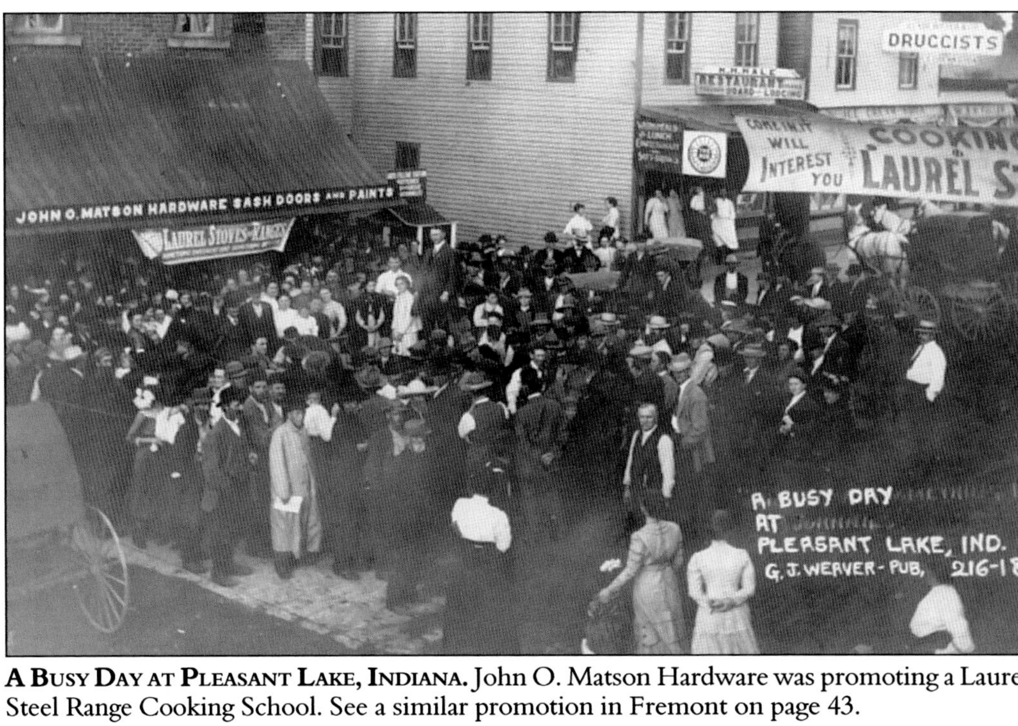

A Busy Day at Pleasant Lake, Indiana. John O. Matson Hardware was promoting a Laurel Steel Range Cooking School. See a similar promotion in Fremont on page 43.

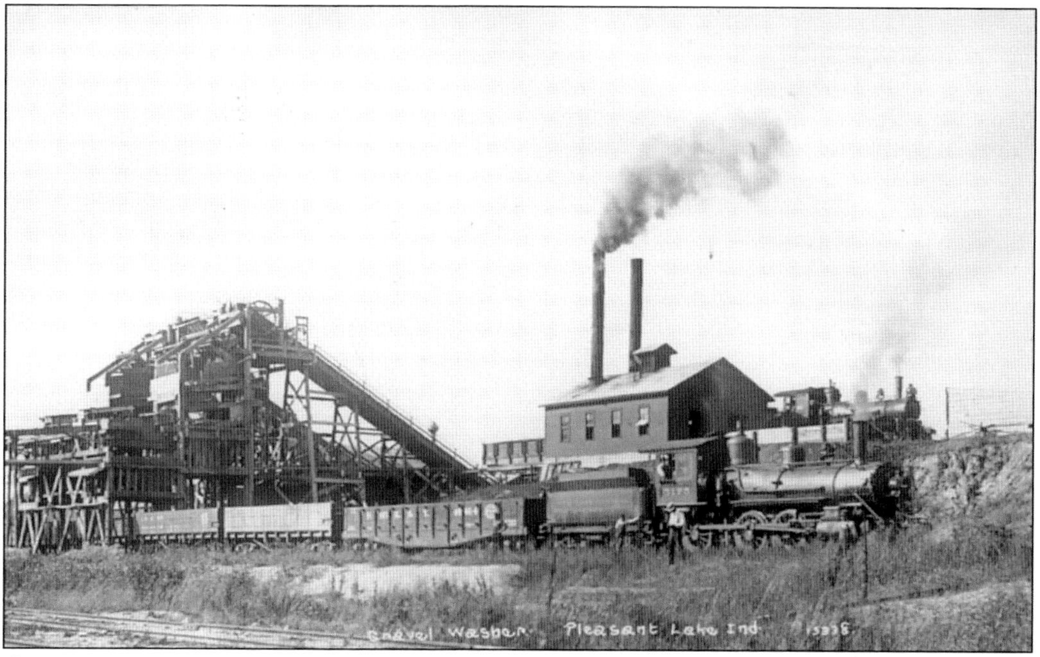

Gravel Washer, Pleasant Lake, Indiana. Gravel was mined, processed, and washed at Pleasant Lake. It was then shipped out on the New York Central Railroad, formerly the Fort Wayne, Jackson & Saginaw Railroad. The engine in the foreground has a New York Central designation on the tender.

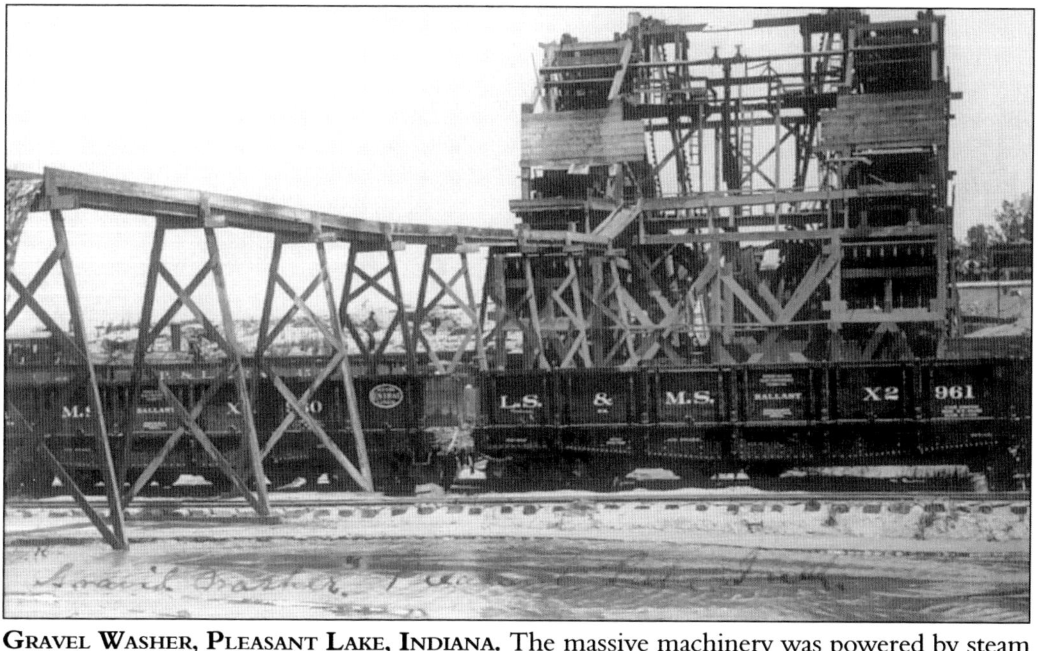

Gravel Washer, Pleasant Lake, Indiana. The massive machinery was powered by steam engines and included facilities for loading the railroad cars. The designation L.S. & M.S. stands for Lake Shore & Michigan Southern Railroad, which was acquired by the New York Central Railroad.

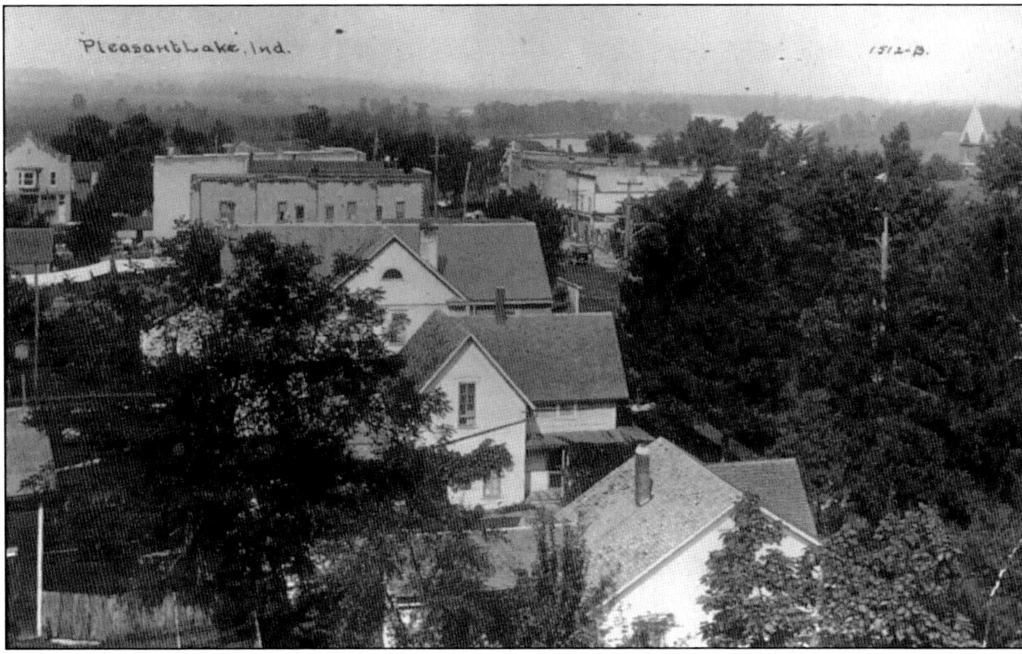

PLEASANT LAKE, INDIANA, c. 1917. This bird's-eye view shows residences and business buildings.

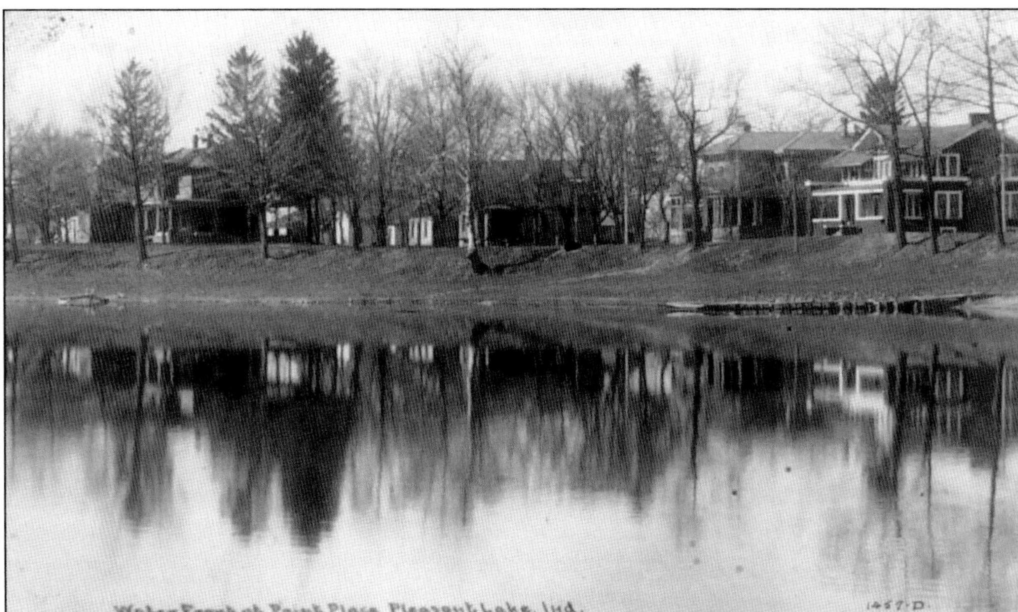

WEBER FRONT AT POINT PLACE, PLEASANT LAKE, INDIANA. Many fine residences were built around the west side of Pleasant Lake.

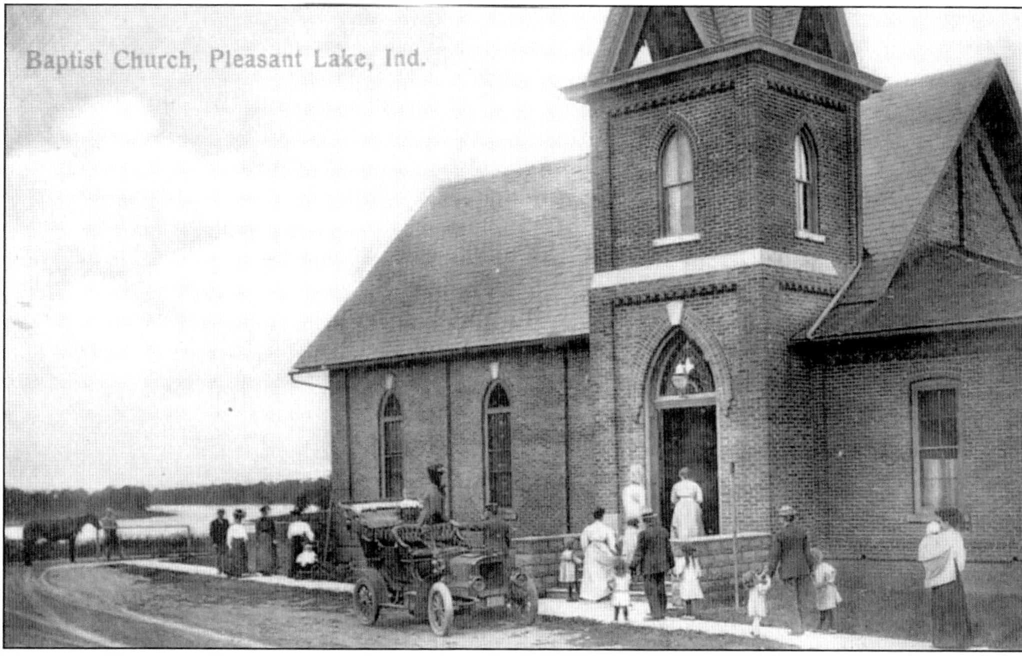

BAPTIST CHURCH, PLEASANT LAKE, INDIANA. An Auburn automobile is at the curb. A hitching rack and the lake can be seen in the background. The message states: "I am helping Mrs. Crowl cook for thrashers. Will be home Saturday night or Sunday."

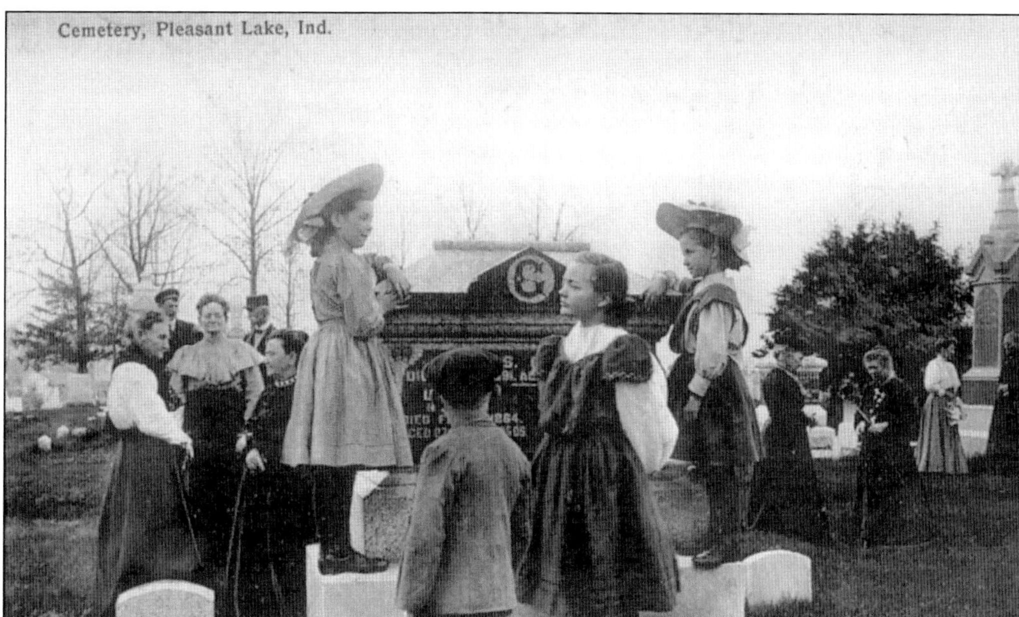

CEMETERY, PLEASANT LAKE, INDIANA. This is a curious scene for a postcard. It was perhaps a Memorial Day Celebration at the cemetery.

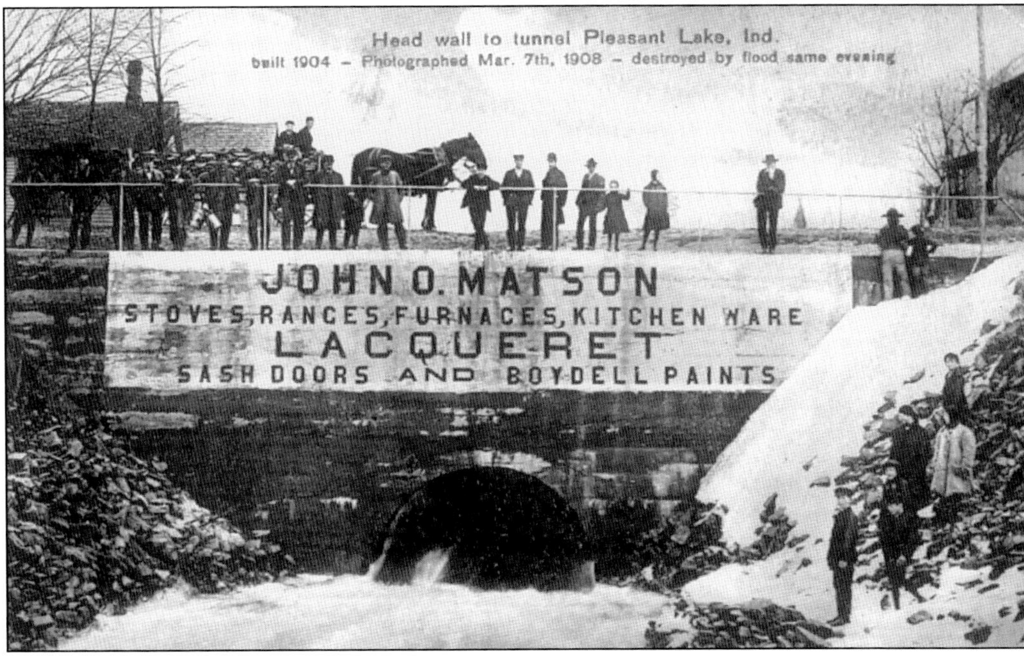

HEAD WALL TO TUNNEL PLEASANT LAKE, INDIANA. This was built in 1904, photographed March 7, 1908, and destroyed by flood the same evening. The spectators were apparently watching the discharge of water during a flood threat. The merchant, John O. Matson, got an extension of his advertising message in the form of a postcard. Before the common use of photographs in newspapers, postcards provided a means of disseminating an image of a catastrophic event.

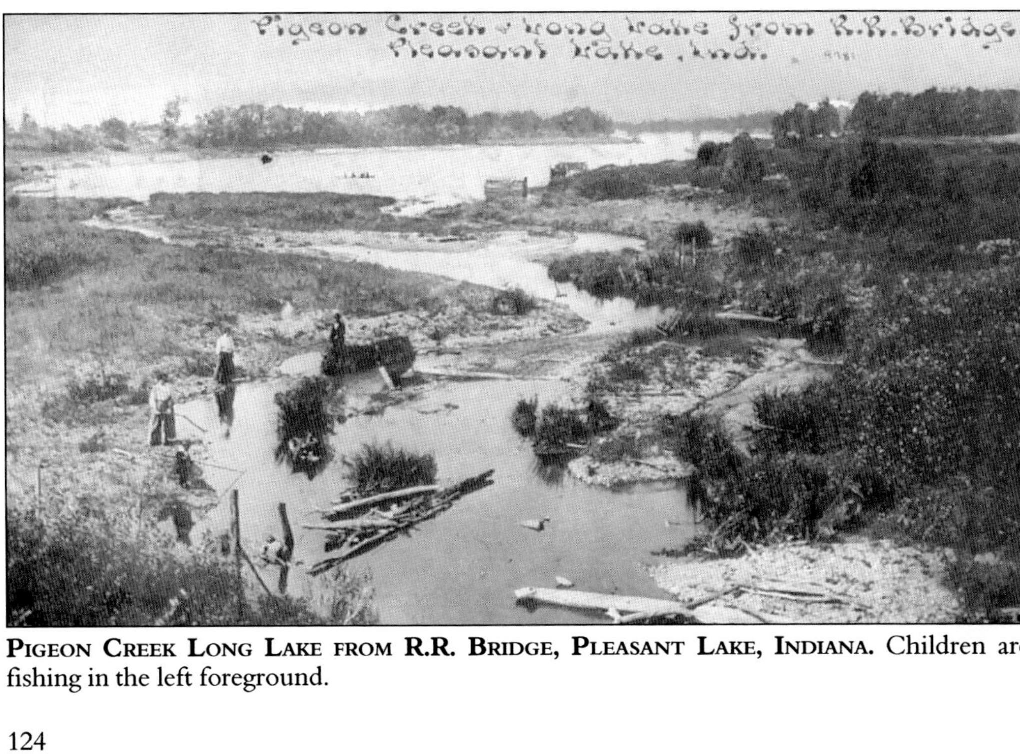

PIGEON CREEK LONG LAKE FROM R.R. BRIDGE, PLEASANT LAKE, INDIANA. Children are fishing in the left foreground.

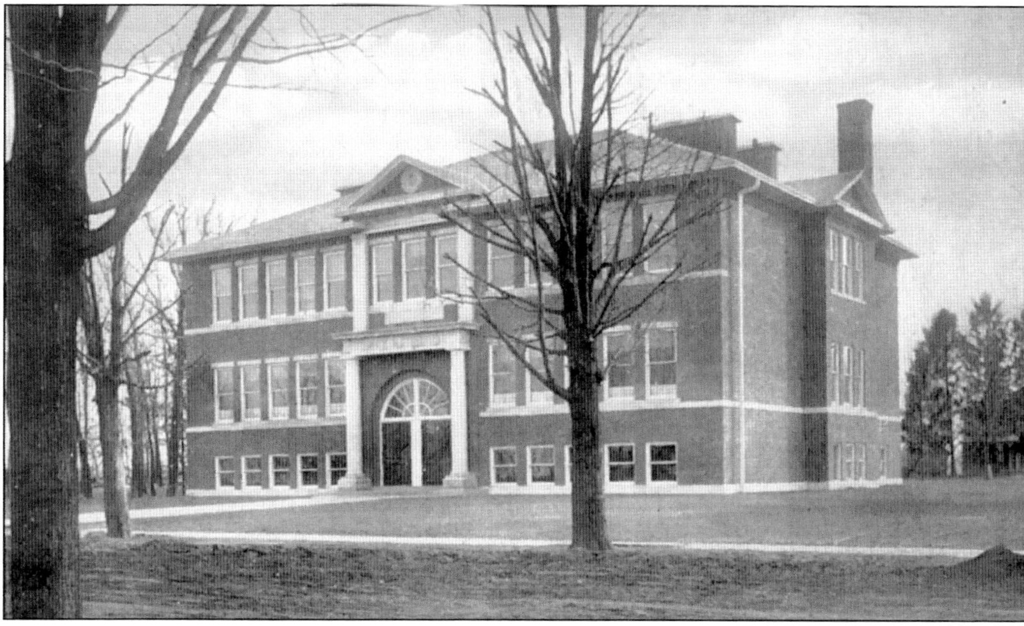

New High School, Pleasant Lake, Indiana. Each community was proud of its school buildings.

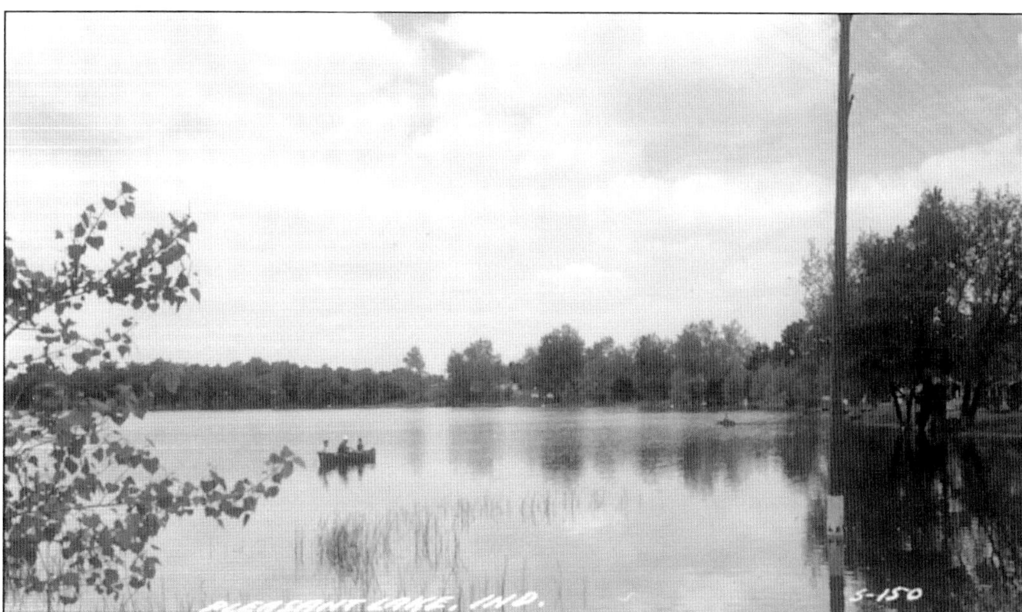

Pleasant Lake, Indiana. Pictured above is a pleasant scene at Pleasant Lake.

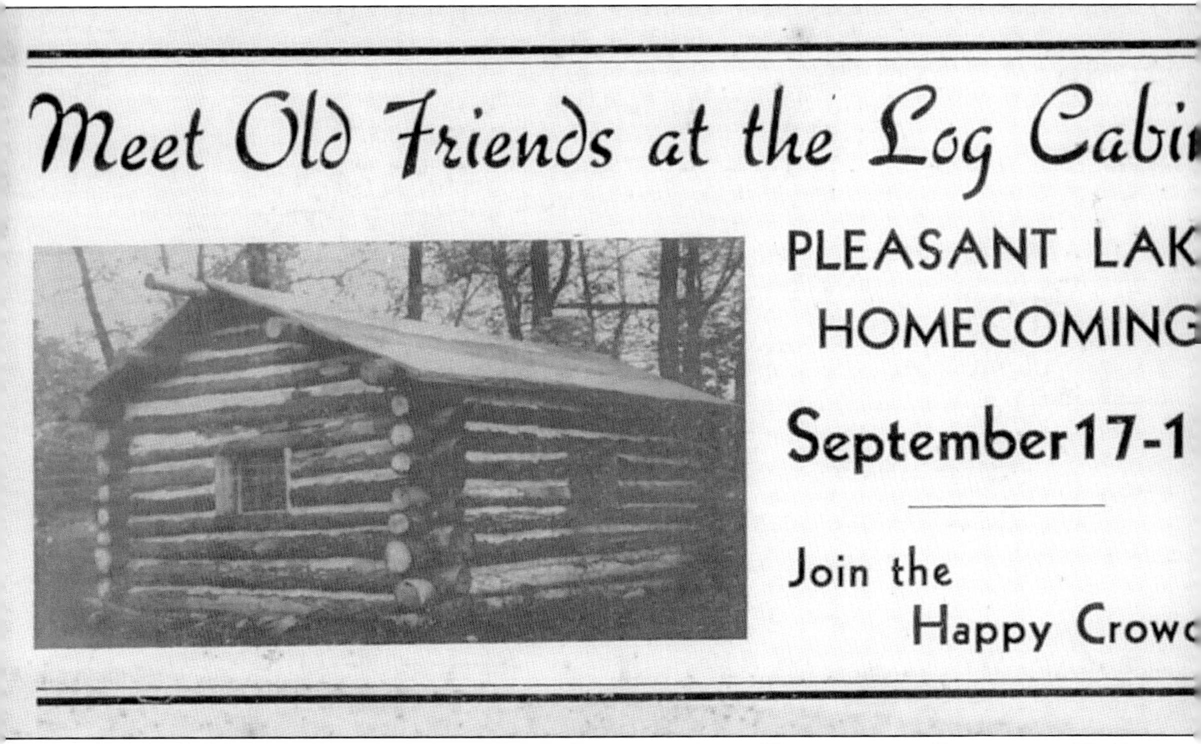

Meet Old Friends at the Log Cabin Pleasant Lake Homecoming, September 17–18, Join the Happy Crowd! An advertising card for the annual homecoming.

Ten

RAY

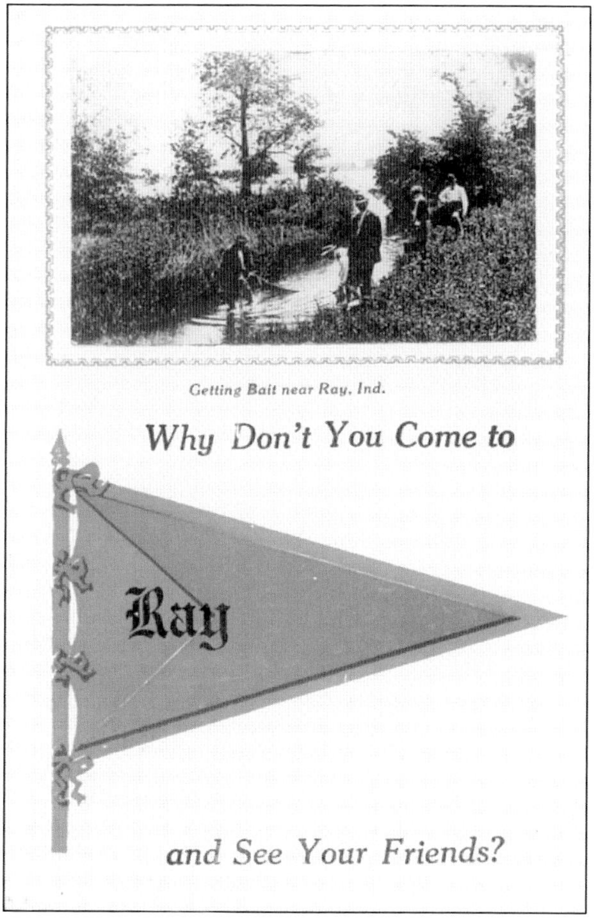

WHY DON'T YOU COME TO RAY AND SEE YOUR FRIENDS? *c.* 1916. Ray is in the extreme northeast corner of Indiana. The photograph is a separate image glued to the card. The photograph's caption is, "Getting Bait near Ray, Ind."

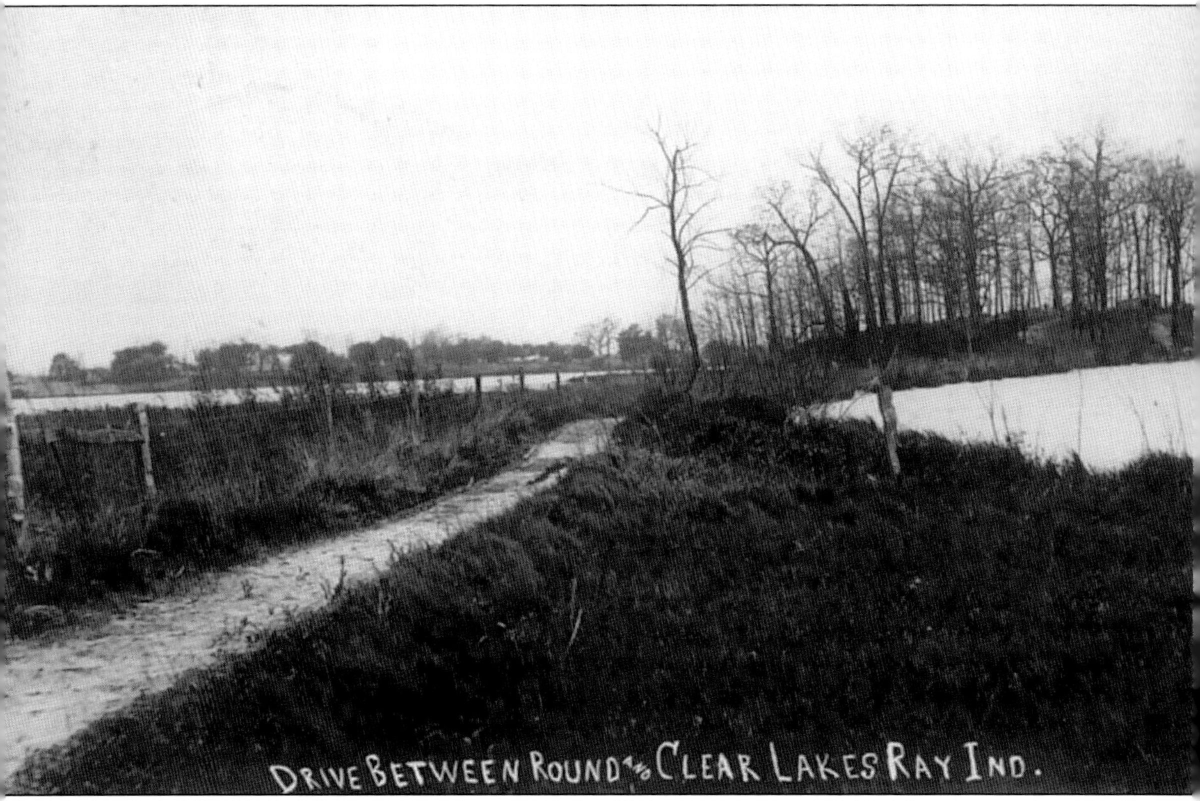

DRIVE BETWEEN ROUND AND CLEAR LAKES, RAY, INDIANA, C. 1910. The message states: "I am here with a very good friend. His brother and wife have a cottage rented here and we are having a great time boat riding and fishing. I had planned quite a while ago to come so cannot visit. You this summer as much as I would like to. Will ans. letter when I go home. Belle."